THE
AFTERMATH

This book was originally planned and produced as a special issue of *Ambio* by the editorial staff and a group of special advisors.

Editor of the Issue: Jeannie Peterson

Manuscript Editors: Don Hinrichsen, William Dampier

Special Advisors: Frank Barnaby (Chief Advisor), Lars Kristoferson, Jan Prawitz, Henning Rodhe, Joseph Rotblat

Special Consultant: Frank von Hippel

Production: Lynn Taylor, Berit Kind, Florence Heneby

Maps: Lynn Taylor

THE
AFTERMATH:

THE HUMAN AND ECOLOGICAL CONSEQUENCES OF NUCLEAR WAR

EDITED BY
JEANNIE PETERSON
FOR *AMBIO*

WITH AN INTRODUCTION BY ALVA MYRDAL

PANTHEON BOOKS, NEW YORK

Based on a special issue of *Ambio,* vol. II, nos. 2–3, 1982.

Library of Congress Cataloging in Publication Data

Nuclear war, the aftermath.
  The Aftermath.

  "A special AMBIO publication."
  "Published under the auspices of the Royal Swedish Academy of Sciences."
  1. Atomic warfare—Addresses, essays, lectures.
I. Kungliga Svenska vetenskapsakademien. II. Ambio.
U263.N8   1983   355′.0217   83-11408
ISBN 0-394-53443-8
ISBN 0-394-72042-3 (pbk.)

Manufactured in the United States of America
First American Edition

FOREWORD

THE AFTERMATH is published in the belief that a realistic assessment of the possible human and ecological consequences of a nuclear war may help to deter such a catastrophe.

It is based on a special issue of the international journal *Ambio,* which is published by the Royal Swedish Academy of Sciences and dedicated to recent work in the interrelated fields of environmental management, technology and the natural sciences. Throughout the years *Ambio* has dealt with the possible consequences of many threats to the environment, such as rising CO_2 levels in the atmosphere, pollution of the world's freshwater resources, the rapid spread of desertification and the accelerating rate of the disappearance of species. However, the impact of a nuclear war would be far more devastating to the biosphere than any other threat that is likely to appear in our time. Moreover, the likelihood of such a war occurring does not seem to be diminishing. In the past innumerable scenarios have been constructed to describe variations on the nuclear war theme. The reference scenario round which this book is built (and which we refer to in the text as the *Ambio* scenario) is not intended to be the "most likely" of these possibilities and it is not intended for use in civil defense planning. It was formulated by the Advisory Group for the Issue.* Their scenario does not describe a "limited" nuclear war because in their view the concept of "limited" nuclear war is fallacious. Once a nuclear war had broken out it would probably be neither containable nor controllable. The *Ambio* scenario was chosen to emphasize the environmental effects of a major nuclear exchange.

The preparation of this study was carried out with limited financial resources and with extraordinary commitment on the part of the *Ambio* staff. They were fortunate in being able to obtain the cooperation, participation, advice and support of a wide range of outstanding authors, advisors and other experts in a variety of fields. The advisors contributed to the planning of the special issue which is the basis of the book, and were involved with the selection of authors and referees and the final evaluation of the contributions. In accordance with the aim of making this a truly international undertaking, the authors represent the USA, the USSR, Eastern and Western Europe and all of them contributed in their personal capacities. The opinions expressed by individual contributors are their own and do not necessarily reflect the views of the Royal Swedish Academy of Sciences, the publishers of *Ambio*.

Since the inception of this project, increasing concern has been expressed in

---

*The *Ambio* Advisory Group included: Frank Barnaby, Professor of Peace Studies at the Free University of Amsterdam; Lars Kristoferson, Scientific Program Officer of the Beijer International Institute for Energy and Human Ecology; Jeannie Peterson, Editor-in-Chief, *Ambio;* Jan Prawitz, Special Assistant for Disarmament to Sweden's Minister of Defence; Henning Rodhe, Professor of Chemical Meteorology at the Arrhenius Laboratory, University of Stockholm; and Joseph Rotblat, Emeritus Professor of Physics at the University of London and founder of the Pugwash Conference on Science and World Affairs. Short biographical notes on contributors appear at the end of the book.

many countries about the threat of nuclear war. It is hoped that this scientific appraisal of the human and ecological consequences of a nuclear war will contribute to the growing realization that nuclear arms represent a risk that cannot be ignored.

The 1980 UN Report on Nuclear Weapons put it succinctly: "As there is no guarantee that the risk of war can be avoided, the need for nuclear disarmament is imperative".

INTRODUCTION
TO THE AMERICAN EDITION

The case against using, further developing, or even doing research for nuclear weapons is compellingly and convincingly set out in this highly expert study, *The Aftermath: The Human and Ecological Consequences of Nuclear War,* organized by the Swedish Academy of Sciences. It describes in a scientifically truthful and concrete way the deadly danger of nuclear war to the environment, to humanity, and to all living species. With the scientific facts now before us, nobody ought to believe that *more* is necessary; the world has long had more than enough of these weapons of mass destruction. Why preparations are still going on for more nuclear weapons is beyond the rational logic of any man or woman.

The vast majority of people in the civilized world are beginning to learn the truth; as so many scientists, already aware of it, are trying to teach it through articles and books. Still, numerous little Edward Tellers continue to produce strong, well-funded propaganda to mislead the public. Their major argument? That a larger and larger nuclear armory is needed to defend "the national interest." You must always climb the ladder to keep the balance of power in your favor; be certain never to be on the lower rung.

But this is the most fundamental and dangerous mistake. It simply leads to spiralling world insecurity at a higher and higher cost. Escalation under any other name is still just that—escalation!

Will those who lead world affairs never understand the truth of this simple fact which millions of ordinary people are now beginning to grasp? Atomic war can never be limited and never be won. Escalation feeds on its own momentum. Its course leads straight to self-destruction.

Alfred Nobel thought his invention of dynamite would ensure that there would be no more war. Hadn't war now become too awful to undertake? Such an illusion has cost millions of lives and billions of dollars. And such an illusion lies at the heart of all the "peaceful" hopes surrounding the invention of the atomic bomb and the first demonstration of its effects at Hiroshima and Nagasaki. In the years just after Hiroshima and Nagasaki, it was believed by many that this "ultimate weapon" would have the paradoxical effect of making peace a certainty in the world. Such was the argument Bernard Baruch used at the United Nations in those years.

However, escalation follows its own laws. Who then could have predicted that a developing spirit of nuclear competition would be a curse, multiplying many times over the rivalries of the two great superpowers? Although it is true that no mass nuclear war has yet happened, this rivalry contains a continually heightened danger that any conflict may escalate into a nuclear holocaust of the type so horrifyingly described in this book. Already the extensive preparations for such warfare are consuming an increasing share of the world's financial resources as well as usurping enormous reserves of human talent and innovative strength. Our society is being militarized and brutalized by it.

As if these effects were not enough, we are now promised "eternal peace" in space, Ronald Reagan's own star wars—one more enormously expensive, intensely competitive, terrifying step towards the blowing up of our whole planet in a global nuclear war. The end effect of this almost three-decade-long spiral of nuclear escalation is now visible: human behavior has been caught in a giant web of potential self-destruction. No scientific study has made this clearer than *The Aftermath*. Let us hope that its sober language and cataclysmic findings will alert not just citizens but more and more scientists to the pressing urgency of the need to put a stop to the present course of events, even if these scientists personally have to be prepared to go on strike.

What we must insist upon today is a complete turnabout in the nuclear arms race. Public opinion increasingly demands it. Experts are calling for it. There is genuine hope in the "movement for a freeze" for a full stop to deployment, construction, and even research on nuclear weapons. In the end, we must have as total an obliteration of nuclear weaponry as humanly possible. We must put an end to the driving forces behind the arms race. We still have time; it is up to us to choose. But this expert study makes it clear why we can wait no longer. Now, very simply, is the time to act.

Alva Myrdal
Stockholm
May 1983

CONTENTS

ONE

THE EFFECTS OF A GLOBAL NUCLEAR WAR: THE ARSENALS

FRANK BARNABY

Five nations are now known to possess nuclear weapons, and several others are believed to be developing them, but the nuclear arsenals of the two superpowers dwarf all the others. Together they total more than 50 000 nuclear warheads, with an explosive power one million times that of the bomb dropped on Hiroshima. Those nuclear stockpiles are now the equivalent of more than three tons of TNT for every person on the earth.

The number of ways in which a global nuclear war might begin is frighteningly large. It could start with a deliberate decision by one of the superpowers to wage war on the other; or by the escalation of a conventional war; or through mechanical error or malfunction in a nuclear weapon system; because of irrational behavior by those controlling nuclear weapons; through an error by humans or computers controlling the nuclear alert and firing system; by the acquisition and use of nuclear weapons by irresponsible governments; or through the use of nuclear weapons by terrorists.

While the danger of a nuclear war starting by accident, miscalculation or madness is ever present, the escalation of a regional conflict fought with conventional arms to a general war fought with nuclear arms is perhaps the most likely—more likely than a direct attack by one superpower on the other. In a world divided into hostile camps the competition for scarce raw materials may become a frequent— perhaps the most frequent—cause of future conflicts, and it is not difficult to imagine a local conflict in a region like the Persian Gulf escalating into a more general confrontation and finally into a full-scale nuclear war. This escalation is more likely if the superpowers supplied the original arms, and if any of the initial combatants possess nuclear arms, and to that extent both the international arms race and the proliferation of nuclear weapons contribute to the possibility of a nuclear war.

Five nations—the USA, the USSR, the UK, France and China—are known to have nuclear weapons; another, India, has detonated a nuclear explosion; and a number of other countries, like Israel and South Africa, are believed to have nuclear devices, although the evidence is inconclusive. But all of the other nuclear powers are miniscule in comparison with the USA and the USSR. While the British, French and Chinese together possess about 1000 nuclear weapons, the superpowers deploy tens of thousands of warheads. The smaller nuclear arsenals are not insignificant. They could wreak unimaginable damage. But we will concentrate in these chapters on the US and Soviet nuclear arsenals simply because they are so huge they totally overshadow the others. Because of the Soviet obsession with military secrecy, most of the information in this and the following discussions comes from western sources. But while there may be differences in emphasis, the policies and strategies of the two superpowers tend to be remarkably similar.

THE SOVIET AND AMERICAN STRATEGIC NUCLEAR ARSENALS

Current operational nuclear weapons have a vast range of explosive power—varying between 100 tons and at least 20 million tons (20 megatons) of TNT equivalent (1). To put these numbers into some sort of perspective, all of the bombs dropped in the eight most violent years of the Vietnam war totalled only about 4 megatons. A single American B-52 strategic nuclear bomber can now carry more explosive power than that used in all the wars in history.

American *strategic* nuclear forces carry about 9500 nuclear warheads, with a total explosive power equivalent to approximately 3400 megatons of high explosive. Soviet *strategic* nuclear forces could deliver about 8400 nuclear warheads, with a total explosive power equivalent to approximately 4100 megatons of high explosive. In the *tactical* nuclear arsenals there are probably about 35 000 nuclear warheads— about 20 000 American and about 15 000 Soviet—each on average several times more powerful than the Hiroshima bomb. These add another 4500 or so megatons of high-explosive equivalent to make a grand total of about 12 000 megatons—the equivalent of about 1 000 000 Hiroshima bombs, or about three tons of TNT for every man, woman and child on earth (2).

Strategic nuclear weapons are deployed on intercontinental ballistic missiles (ICBMs), submarine-launched ballistic

2

missiles (SLBMs), and strategic bombers. Soviet and American ICBMs have ranges of about 11 000 kilometers (6875 miles), modern SLBMs have ranges of about 7000 kilometers (4340 miles) and strategic bombers have ranges of about 12 000 km (7440 miles). Range is the main distinguishing feature between strategic and tactical nuclear weapons, the former having long (intercontinental) ranges, although the existence of intermediate range missiles (*eg* the SS-20 or cruise missile) confuses the distinction between different types of weapons.

Some ballistic missiles carry multiple warheads. Modern multiple warheads are independently targetable on targets hundreds of kilometers or miles apart. These are called multiple independently targetable re-entry vehicles or MIRVs.

Strategic bombers carry free-fall nuclear bombs and air-to-ground missiles fitted with nuclear warheads. The most modern of these missiles now being tested is the American air-launched cruise missile (ALCM) which has a range of about 2500 kilometers (1563 miles).

The United States now has 1628 ballistic missiles (1052 ICBMs and 576 SLBMs) of which 1070 (550 ICBMs and 520 SLBMs) are fitted with MIRVs. Some 340 B-52s are operational as long-range strategic bombers.

The Soviet Union has deployed 2348 ballistic missiles (1398 ICBMs and 950 SLBMs), of which about 1074 (818 ICBMs and 256 SLBMs) are MIRVed. About 150 of its long-range bombers are probably assigned strategic roles.

Tactical nuclear weapons are deployed in a wide variety of systems—including howitzer and artillery shells, ground-to-ground ballistic missiles, free-fall bombs, air-to-ground missiles, anti-aircraft missiles, atomic demolition munitions (land mines), submarine-launched cruise missiles, torpedoes, naval mines, and anti-submarine rockets. Land-based systems have ranges varying from about 12 kilometers or 7.4 miles (artillery shells) to a few thousand kilometers (intermediate range ballistic missiles). The explosive power of these warheads varies from about 100 tons to about one megaton.

The USA deploys tactical nuclear weapons in Western Europe, Asia, and the United States and with the Atlantic and Pacific fleets. The USSR deploys its tactical nuclear weapons in eastern Europe, in the western USSR, and east of the Urals.

FUTURE DEVELOPMENTS IN THE NUCLEAR ARSENALS

Although present plans call for significant increases in the number of warheads in the Soviet and American arsenals over the next few years, mainly because of the deployment of more MIRVed ICBMs and SLBMs and cruise missiles, the most important developments in nuclear weapons in the forseeable future will be qualitative improvements. There are now so many nuclear weapons in the arsenals that any further increases in numbers would make no sense, from a military or from any other point of view. This has been true for many years.

The most important qualitative advances in nuclear weapons are those which improve the accuracy and reliability of nuclear weapon systems. Some of these new weapons will be seen as suitable for *fighting* rather than for *deterring* a nuclear war. Very accurate and reliable ballistic missiles can deliver warheads on smaller —and therefore many more—military targets than less accurate ones can. In other words, the day may be coming when one country might hope to destroy its enemy's nuclear retaliatory capability by striking first.

In this context it is not necessary for one side to possess the ability to completely destroy the other's retaliatory capacity for such a first strike to be considered feasible. It is sufficient for the attacker to *believe* that a surprise attack will deplete the enemy's capacity to retaliate to the point where the attacker's casualties will be "acceptable" for a given political goal.

3

Such reasoning is extremely dangerous, but in times of crisis political leaders are more apt to give credence to their military chiefs than to their scientific advisers. As a result, calculations of casualties are likely to be based on erroneous assumptions about the military performance of both sides, assumptions which emphasize estimates of prompt deaths but which ignore the uncertain long-term effects of a nuclear war, even though those effects may ultimately be more lethal. In addition, the serious sociological and psychological consequences of the total loss of social and technical services are likely to be ignored.

For many years official doctrines, at least in the US, have been based on nuclear deterrence through "mutually assured destruction" (MAD), but over much of the past decade there has been a movement toward strategies and policies suitable for fighting, rather than deterring, a nuclear war. There is every reason to believe the USSR is following the US in developing a nuclear fighting policy. One of the reasons for this change in nuclear strategies is the development of new weapons.

Some believe that Soviet nuclear strategy has always had a stronger emphasis on counterforce than US strategy, even though Soviet missiles have been less accurate and reliable than their American counterparts. As the Russians improve the quality of their missiles, their nuclear fighting doctrine will probably become more refined. And the more the two great powers adapt to counterforce doctrines and integrate many types of nuclear weapons into their military tactics and strategies, the greater will be the probability of a nuclear war, because the idea that such war is both "fightable and winnable" will gain ground. Statements made by President Reagan, Secretary of State Haig and Secretary of Defense Weinberger imply that this type of thinking is quite advanced in the USA. The situation is no doubt similar in the Soviet Union.

MODERNIZATION OF USA AND SOVIET STRATEGIC NUCLEAR WEAPONS

The accuracy of a nuclear warhead is normally measured by its CEP (circular error probable), the radius of the circle centered on the target within which half of a large number of warheads, fired at the target, will fall. In both the USA and the USSR, the CEPs of ICBMs and SLBMs are being continually improved. In the USA, for example, improvements are being made in the computer of the NS-20 guidance system in the Minuteman III ICBMs, involving better mathematical descriptions of the in-flight performances of the inertial platform and accelerometers, and better pre-launch calibration of the gyroscopes and accelerometers. With these guidance improvements, the CEP of the Minuteman III will probably decrease from about 350 meters (1155 feet) to about 200 meters (660 feet). At the same time the Mark 12 re-entry vehicle and the W62 170-kiloton nuclear warhead are being replaced with the Mark 12A re-entry vehicle and the W78 350-kiloton nuclear warhead. The plan is to put the new warheads on 300 of the existing 550 Minuteman III missiles. The Mark 12A will have roughly the same weight, size, radar cross-section and aerodynamic characteristics as the Mark 12.

Mark 12A warheads with the higher accuracy will be able to destroy Soviet ICBMs in silos hardened to about 10 megapascals (1500 pounds per square inch) with a probability of success of about 57 percent for one shot and about 95 percent for two shots. Superior arming and fusing devices will provide more control over the height at which the warhead is exploded and hence the damage done.

The upgraded land-based ICBM force will significantly increase US nuclear-war fighting capabilities. These will be further increased by the MX missile system, now under development.

4

Table 1. Additions and Replacements to US Nuclear Weapon Stockpile 1982–1992.

Number of Nuclear Weapons	Weapon Systems
4 348*	Air-launched cruise missiles
1 728*	Trident C4 missiles
49	Trident Submarines Mirv X8
380*	Lance (Neutron weapons)
800*	8″ artillery shells (Neutron weapon)
1 000*	Weapon system B61 Bombs
165	Pershing II
560	Ground-launched cruise missiles
2 000	B-83 Bombs
3 000	155 mm artillery shells
500	Standard Missile II Extended Range
384	Submarine-launched cruise missiles
1 200–1 680	B-5 missiles for at least 5 Trident submarines Mirv X 10–14
1 000	MX
17 065–17 545	**Total Nuclear Weapons**

* Weapons in production now.
1. Approximately 10 000 existing weapons will be retired over the decade resulting in a net gain of approximately 6000–7000 weapons.
2. Programs nearing completion: 1083 Mark 12 A for 900 weapons on 300 Minuteman III; 1740 Trident C4 missiles for 12 Poseidon submarines.
Source: Center for Defense Information. Based on US Department of Defense plans for new delivery systems.

The MX system includes both a new ICBM and a related basing scheme. The guidance for the MX missile will probably be based on the advanced inertial reference sphere (AIRS), an "all-attitude" system which can correct for movements of the missile along the ground before it is launched. A CEP of about 100 meters (328 feet) should be achieved with this system. If the MX warhead is provided with terminal guidance, using a laser or radar system to guide the warhead on to its target, CEPs of a few tens of meters (yards) may be possible. Each missile will probably carry ten warheads, the limit allowed in the Salt II treaty.

The launch-weight of the MX will probably be about 86 000 kilograms (*ca* 95 tons), about 2.4 times more than that of the Minuteman III, and the throw-weight will probably be about 3500 kilograms (*ca* 4 tons). The three MX booster stages will use advanced solid propellants, very light motor cases, and advanced nozzles to produce nearly twice the propulsion efficiency of the Minuteman.

In October 1981, President Reagan described in some detail his long-range strategic policy. His statement included a modernization plan for American strategic nuclear forces emphasizing improvements in strategic bombers and submarine-launched ballistic missiles (SLBMs). The final decision on the method of basing the new MX intercontinental ballistic missile (ICBM) is postponed. The President, in other words, has finally rejected the idea of putting MX missiles in multiple protective shelters. This mobile basing scheme, as envisaged by the Carter Administration, involved shuttling 200 MX missiles between 4600 fixed horizontal shelters. This mobility would, it was assumed, ensure the survival of many of the MX missiles in a surprise Soviet attack. It is widely (but probably incorrectly) believed that the Soviets will be able to destroy 90 percent or so of existing US ICBMs in the early 1980s.

In the meantime, alternative mobile basing systems for the MX missile are to be investigated. These will include the use of

5

aircraft capable of flying for long periods over oceans, each carrying an MX missile for airborne launch, and deep underground-silo basing in which MX missiles would be placed in holes up to 1000 meters deep. One or both of these concepts could be deployed along with MX missiles in existing silos defended by anti-ballistic missiles.

The perception of ICBM vulnerability may well lead to the deployment of launch-on-warning systems. In such a system, enemy missiles in flight would be detected by early-warning satellites soon after they are launched. Satellite signals would be transmitted to computers which would fire the threatened ICBMs before the enemy missiles landed. In other words, the nuclear holocaust could be launced by computer without any human decision. The deployment of a launch-on-warning system would be highly dangerous—perhaps the ultimate madness.

The most formidable of Soviet ICBMs is the SS-18, or the RS-20 in Soviet terminology. This is thought to have a CEP of about 500 meters (1625 feet). This accuracy will probably soon improve to about 250 meters (813 feet). Each SS-18 warhead probably has an explosive power equivalent to about 500 kilotons. With the higher accuracy, this would give the warhead about a 55 percent chance of destroying a US Minuteman ICBM in its silo. Two warheads fired in succession would have about a 95 percent chance of success.

The USSR also has the SS-19 ICBM (the RS-18). This is thought to be more accurate than the SS-18 and to be equipped with a similar warhead. Some of both the SS-18 and -19s are MIRVed. So far a total of more than 600 SS-18s and -19s have been deployed. If these were MIRVed to the extent allowed by the SALT II Treaty, they would be equipped with a total of about 4000 warheads. The other Soviet MIRVed ICBM, the SS-17 (or RS-16), has been tested with four warheads, but so far 150 SS-17s have been deployed. According

to US sources, the USSR is developing at least two new types of ICBM.

The Soviet MIRVed strategic missile force is clearly an increasing threat to the 1000-strong US Minuteman ICBM force as the accuracy and reliability of the Soviet warheads are improved. The USSR could, under SALT II, double the number of warheads on its ICBMs to about 8000.

The quality of strategic nuclear submarines and the ballistic missiles they carry is also being continuously improved. In the USA, for example, the present Polaris and Poseidon strategic nuclear submarine force is being augmented, and may eventually be replaced, by Trident submarines. The Polaris submarines now operating will be phased out by the end of 1982. Thirty-one Poseidon submarines are now operating.

Trident submarines will be equipped with a new SLBM, the Trident I, the successor of the Poseidon C-3 SLBM. Yet another SLBM, the Trident II, is currently being developed for eventual deployment on Trident submarines.

In the meantime, Trident I missiles will also be deployed on Poseidon submarines. The first of 12 Poseidons to be modified to carry Trident I missiles went to sea in October 1979; the others should be ready by 1984.

The first Trident submarine, the USS *Ohio*, became operational in 1981. At least 8 Trident submarines (which have already been ordered) are likely to become operational during the 1980s, but the ultimate size of the Trident fleet has yet to be decided.

The Trident displaces 18 700 tons when submerged. The enormous size of the Trident can be judged from the fact that it is twice as large as a Polaris/Poseidon submarine, which has a submerged displacement of about 8300 tons, and is as large as the new British through-deck cruiser (displacement 19 500 tons).

Each Trident will carry 24 SLBMs. The Trident I SLBM is designed to have a maximum range of 7400 kilometers (4590 miles) when equipped with eight 100-kiloton MIRVed warheads. Even longer ranges can be achieved if the missile has a smaller payload. The Poseidon SLBM, which it replaces, can carry up to fourteen 40-kiloton MIRVed warheads, but has a maximum range of only 4600 kilometers (2850 miles). With the longer-range missile, Trident submarines will be able to operate in many times more ocean area and still remain within range of its targets. The long-range missiles will also allow Trident submarines to operate closer to US shores and still reach their targets, giving the submarines greater protection against Soviet anti-submarine warfare (ASW) activities.

Trident I, a two-stage solid propellant rocket, is provided with a stellar-aided inertial guidance system to provide course corrections. The CEP of the Trident SLBM is probably about 500 meters (1625 feet) at a maximum range, whereas that of the Poseidon SLBM is about 550 meters (1788 feet), and that of the Polaris I SLBM is about 900 meters (2925 feet). The development and deployment of mid-course guidance techniques for SLBMs and the more accurate navigation of missile submarines will steadily increase the accuracy of the missiles.

SLBM warheads may eventually be fitted with terminal guidance, using radar, laser or some other device to guide them to their targets after re-entry into the Earth's atmosphere. This could give CEPs of a few tens of meters or yards. SLBMs will then be so accurate as to cease to be only deterrence weapons aimed at enemy cities and become nuclear fighting weapons.

The most modern Soviet SLBM is the 7400 kilometer (4590 mile) range SS-N-18, equipped with three 200-kiloton MIRVs. So far, 256 SS-N-18s have been put to sea, 16 on each of 16 Delta-class submarines, the most modern operational Soviet strategic nuclear submarines. The other main Soviet SLBM is the SS-N-8, with a range of 8000 kilometers (4960 miles) and a single 1-megaton warhead. Two hundred and

eighty SS-N-8s are deployed on 22 Delta-class submarines.

The USSR also operates 24 Yankee-class strategic nuclear submarines, each carrying 16 SS-N-6 SLBMs, a 3000 kilometer (1860 mile) range missile carrying either a 1-megaton warhead or two 200-kiloton warheads. In all, the USSR has 950 SLBMs, 256 of them MIRVed.

The USSR is developing a new ballistic-missile-firing submarine—the Typhoon—which is apparently even bigger than the American Trident, with a displacement of 25 000 tons submerged. A new SLBM, the SS-N-20, has been tested, presumably for deployment on the Typhoon.

On the US side, President Reagan plans to resume the development and production of the B-1B Strategic bomber (called the long-range combat aircraft) and to accelerate the production of air-launched cruise missiles. The Reagan plan calls for the procurement of 100 B-1B bombers. The first bombers should be operational in 1986, with a strategic fleet of 90 aircraft operational in 1988 or 1989. According to current plans the B-1B will have a maximum take-off weight of 477 000 pounds and be powered by four 30 000-pound-thrust turbo-fan engines.

The Reagan plan also involves the development of an advanced technology bomber, called the Stealth aircraft. By incorporating a number of technologies, the bomber is to be given a very small radar cross-section to enable it to penetrate enemy air-defence systems with much reduced risk of detection. The Stealth aircraft may fly for the first time in 1984 and is scheduled for operation in the early 1990s. The B-1B bomber program may therefore be obsolete soon after it becomes operational.

The current US strategic bomber force will be modernized by equipping B-52 strategic bombers with air-launched cruise missiles (ACLMs). The B-1B will also carry probably 30 ALCMs, small, long-range, sub-sonic, very accurate, nuclear-armed,

7

Table 2. US strategic delivery capability (Mid. 1982)

Vehicle	Number of delivery vehicles deployed	Number of warheads per delivery vehicle	Total delivery capability (number of warheads)	Total yield per delivery vehicle (Mt)	Total delivery capability (Mt)	Estimated CEP (m)
MIRVed vehicles						
Minuteman III	350	3	1 050	0.51	18p	300
Minuteman III (Mk 12A)	200	3	600	1.05	210	200
Poseidon C-3[a]	320	10[b]	3 200	0.4	128	500
Trident C-4[a]	200	8	1 600	0.8	160	500
Sub-total	1 070		6 450		678	
Non-MIRVed vehicles						
B-52 (SRAMS + bombs)	150[c]	12[d]	1 800	5.6	840	180
B-52 (bombs)	190[c]	4[d]	760	4	760	180
Titan II	52	1	52	9	468	1 300
Minuteman II	450	1	450	1.5	675	400
Sub-total	842		3 062		2 743	
TOTAL	**1 912**		**9 512[e]**		**3 421**	

[a] SLBM.
[b] Average figure.
[c] Including heavy bombers in storage, etc. there are 573 strategic bombers.
[d] Operational loading. Maximum loading per aircraft may be eleven bombs, each of about one megaton.
[e] Of these, 6 952 are independently targetable warheads on ballistic missiles (2 152 on ICBMs and 4 800 on SLBMs.) Ballistic missiles carry 53 % of the megatonnage, 45 % on ICBMs and 8 % on SLBMs, and bombers carry 47 %.
Source: Material based on SIPRI Yearbook, 1982.

winged vehicles. ALCMs can be launched against Soviet targets by bombers penetrating Soviet defenses or from outside Soviet territory.

According to current plans, ALCMs should become operational in 1982, when the first B-52 G squadron is loaded with cruise missiles under the aircraft's wings. Full operational capability is planned for 1990, when all 151 B-52G aircraft will be loaded, each with 12 ALCMs under the wings and 8 in the bomb bays. ALCMs will about double the number of nuclear weapons these aircraft carry.

Current US ballistic missiles carry 6952 independently targetable warheads. Of these missile warheads, 4800 are sea-based—3200 on Poseidon SLBMs and 1600 on Trident SLBMs. US ballistic missiles have a total explosive yield of about 1820 megatons, of which about 300 megatons are carried by SLBMs. US sea-based strategic nuclear forces account therefore for about 70 percent of the missile warheads.

If all US strategic warheads, on bombers and missiles, are included the sea-based forces account for about 50 percent of the total (Table 2).

Almost all Soviet strategic nuclear warheads are deployed on ballistic missiles; the USSR operates no more than 150 strategic bombers and there is no evidence that they are assigned an intercontinental role. There are said to be about 7300 independently targetable Soviet missile warheads. Of these, about 1460, or 20 percent, are probably carried by SLBMs, while the rest are on ICBMs. The SLBM warheads probably have a total explosive yield of about 740 megatons, or 18 percent of the total Soviet strategic megatonnage. According to US sources, the Soviet Union normally has only about one-seventh of its strategic submarines (about ten boats) at sea at any one time. Thus the land-based ICBM-force is at present by far the most important component of the Soviet strategic nuclear arsenal (Table 3).

8

Table 3. Soviet strategic missile delivery capability (Mid. 1982)*

Vehicle	Number of delivery vehicles deployed	Number of warheads per delivery vehicle	Total delivery capability (number of warheads)	Total yield per delivery vehicle (Mt)	Total delivery capability (Mt)	Estimated CEP (m)
MIRVed vehicles						
SS-17	150	4	600	2	300	300–600
SS-18	308	8	2 464	5	1 540	300–600
SS-19	360	6	2 160	3	1 080	330–450
SS-N-18[a]	256	3	768	0.6	154	550–1 000
Sub-total	1 074		5 992		3 074	
Non-MIRVed vehicles						
SS-11	230	1	230	1	230	1 000–1 800
SS-11 (MRV)	290	3	870	0.6	174	
SS-13	60	1	60	1	60	
SS-N-5[a]	18	1	18	1	18	
SS-N-6[a]	102	1	102	1	102	1 000–2 500
SS-N-6[a] (MRV)	272	3	816	0.6	163	1 400
SS-NX-17[a]	12	1	12	1	12	500
SS-N-8[a]	290	1	290	1	290	1 000–1 500
Sub-total	1 274		2 398		1 049	
TOTAL	**2 348**		**8 390[b]**		**4 123**	

[a] SLBM.
[b] Of these, 7 266 are independently targetable (5 804 on ICBMs and 1 462 on SLBMs). ICBMs carry 82 % of the total megatonnage, and SLBMs carry the remaining 18 %.
Source: Material based on SIPRI Yearbook, 1982.

Table 4. Probable US strategic delivery capability in 1985

Vehicle	Number of vehicles deployed	Number of warheads per delivery vehicle	Total delivery capability (number of warheads)	Total yield per delivery vehicle (Mt)	Total delivery capability (Mt)	CEP (m)
MIRVed vehicles						
Minuteman III (Mk 12)	236	3	708	0.51	120	200
Minuteman III (Mk 12A)	300	3	900	1	300	200
Poseidon C-3[a]	336	10[b]	3 360	0.4	134	500
Trident I[a]	160	8	1 280	0.8	128	500
Trident II[a]	168	8	1 344	0.8	134	500
B-52 with ALCM	120	20	2 400	4	480	150
Sub-total	1 320		9 992		1 296	
Non-MIRVed vehicles						
B-52 (SRAM, bombs)	150	12[c]	1 800	5.6	840	180
B-52 (bombs)	76	4[c]	304	4	304	180
Titan II	53	1	53	9	477	1 300
Minuteman II	450	1	450	1.2	540	400
Sub-total	729		2 607		2 161	
TOTAL	**2 049**		**12 599[d]**		**3 457**	

CEP – Circular error probable
ALCM – air launched cruise missile
SRAM – short range attack missile

[a] SLBM.
[b] Average.
[c] Operational. Maximum loading per aircraft may be eleven bombs, each of about one megaton.
[d] Of these, 8 095 are independently targetable warheads on ballistic missiles (2 111 on ICBMs, and 5 984 on SLBMs). Ballistic missiles carry 54 % of the total megatonnage, 41 % on ICBMs and 13 % on SLBMs.

Table 5. Probable maximum Soviet strategic delivery capability in 1985

Vehicle	Number of vehicles deployed	Number of warheads per delivery vehicle	Total delivery capability (number of warheads)	Total yield per delivery vehicle (Mt)	Total delivery capability (Mt)
MIRVed vehicles					
SS-17	200	4	800	2	400
SS-18	308	10	3 080	5	1 540
SS-19	450	6	2 700	3	1 350
SS-N-18[a]	176	7	1 232	1.4	246
New MIRVed SLBM	180	14[b]	2 520[b]	2.8	504
Sub-total	1 314		10 332		4 040
Non-MIRVed vehicles					
SS-11 (MRV)	60	3	180	0.6	36
New ICBM	300	1	300		[d]
SS-N-6 (MRV)[a]	352	3	1 056	0.6	211
SS-N-8[a]	268	1	268	1	268
Sub-total	980		1 804		515
TOTAL	**2 294**		**12 136[c]**		**4 555–9 055[d]**

[a] SLBM.
[b] Maximum allowed.
[c] Of these, 10 484 are independently targetable warheads (6 112 on ICBMs and 4 372 on SLBMs).
[d] If the new ICBM has a 15 megaton warhead the total megatonnage will be 8 641.

The numbers of nuclear weapons that will probably be carried by Soviet and American strategic nuclear weapon systems are shown in Tables 4 and 5.

NEW TACTICAL NUCLEAR WEAPONS

Many of the 7000 or so tactical nuclear weapons in NATO countries in Western Europe were put there during the late 1950s and early 1960s. Since nuclear weapons have a lifetime of about 20 years, these are about due for replacement. In the meantime, new types of nuclear weapons have been developed and the plan is to replace the old nuclear weapons with some of these new types.

Among the new types of nuclear weapons planned for NATO are Pershing II missiles and ground-launched cruise missiles. These weapons are so accurate as to be perceived as nuclear fighting weapons.

The SS-20

Although less accurate than the American weapons, the Soviet SS-20 intermediate-range ballistic missile is accurate enough,
10

or will soon be made so, to be regarded as a nuclear-war fighting weapon, given the large explosive yield of its warhead.

The Soviet SS-20, a two-stage mobile missile, was first deployed in 1977. Between 250–300 were deployed in mid-1982, about 60 percent targeted on Western Europe and the rest targeted on China (3). The missile carries three MIRVs. With these warheads its range is said to be about 5000 km.

The yield of each SS-20 warhead is estimated by Western sources to be between 150 and 500 kilotons and the accuracy (CEP) is said to be about 400 meters (1320 feet).

The Pershing II Missile

The Pershing II missile is planned to replace the Pershing I missile, first deployed in 1962. Pershing II will use the same rocket components as Pershing I. But there the similarity ends. Pershing II will be provided with a formidable new guidance system called RADAG. In the terminal phase of the trajectory, when the warhead is getting close to the target, a video radar scans the target area and the image is compared with a reference image stored in the computer carried by the warhead before the missile is launched. The computer operates aerodynamic vanes which guide the warhead on to the target with accuracy unprecedented for a ballistic missile with a range of about 1700 kilometers (1063 miles). The accuracy (CEP) of Pershing II is about 45 meters (147 feet). Pershing II has double the range of Pershing 1 (750 kilometers/469 miles) because it has new rocket motors and uses a new highly efficient solid fuel. The missile is the only NATO ballistic missile able to penetrate a significant distance into the USSR—it could, for example, reach Moscow from the Federal Republic of Germany.

The Ground-launched Cruise Missile (GLCM)

NATO also decided to deploy in Europe 464 GLCMs. The GLCM will carry a lightweight 200-kt nuclear warhead. These missiles are not only very accurate, with CEPs of about 40 m (130 feet), but are relatively invulnerable, although flying at sub-sonic speeds, because of their very small radar cross-section.

The replacement of existing tactical nuclear weapons with new types is likely to reduce somewhat the total number deployed, but the reduction is unlikely to be very significant. Over the next few years the number deployed in NATO countries in Western Europe may, for example, decrease from about 7000 to about 6000. A similar reduction may occur on the Warsaw Pact side.

The Sea-launched Cruise Missiles

The Reagan Administration also plans to deploy modern nuclear-armed Tomahawk cruise missiles on attack submarines. These missiles are the same as those scheduled for deployment on land (ground-launched cruise missiles). Tomahawks will be mounted in launchers attached externally

to the pressure hulls of the submarines. Each boat will carry 12 cruise missiles.

The US Navy plans to procure 1720 Tomahawks between Fiscal Year 1983 and Fiscal Year 1987. Some of these missiles will be deployed on surface ships. About half of those deployed will be for attacking land targets and the rest for attacking enemy ships.

Because cruise missiles will be deployed in a variety of weapon systems—tactical and strategic—and may be equipped with conventional and nuclear warheads they will be exceedingly difficult, if not impossible, to verify. Their deployment will therefore greatly complicate the negotiations of future strategic arms control treaties.

Types of Nuclear Weapons

The basic nuclear weapon is the fission bomb, or A-bomb as it was first called. A fission chain reaction is used to produce an incredible amount of energy in a very short time—roughly a millionth of a second—and therefore a very powerful explosion.

The fission occurs in a heavy material, uranium or plutonium. The atomic bombs built so far have used the isotopes uranium-235 or plutonium-239 as the fissile material (1). A fission occurs when a neutron enters the nucleus of an atom of one of these materials, which then breaks up or fissions. When a fission occurs a large amount of energy is released, the original nucleus is split into two radioactive nuclei (the fission products), and two or three neutrons are released. These neutrons can be used to produce a self-sustaining chain reaction. A chain reaction will take place if at least one of the neutrons released in each fission produces the fission of another heavy nucleus.

There exists a critical mass for uranium-235 and plutonium-239—the smallest amount of the material in which a self-sustaining chain reaction (and hence a nuclear explosion) will take

11

place. The critical mass depends on the nuclear properties of the material used for the fission (whether, for example, it is uranium-235 or plutonium-239); the density of the material (the higher the density the shorter the average distance travelled by a neutron before causing another fission and therefore the smaller the critical mass); the purity of the material (if materials other than fissile ones are present some neutrons may be captured by their nuclei instead of causing fission); and the physical surrounding of the material (if the material is surrounded by a medium like natural uranium, which reflects neutrons back into the material, some of the neutrons may be used for fission which would otherwise have been lost, thus reducing the critical mass).

The critical mass of, for example, a bare sphere of pure plutonium-239 metal in its densest phase, would be about 10 kilograms (22 pounds), about the size of a small grapefruit. If the sphere were surrounded by a natural uranium neutron reflector of about 10 centimeters (4 inches), the critical mass would be reduced to about 4.4 kilograms (10 pounds), a sphere of radius of about 3.6 centimeters (1.4 inches), about the size of an orange. Using a technique called implosion, in which conventional explosive lenses are used to compress a mass slightly less than critical to a mass which is slightly greater than critical, a nuclear explosion could be achieved with less than 2 kilograms (4.4 pounds) of plutonium-239. A 2-kilogram sphere of plutonium-239 would have a radius of about 2.8 centimeters (1.1 inches), smaller than a tennis ball.

In the atomic bomb which destroyed Nagasaki, about 8 kilograms (18 pounds) of plutonium (which contained more than 90 percent plutonium-239) were used, in the form of two gold-clad hemispheres of plutonium metal. The plutonium was surrounded by a tamper which had two functions. First, to reflect back into the plutonium some of the neutrons which escaped through the surface of the core, allowing some reduction in the mass of plutonium needed for a nuclear explosion. Second, and more importantly, because the tamper was made of heavy material, its inertia helped hold together the plutonium during the explosion to prevent the disintegration of the fissile material and obtain greater efficiency.

In a nuclear explosion exceedingly high temperatures (hundreds of millions of degrees Celsius) and exceedingly high pressures (millions of atmospheres) build up very rapidly (in about one-half of a millionth of a second, corresponding to the time taken for about 55 generations of fission). The mass of the fissile material therefore expands at very high speeds, initially at a speed of about 1000 kilometers (625 miles) a second. In much less than a millionth of a second the size and density of the fissile material have changed so that the mass becomes less than critical and the chain reaction stops. The designer of a nuclear weapon must aim at keeping the fissile material together, against its tendency to fly apart, long enough to get sufficient generations of fission to produce an explosion strong enough for his purpose.

In the Nagasaki bomb the plutonium core was surrounded by chemical explosives arranged as explosive lenses focussed on the center of the plutonium sphere. When these lenses were detonated the sphere was compressed uniformly by the implosion. The compression increased the density of the plutonium so that the subcritical mass was made super-critical. The complete detonation of 1 kilogram (2.2 pounds) of plutonium would produce an explosion equivalent to that of 18 kilotons of TNT. The 8 kilograms of plutonium in the Nagasaki bomb produced an explosion equivalent to that of 22 kilotons of TNT. Its efficiency was therefore only about 15 percent.

The final component in the Nagasaki bomb was the "initiator" used to initiate the fission reaction in the plutonium at precisely the right moment during the explosion of the chemical explosive lenses. The initiator consisted of a hollow sphere placed at the center of the plutonium core. Inside the initiator were some polonium and beryllium, two elements which produce neutrons when intimately mixed. The two substances were placed separately on opposite sides of the initiator. At the moment of implosion the initiator was crushed, the beryllium and polonium mixed and a pulse of neutrons given off when the plutonium was super-critical. The timing of the detonation of the explosive lenses is crucial for the efficient operation of an implosion bomb. Microsecond precision is essential.

A major problem in designing this type of nuclear weapon for maximum efficiency is to prevent the chain reaction from being started before the maximum achievable super-criticality is reached, an eventuality called pre-initiation. If this occurs it will reduce the explosive power, or the yield, of the explosion and will also make the yield uncertain.

12

Pre-initiation is most likely to be caused by a neutron from spontaneous fission—fission that occurs without the stimulus of an external neutron—in the fissionable material. In 8 kilograms (18 pounds) of plutonium-239 the average time between spontaneous fissions is only about three millionths of a second. The assembly of a plutonium bomb must therefore be rapid and implosion is necessary. In uranium, however, the average time between spontaneous fissions is much greater and so a gun method can be used to assemble critical mass in a nuclear weapon.

In the Hiroshima bomb, for example, a sub-critical mass of uranium-235 was fired down a "cannon barrel" into another sub-critical mass of uranium-235 placed in front of the "muzzle". When the two masses came together they formed a super-critical mass which exploded.

About 60 kilograms (132 pounds) of uranium-235 were used in the Hiroshima bomb, of which about 700 grams (1.5 pounds) were fissioned. The average time between spontaneous fissions was about one-fiftieth of a second—adequate for the gun technique. The yield of the Hiroshima bomb was equivalent to that of about 12.5 kilotons of TNT.

Although designs based on the Hiroshima and Nagasaki bombs might still be used by countries beginning a nuclear weapon program, they are crude compared with current American and Soviet nuclear warheads. The Nagasaki bomb, for example, was about 3 meters (10 feet) long, 1.5 meters (5 feet) wide, and weighed about 4500 kilograms (9900 pounds). A modern American warhead weighs about 100 kilograms (220 pounds) and has an explosive power of about 350 kilotons of TNT. Yield-to-weight ratios, the standard measure of the efficiency of a bomb, have gone from about 5000 for the Nagasaki bomb to about 3.5 million for today's best nuclear warheads. The latter figure is, in fact, close to the theoretical maximum attainable. Another indication of the sophistication of modern nuclear warheads is that they are used in 8-inch artillery shells.

H-bombs

The next significant advance in warhead design after the Nagasaki bomb was the "boosted weapon," in which fusion was used to obtain nuclear explosions with yields in the 100 000 ton (100-kiloton) range. The maximum explosive yield achievable by pure fission weapons is lim-

ited to a few tens of kilotons by the critical mass.

The fusion process is the opposite of fission. In fusion, light nuclei are formed (fused) into heavier ones. In nuclear weapons the heavier isotopes of hydrogen—deuterium and tritium—are fused together to form helium. The reaction produces energy and is accompanied by the emission of neutrons. There is no critical mass for the fusion process and therefore in principle there is no limit to the explosive yield of fusion weapons—or H-bombs as they are often called.

Fission is relatively easy to start—one neutron will initiate a chain reaction in a critical mass of fissile material. But fusion is possible only if the component nuclei are given a high enough energy to overcome the repulsive electric force between them due to their like positive charges. In the H-bomb this energy is provided by raising the temperature of the fusion material. Hence H-bombs are also called thermonuclear weapons.

In order to make the deuterium-tritium fusion reaction work, a temperature of a hundred million degrees Centigrade or so is required. This can be provided only by an A-bomb in which such a temperature is achieved at the moment of the explosion. An H-bomb, therefore, consists of a fission stage, which is an A-bomb acting as a trigger, and a fusion stage, in which hydrogen is ignited by the heat produced by the trigger.

The energy released from an H-bomb comes from the fission trigger and the fusion material. But if the fusion weapon is surrounded by a shell of uranium-238 the high-energy neutrons produced in the fusion process will cause additional fissions in the uranium shell. This technique can be used to enhance considerably the explosive power of an H-bomb. Such a weapon is called a fission-fusion-fission device. On average, about half of the yield from a typical thermonuclear weapon will come from fission and the other half from fusion.

H-bombs are much more difficult to design than A-bombs. The problem is to prevent the A-bomb trigger from blowing the whole weapon apart before enough fusion material has been ignited to give the required explosive yield. Sufficient energy has to be delivered to the fusion material to start the thermonuclear reaction in a time much shorter than the time it takes for the explosion to occur. This requires that the energy be delivered with a speed approaching the speed of light (4). It is this requirement that makes the design of an H-bomb much more sophisticated than that of an A-bomb.

13

The first use of fusion was in a boosted weapon in which some fusion material was placed at the center of the plutonium sphere in an ordinary atomic bomb. The fusion energy produced by the explosion of the A-bomb increased the yield of the weapon several fold. But in a proper H-bomb in which, by an appropriate design, a much larger amount of material is made to undergo fusion, very large yields have been obtained. For example, the Soviet Union exploded an H-bomb in 1962 with a yield equal to that of 58 million tons of TNT (58 megatons), equivalent to about 3000 Nagasaki bombs. Even higher yields could be obtained. Such huge bombs, however, make little sense. The largest city would be completely devastated by an H-bomb of 10 megatons or so.

References and Notes

1. The total amount of highly-enriched uranium produced for nuclear weapons since World War II is roughly 1500 tons. To get this material about 2.5 million tons of natural uranium have been mined and processed. In addition, about 150 tons of plutonium have been produced worldwide for nuclear weapons.

2. The data in this chapter are drawn mainly from Stockholm International Peace Research Institute publications and data files. See in particular *World Armaments and Disarmament: SIPRI Yearbook 1982*, Taylor and Francis, London, and *Tactical Nuclear Weapons: Perspectives for Europe*, Taylor and Francis, London, 1978, both available from SIPRI, Bergshamra, S 17173, Solna, Sweden.

3. The Soviet Union has announced that no further SS-20 missiles will be deployed west of the Urals for the time being.

4. Professor J Rotblat has described the technique used thus: "The solution to the problem lies in the fact that at the very high temperature of the fission trigger most of the energy is emitted in the form of X-rays. These X-rays, travelling with the speed of light, radiate out from the center and on reaching the tamper (sorrounding the fusion material) are absorbed in it and then immediately re-emitted in the form of softer X-rays. By an appropriate configuration of the trigger and the fusion material it is possible to ensure that the X-rays reach the latter almost instantaneously. If the fusion material is subdivided into small portions, each surrounded with a thin absorber made of a heavy metal, the bulk of the fusion material will simultaneously receive enough energy to start the thermonuclear reaction before the explosion disperses the whole assembly".

TWO

THE EFFECTS OF NUCLEAR WEAPONS

FRANK BARNABY AND JOSEPH ROTBLAT

At least 40 percent of the population of Hiroshima and 26 percent of the population of Nagasaki were killed in the nuclear attacks on those two cities. Modern nuclear weapons are much more powerful, and the casualties today would be far higher.

It might be appropriate to begin a description of the effects of nuclear weapons by describing what we know from their use on Hiroshima and Nagasaki. The bomb which obliterated Hiroshima on August 6, 1945 was dropped at 8.15 AM and exploded 510 meters above the center of the city, with an explosive power said to be about 12 000 tons (12 kilotons) of TNT, although recent studies suggest a somewhat higher figure. This explosion was several thousand times more powerful than that produced by any previous bomb. Such is the efficiency of even a primitive nuclear weapon.

"Little Boy" was a crude device—nearly 3 meters long and weighing over 4000 kilograms. A modern designer could produce a nuclear weapon having a yield of a hundred kilotons or more with, say, 20 kilograms of uranium-235, one-third of the amount used in the Hiroshima bomb. And if he used it to trigger a hydrogen bomb, he could produce an explosion a thousand times more powerful still.

The atomic bomb used to destroy Nagasaki exploded 500 meters above the city at 11.02 AM on August 9, 1945. It is thought to have had a yield of some 22 kilotons. "Fat Man" was about 3 meters long, 1.5 meters wide, and weighed 4500 kilograms.

THE NUMBER OF PEOPLE KILLED

Hiroshima is built on a plateau: the city was damaged symmetrically in all directions. The damage to Nagasaki, built on mountainous ground, varied considerably according to direction. But the death rate at given distances from the hypocenter (the point on the ground directly below the center of the explosion) was about the same in both cities.

Almost all of those within 500 meters of the hypocenters when the bombs exploded were killed; about 60 percent of those within 2 kilometers died. About three-quarters of the deaths occurred in the first 24 hours, but people were dying from the acute effects of the bombs for weeks, months and even years afterwards.

16

The number of people in Hiroshima at the time of the bomb is not clear. Tens of thousands of troops and Korean forced laborers were there, for example, but the exact number is unknown. The best estimate is that about 350 000 people were in the city.

By the end of 1945, 140 000 of these people—or approximately 40 percent of the population—had died, but even this high figure is almost certainly an underestimate. Many thousands of people were found to be unaccounted for in the 1950 National Census. The number that initially survived but died in the next few years is unknown. And so is the fate of the very large number of people who came into Hiroshima within the first week of the bombing.

About 280 000 people are thought to have been in Nagasaki when the bomb exploded. According to the best estimate, some 74 000 or 26 percent died by the end of 1945. There were many Koreans in Nagasaki too, and the exact number of them killed by the bomb is not known. The number of Nagasaki A-bomb victims who died after the end of 1945 is also not known.

The number of people killed by "Little Boy" and "Fat Man" probably greatly exceeds a quarter of a million, a staggeringly high death rate, but its exact value may never be known.

BLAST

Those killed immediately were mainly either crushed or burned to death. The combined effect of thermal radiation and blast was particularly lethal. Many of those burned to death in collapsed buildings would have escaped with only injuries had there been no fires. But as it happened, an area of 13 square kilometers in Hiroshima and 7 square kilometers in Nagasaki was reduced to rubble by blast and then to ashes by fire. The difference in area was due mainly to the different terrain.

Atomic bomb damage Hiroshima 26 October 1945.   Photo: National Archives, Washington, D.C.

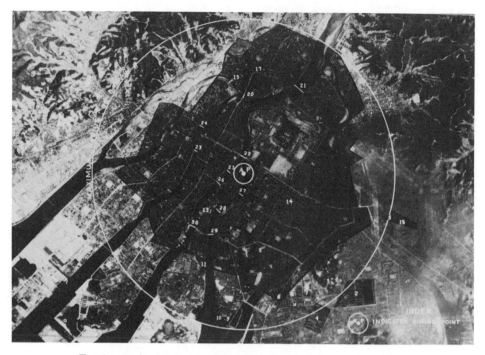

Total area devastated by the atomic bomb strike on Hiroshima.
Photo: National Archives, Washington, D.C.

The "Little Boy" which fell on Hiroshima.   *Photo: Popperfoto, London*

About one-half of the energy generated by the atomic bomb was given off as blast. The front of the blast moved as a shock wave—a wall of high-pressure air, spreading outward at a speed equal to or greater than that of sound. It travelled about 11 kilometers in 30 seconds.

The shock wave was followed by a hurricane-force wind. But as the shock wave travelled outward, the pressure behind it fell below atmospheric pressure and eventually the air flowed in the inward direction. Thus, a supersonic shock wave was followed by an exceedingly powerful wind and then, after a deathly instant of stillness, a violent wind blew in the opposite direction.

At Hiroshima all buildings within 2 kilometers of the hypocenter were damaged beyond repair by a blast of up to 3 tons (35 kPa) per square meter. Casualties due to blast were particularly severe within about 1.3 kilometers of the hypocenter, where the blast reached a pressure of 7 tons per square meter.

FIRE

About one-third of the total energy generated by the bombs was given off as heat. The fireballs produced by the nuclear explosions instantly reached temperatures of the same magnitude as that of the sun (several million degrees Centigrade). The fireballs grew to their maximum diameters of about 400 meters within a second, when the surface temperatures were about 5000°C.

At a distance of 500 meters from the hypocenter in Hiroshima the thermal radiation received in the first three seconds was about 600 times as searing as the sun on a bright day. Even at a distance of 3 kilometers from the hypocenter, the heat in the first 3 seconds was about 40 times more than that from the sun. The heat at Nagasaki was even more intense, twice that at Hiroshima.

The heat was sufficient to burn exposed human skin at distances as great as 4 kilo-

meters from the hypocenters. Many people caught in the open within about 1.2 kilometers from the hypocenters were burned to death; a lot were simply vaporized.

Violent firestorms raged in Hiroshima and Nagasaki. The one in Hiroshima was particularly severe, lasting for half a day. It completely consumed every combustible object within two kilometers from the hypocenter.

Moisture condensed around rising hot ash particles as they came into contact with cold air. Heavy rain consequently fell in regions of the two cities. But not clean rain. The liquid which fell was highly radioactive and oily, known to this day as "black rain".

Hiroshima had about 76 000 buildings before the bomb was dropped. Two-thirds were destroyed by fire. A quarter of Nagasaki's 51 000 buildings were totally destroyed, and many more seriously damaged. In the midst of such extensive damage, effective fire-fighting was impossible. In any case, there was no water.

IONIZING RADIATION

About 15 percent of the energy generated by the bombs was given off as ionizing radiation, about a third of which, known as initial radiation, was emitted within 1 minute of the explosion. The remainder, called residual radiation, was emitted from radioactive materials (fallout). The initial radiation dose at the hypocenter in Hiroshima was of the order of 100 000 rads. In Nagasaki the dose at this distance was several times greater.

One-half of a large number of people receiving a whole-body radiation dose of about 450 rads (air dose) will die within a month or so. Virtually all of those exposed to whole-body radiation of 700 rads or more will die quickly. People exposed in the open within about a kilometer of the Hiroshima and Nagasaki bombs are thought to have received doses exceeding 1000 rads.

19

Generally those exposed to large doses of radiation rapidly became incapacitated, and suffered from nausea and vomiting, the first symptoms of radiation sickness. They later vomited blood, developed a high fever, had severe diarrhea and much bleeding from the bowels. They usually died within about 10 days. Smaller doses of radiation produced a wide variety of symptoms, including nausea, vomiting, diarrhea, bleeding from the bowels, gums, nose and genitals. There was often a total loss of hair, fever, and a feeling of great weakness. Resistance to infection was markedly decreased. Septicemia (blood-poisoning) was a frequent cause of death.

LATE EFFECTS

Most of the survivors of Hiroshima and Nagasaki still alive at the end of 1945 appeared to be reasonably healthy. But later a variety of illnesses—including eye diseases, blood disorders, malignant tumors and psychoneurological disturbances—began to appear.

These long-term effects are the unique consequences of the atomic bombs in Hiroshima and Nagasaki, where there was little local fallout.

Leukemia among survivors increased during the first two decades, when the mortality rate in the high dose group reached a level about 30 times higher than that of non-exposed Japanese. Thirty-seven years later, it still has not fallen to the national average. The incidence of other malignant tumors—thyroid, breast, lung, bone, alimentary tract and so on —has been higher among survivors than among the non-exposed, and is still growing.

Children born to women pregnant when the bombs exploded show an increase in some congenital malformation, particularly microcephaly (abnormally small size of the head), resulting in mental retardation. We know from experiments with animals and other evidence that genetic damage is undoubtedly caused by radiation. But, sur-

20

prisingly, there is an apparent absence of genetic damage in survivors exposed to radiation from the atomic bombs dropped on Hiroshima and Nagasaki.

A number of reasons have been suggested by experts for this absence. Among them:

- the number of survivors involved, and the radiation doses received by them, are such that too few of the children examined showed genetic effects (even though these may have been present) to be statistically significant;
- the research methods used to search for effects are insufficiently sensitive;
- the mutations induced will show up only in second, or even later, generations; and
- there may have been a large number of spontaneous abortions.

The absence of observed genetic abnormalities certainly does not mean that radiation does not produce genetic damage.

THE EFFECTS OF BLAST, HEAT AND RADIATION

Because nuclear weapons have so many yields, sizes, and designs, the proportion of the energy given off as blast, heat, and radiation can differ considerably. The energy distribution would also depend on where the nuclear weapon was exploded— under water, on the surface of the earth, or in the atmosphere. For example, an explosion on or near the ground would produce much radioactive fallout so that the radiation effect would be enhanced.

But, as a rule of thumb, we can say that roughly half of the energy given off by a typical nuclear weapon would be blast, about a third heat, and the remainder ionizing radiation. Blast would cause the greatest number of immediate casualties and the greatest physical damage if the nuclear weapon were exploded over a population center.

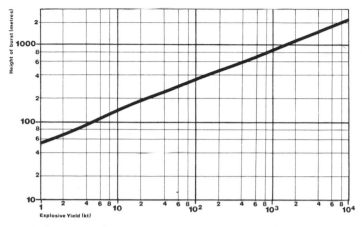

Figure 1. Maximum height of nuclear burst for occurrence of appreciable local fallout.

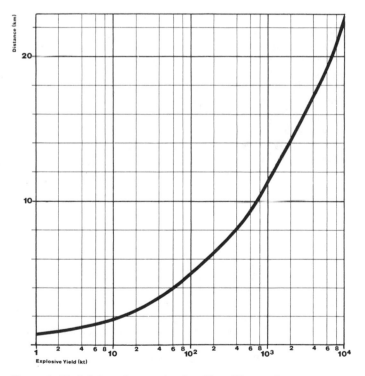

Figure. 2. Slant distance from nuclear burst for a 50 percent probability of third degree burns.

21

Thermal Radiation

Any body at an elevated temperature emits electromagnetic radiation; at the high temperature of a nuclear explosion the radiation lies in the soft X-ray region of the electromagnetic spectrum. About 75 percent of the total energy released may be carried by these X-rays. At this stage there is relatively little radiation in the visible region. However, soft X-rays are easily absorbed in the surrounding air. For explosions at not too high altitudes the absorption would be practically complete within a few meters. The air, being at a lower temperature, will re-radiate energy of longer wave-length, and thus there will be a gradual transition from X-ray to the emission of ultraviolet, visible and infrared radiation. This process will lead to the formation of a luminous mass of air, the so-called fire-ball. Immediately after its formation, the fire-ball begins to grow and to rise in the air; as its mass increases, its temperature drops sufficiently for the fire-ball not to emit visible radiation any longer. The size of the fire-ball depends on the yield of the weapon. For a one-megaton bomb the radius of the fire-ball at maximum brilliance is about 1200 meters.

For aerial explosions the altitude of the burst and the size of the fire-ball have an important bearing on the magnitude of the local fallout. If the fire-ball touches the ground, then the soil and other materials are vaporized and taken up with the fire-ball. The strong after-winds cause huge quantities of dirt and debris to be sucked up. They mix with the radioactive fragments of the bomb and form particles of various sizes which move upwards as well as spreading out. Later they begin to fall to the ground, at rates and distances which depend on the size of the particles and the velocity of the wind. This deposition of radioactivity constitutes the local fallout. On the other hand, if the bomb was exploded at such a height that the fire-ball never touches the ground there will be much less local fallout and perhaps none at

all. The maximum height of the burst for which there would be appreciable local fallout is plotted in Figure 1 as a function of the yield of the bomb; for every ten-fold increase in yield, the altitude of the burst must increase by a factor of 2.5 before appreciable local fallout ceases to be produced; but small amounts of fallout may occur even with bursts at greater heights.

The thermal radiation from the fire-ball can cause fatal or severe burns and start fires over a large area; its range depends on the yield of the bomb and, to a lesser extent, on the atmospheric conditions. With fairly good visibility the heat wave can cause casualties at distances much greater than those produced by the blast and the initial ionizing radiations, although well within the area of local fallout. Figure 2 shows the distance at which there is a 50 percent probability of lethal third degree burns being suffered by persons caught in the path of the thermal radiation, as a function of the explosive yield. The data apply to explosions at low altitudes and a visibility of about 20 kilometers. Thus, for 10 kilotons the distance is about 2 kilometers, while for 10 megatons it is more than 22 kilometers. The 50 percent chance of survival assumes that the burn is the only injury, and that the person will receive medical treatment. Under war conditions this is unlikely to be the case; if the person was also exposed to a significant but non-lethal dose of radiation, the chances of survival will be much less than 50 percent.

Blast Wave

If the fire-ball touches the ground a crater is formed in which everything is vaporized. The size and depth of the crater depend on the yield of the bomb, on the height above ground of the burst, and on the nature of the soil.

Crater formation will occur when the height of the burst is less than about one tenth of the maximum radius of the fire-ball. For a surface explosion the diameter of the crater in dry soil, or dry soft rock, is 45 meters for a 1-kiloton yield, and it increases by a factor of 2 for every ten-fold increase in yield.

At much larger distances casualties and deaths result from direct and indirect injuries produced by the shock wave. The human body can withstand quite high pressures, double the normal atmospheric pressure, but most blast deaths occur from indirect effects, from the collapse of buildings, from flying objects or from falling debris. It is generally assumed that an overpressure (excess of pressure above atmospheric) of 35 kPa (five pounds per square inch) is the relevant value for calculating the "lethal area" for blast effects. This is defined as the circular area in which the number of survivors is equal to the number of persons killed by the blast outside the area. For a given explosive yield there is an optimum height of burst for which a given overpressure will extend furthest from ground zero. For example, for a 1-kiloton bomb, the greatest extension of a 35 kPa overpressure will occur if the detonation is at a height of about 320 meters. For other yields, the optimum height goes up as the cube root of the yield.

weapon. For example, for a 1-megaton bomb the lethal distance is nearly 5 kilometers.

INITIAL RADIATION

Neutrons

Neutrons are emitted by both fission and fusion reactions. Therefore the total number of neutrons produced at the instant of the explosions is proportional to the total energy released, whether it came from a fission, fusion or a fission-fusion-fission bomb. However, in any of these types of bombs the interactions between the neutrons and the materials of the bomb itself considerably modify both the number and the energy distribution of the neutrons which are emitted after the explosion. Thus the radiation hazards due to neutrons vary widely, even for bombs from the same family.

For example, the two fission bombs detonated over the Japanese cities were thought to differ greatly in their neutron emission. In the Nagasaki bomb, which was detonated by the implosion technique, large amounts of hydrogenous material surrounded the plutonium, mainly in the

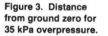

Figure 3. Distance from ground zero for 35 kPa overpressure.

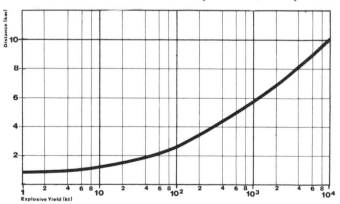

Figure 3 shows the distance at which a peak overpressure of 35 kPa will occur, for bombs exploded at a height of 300 meters, as a function of the explosive yield of the

plastic explosive charges which initiated the implosion. Hydrogen is very effective in slowing down fast neutrons and in absorbing slow neutrons, so that there would be hardly any neutron component in the radiation emitted from the Nagasaki bomb; the radiation exposure would therefore be due to gamma-rays. By contrast in Hiroshima, where the gun assembly was used, the iron of the gun attenuated the gamma-rays more than the neutrons; consequently the latter were believed to have contributed a significant proportion (about 20 percent) to the dose received by the population. Due to the high radio-biological efficiency of the neutrons the long-term radiation effects among the Hiroshima survivors were believed to have been caused by neutrons more than by gamma-rays. However, a recent analysis of the dosimetry suggests that even in Hiroshima neutrons contributed very little to the dose.

Fission and fusion bombs differ in the initial number of neutrons produced per unit of explosive power, as well as in their energy distribution. For a given explosive yield, the number of neutrons produced in fusion reactions is about ten times greater than in fission reactions.

However, as already indicated, immediately after their production and before the bomb breaks up, the neutrons make numerous collisions with the atomic nuclei of the materials of the bomb; in these collisions they lose energy and some neutrons are captured by nuclei with the emission of gamma-rays. The result is that with both fission and fusion bombs, we end up with a continuous spectrum of neutron energies, although still with a larger component of high energy neutrons in fusion than in fission bombs.

Depending on the amount and type of material used in the assembly of the bomb, the total number of neutrons actually emitted after the explosion may vary by several orders of magnitude for bombs of the same explosive yield. The neutron emission can be deliberately made much smaller or much larger, depending on the decision about the type of damage it is intended to inflict. In particular, bombs can be de-

signed such that most of the damage is due to neutrons (the neutron bomb).

When the neutrons reach the human body they are partially absorbed, and in this way deliver a dose of radiation. For the same number of neutrons the dose delivered varies with the energy of the neutrons; therefore to determine the dose at a given distance calculations have to be made which take into account the spectrum of energies as it varies with distance. The result of such calculations is presented in Figure 4, which gives the neutron dose (in tissue at the surface of the body) as a function of the slant distance for a 1-kiloton bomb. The slant distance takes into account the height of the burst above ground *ie* the distance measured obliquely from the point of the explosion in the air to a given point on the ground. The curves of Figure 4 apply to an air burst at a height greater than 100 meters. For a surface

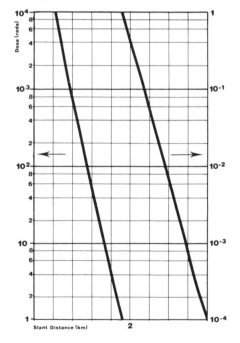

Figure 4. Neutron dose (surface tissue) per kiloton as a function of slant distance.

burst the dose values should be multiplied by 0.5 (because half of the neutrons are absorbed in the ground); for intermediate heights a proportionate factor between 0.5 and 1 should be applied.

Since for a given type of bomb assembly the number of neutrons is proportional to the explosive yield, the neutron dose for a bomb of any other yield can be read off these curves simply by multiplying the explosive yield. Thus a 1 megaton thermonuclear bomb would deliver, at a slant distance of 1 kilometer, a dose of 200 000 rads; at 2 kilometers the dose would be 700 rads.

These two figures illustrate the rapid decrease of the neutron dose with distance due to the exponential absorption; the casualties from neutron radiation will decrease with distance much more quickly than casualties due to mechanical or thermal effects.

Gamma-rays

The gamma-rays emitted during the first minute after the explosion originate from several nuclear processes, but in a fission bomb the initial gamma-ray dose arises mainly from radiative capture. Neutrons colliding with the nuclei of nitrogen atoms in the air undergo capture, resulting in the release of energy in the form of gamma-rays. For large thermonuclear weapons, the predominant source of initial gamma radiation is fission-product decay. (Most of the fission products emit gamma rays during their radioactive decay.) This is because of the hydrodynamic enhancement of the gamma radiation, and arises from the continuous time of emission of the gamma-rays from the fission products. The gamma-rays from the other sources are all emitted before the shock wave and travel a long distance ahead of it, in air which is still at normal density. However, the gamma-rays from the fission products which are emitted later do not reach distant points until after the shock wave has passed. Following the shock wave there is a period when the air density is low; gamma-

rays travelling through it are much less attenuated, and therefore greater intensities can be reached at longer distances. Had these gamma-rays travelled through air of normal density, a weapon of a much higher explosion yield would have been required to produce the same dose at a given distance. For this reason, the hydrodynamic enhancement is usually expressed in terms of an increase in the effective yield of the weapon. Table 1 shows the calculated "effective" yields of thermonuclear weapons for three actual yields at different distances from the explosion. As is seen, at large distances, the effective yield of a weapon can be several thousand times higher than the actual yield, so far as the exposure to gamma-rays is concerned.

Table 1. "Effective" yield of nuclear bombs (low air bursts) through hydrodynamic enhancement of gamma-rays.

Actual yield (Mt)	Distance (km)	Effective yield (Mt)
0.1	1	0.25
	2	0.35
	3	0.40
1	2	20
	3	30
	4	40
10	3	7 000
	4	20 000
	5	40 000

The attenuation of gamma-rays in passing through the air has the same character as that for neutrons, namely an exponential fall-off in intensity superimposed on an inverse square reduction, but the rate of absorption is less than for neutrons. Figure 5 gives the gamma-ray dose, as a function of slant distance for a fission bomb of 1-kiloton yield. Due to the hydrodynamic enhancement factor, which increases in importance with yield and distance, one cannot use the curves of this figure to calculate the gamma-ray doses from weapons of higher yield, and separate curves have to be drawn for each yield.

25

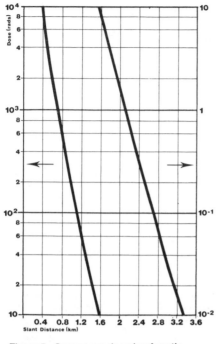

Figure 5. Gamma-ray dose (surface tissue) from a 1 kiloton bomb as a function of slant distance.

Figure 6 shows several such curves for fission bombs (Figure 6a), and thermonuclear bombs (Figure 6b). The data apply to bursts at a height not less than 100 meters. For surface bursts the doses have to be multiplied by a factor which varies from 2/3 (for a 1-kiloton bomb) to 3 (for a 20 megaton weapon).

Combined doses from neutrons and gamma-rays

Both components of the initial radiation, neutrons and gamma-rays, contribute to the total dose which a person may receive. Due to their different rates of attenuation in air, the relative contributions to the tissue dose, measured at the surface of the body, vary with distance from the explosion. At short distances, the neutron dose is greater than that from the gamma-rays; with increasing distance the gamma-ray dose progressively becomes the dominant

26

contributor. For weapons of high yield, and at long distances, when the hydrodynamic enhancement factor is large, the dose is almost entirely due to gamma-rays.

Neglecting the difference in biological effectiveness between neutrons and gamma-rays, the data in Figures 4 and 6 can be used to calculate the distance at which a given total dose would be received from a weapon of a given yield. Figure 7 shows such a curve for a total tissue-surface dose of 450 rads; this is the dose which would be lethal to 50 percent of healthy adults exposed. Under war conditions it is likely that the majority of persons exposed to such a dose would die from the acute effects of radiation. In this sense, the curve on Figure 7 can be considered as defining the lethal distance for acute radiation effects.

A comparison of this curve with those of Figures 2 and 3, which give the lethal distances for thermal and blast effects, shows that for radiation the lethal distances increase much more slowly with explosive yield. The reason for this is the exponential character of the absorption of neutrons and gamma-rays, which causes a much faster reduction with distance of the radiation effect than for thermal or mechanical damage. As a result of this, for large bombs, when the heat and blast effects reach long distances, the injurious action of neutrons and gamma-rays occurs in an area already devastated by the heat or blast waves. For small bombs, the reverse holds: the lethal action of radiation covers a larger area than that affected by the other effects. This can be seen in Table 2, which gives the lethal areas for blast, heat and radiation effects, for bombs of various yields, when exploded at low heights above ground.

FALLOUT

The radioactive products of fission may be deposited on the ground at distances well beyond the range of destruction and casualties caused by the blast, heat and the initial radiation. They may reach these re-

Table 2. Areas of lethal damage from various effects (in km²).

Type of damage	Explosive yield				
	1 kt	10 kt	100 kt	1 Mt	10 Mt
Blast	1.5	4.9	17.7	71	313
Heat	1.3	11.2	74.2	391	1 583
Radiation	2.9	5.7	11.5	22	54

gions and present a radiation hazard long after the explosion. With high yield bombs, a single detonation may contaminate a huge area with radioactivity and make it uninhabitable for a long time. Fallout is therefore a major and unique effect of nuclear weapons and of particular interest to us here.

It should be noted that *all* nuclear weapons detonated in the air give rise to fallout, but where and when it occurs depends primarily on the altitude of the explosion. With explosions in the air at altitudes such that the fire-ball does not touch the ground the fission products, which are initially in gaseous form, rise with the fireball to great heights into the troposphere or stratosphere. When the temperature of the fire-ball becomes sufficiently low, the radioactive materials form particles through condensation and coagulation. These particles are very small and as a result their descent is very slow; it may take many months before they come down to the ground. By that time they have been carried by stratospheric winds round the globe. Under such conditions there is no fallout, or very little, in the vicinity of the explosion. This is the fallout referred to as "global" or "delayed" fallout.

With surface explosions, or at altitudes low enough for the fire-ball to touch the ground (Figure 1), huge quantities of earth and debris are sucked up with the fire-ball together with the fission products. As the fire-ball cools, the radioactivity condenses on the particles of the ground material; many of these are large particles and they come down by the force of gravity within a day or so, at distances not too far from the burst, some hundreds of kilometers. This

constitutes the "local" or "early" fallout. The extent and location of the early fallout depend primarily on the meteorological conditions, *eg* the velocity and direction of the wind. They also depend on precipitation conditions; the particles may come down to earth with the rain or snow, which is referred to as "rain-out" or "snow-out".

In addition to surface bursts and air bursts, sea bursts occur when submarine targets are hit by nuclear warheads. Radioactive fission products in submarine blasts would mainly be absorbed by the water, but some would escape to produce radioactive materials carried in a cloud of fog-spray which could drift in over land, adding to the exposure of the public. Submarine blasts would not add to the global or "delayed" fallout, as the materials would fall back into the water or onto local land areas.

These different types of fallout create radiation hazards to man of entirely different magnitudes: a large hazard to a relatively small number of people from local fallout, and a much smaller hazard to much larger populations in remote countries, from the global fallout.

In addition to the fission products, the fallout contains the uranium and plutonium which did not undergo fission, and the tritium from fusion reactions. Radioactivity induced by neutrons in the weapon materials also contributes to the content of the fallout. Moreover, there is some residual radiation from the radioactivity induced by the neutrons on the ground, and in walls of buildings. However, the radioactivity from the fission product is by far the most important contributor to the radiation hazard.

DECAY OF EARLY FALLOUT

Fission of uranium or plutonium results in the formation of radioactive nuclides, which break up with the emission of radiation and are transformed into other nuclides, often also radioactive. Altogether some 300 different radioactive nuclides are formed in fission, each decaying exponen-

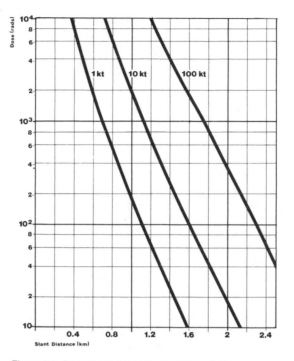

Figure 6a. Gamma-ray doses (surface tissue) as a function of slant distance for fission bombs of specified yield.

tially with time, with half-lives ranging from a fraction of a second to many millions of years. For the whole mixture of fission products the decay of activity with time is highly complex, but it has been found empirically that during the first six months after the explosion, the activity, and therefore the rate at which the radiation dose is delivered, decays approximately according to a power law such that for every sevenfold increase in time, the dose rate decreases by a factor of 10. For example, at the end of one week the dose rate is 10 times smaller than it was after one day; after seven weeks it is 100 times smaller than after one day.

Table 3 gives the average dose rates due to the gamma-rays from early fallout, at different times after an explosion. The dose rates in the table are with reference to the dose rate at one hour, at which time it

28

was assumed to be 100 rads per hour. If in any actual situation the dose rate at one hour, or at any other time, is known, then the dose rates at other times can be obtained simply by proportion.

It should be noted that the variation of dose rate with time, as given in Table 3, is valid only after the fallout is complete at a given place, and on condition that no additional material is brought into the location by another explosion, and that none is lost by weathering.

The total dose received by a person is obtained by multiplying the dose rate by the time of exposure. However, since the dose rate rapidly decreases with time, the calculation of the total dose involves an integration over the relevant values of dose rates. The result of such integration is presented in Figure 8 which gives the accumulated dose (in rads), starting from

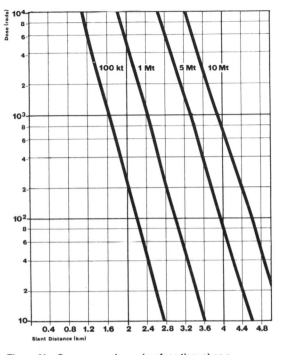

Figure 6b. Gamma-ray doses (surface tissue) as a function of slant distance for thermonuclear bombs of specified yield.

one minute after the explosion up to the given time, assuming that the dose rate at one hour is 100 rads per hour. For other values of the dose rate, the values in Figure 8 have to be multiplied by the actual dose rate at one hour.

Figure 8 also allows the calculation of the total dose received by a person who enters a given fallout locality at a certain time after the explosion and remains in it for a certain period. This dose is given by the difference in the ordinates corresponding to the times of entry and exit.

As is seen from Figure 8, the total accumulated dose tends towards a finite limit, namely 930 rads if the dose rate at one hour is 100 rads per hour. This value, 930 rads, gives the infinity dose, that is the total dose accumulated starting from one minute after the explosion until an infinite time.

The method of dose calculation outlined above applies only to a single detonation. If the fallout is caused by several bombs, exploded at different times, the variation of dose rate with time will be quite differ-

Table 3. Dose rates from fallout at various times after an explosion.

Time (hours)	Relative dose rate (rads/hour)
1	100
2	40
4	15
6	10
12	5.0
24	2.4
36	1.6
48	1.1
72	6.2×10^{-1}
100	3.6×10^{-1}
200	1.7×10^{-1}
500	5.0×10^{-2}
1 000	2.3×10^{-2}

29

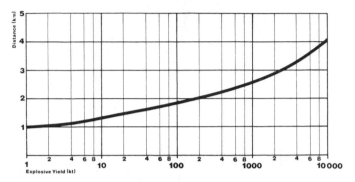

Figure 7. Distances for lethal radiation doses (neutrons plus gamma-rays).

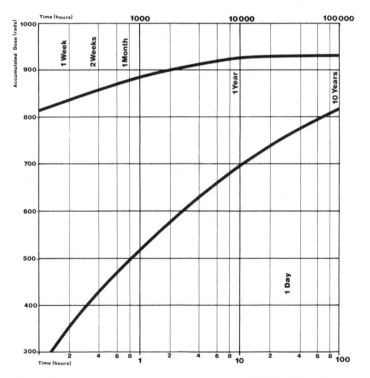

Figure 8. Accumulated dose from local fall-out as a function of time after a nuclear explosion.

ent from that given in Table 3, and a single measurement of the dose rate in that locality would not be sufficient to calculate the accumulated dose.

DISTRIBUTION OF EARLY FALLOUT

As already mentioned, if the fire-ball touches the ground, vaporized earth particles are scooped up with the fire-ball to a great height; the fission products, together with other radioactive materials, then condense on these particles and begin to descend to the ground. The particles have a variety of sizes, from less than 1 micrometer to over 1 millimeter in diameter, with a peak in the distribution at about 50 micrometers. The heaviest particles begin to fall back very soon in the immediate vicinity of the burst. The lighter particles stay in the air for a longer period, and may be carried by the wind for very great distances before descending to the ground, the smallest particles travelling furthest. The radioactive materials which are deposited within 24 hours after the explosion, constitute the "early" fallout. It is reckoned that about 60 percent of the total radioactivity is contained in the early fallout.

For a given bomb the distance travelled by the fallout particles, the time of their deposition, and the locality where it will occur, are primarily dependent on the speed and direction of the wind. As the particles are carried further away by the wind they spread out over larger areas so that the dose rate to which they give rise is rapidly reduced with the distance; this decrease is in addition to the radioactive decay which occurs during the time before the fallout particles reach the ground. Under steady wind conditions, with no change in direction with height, at any given time after the explosion the radioactivity will have spread itself in such a way that the lines joining all points with the same dose rate will be cigar-shaped. Figure 9 a shows several such contours for the fallout from a 2 megaton bomb, with a 50 percent fission content, at 18 hours after

the explosion when the wind speed was 24 kilometers per hour. Figure 9 b shows the contours of the total dose which would result from exposure at these dose rates.

These figures are intended to illustrate the situation in a grossly simplified manner only. In reality the picture is much more complex because many factors may disturb the pattern of the fallout. First of all, the wind may change in speed or in direction, and this would distort the shape of the contours. Then, there may be scavenging of the fallout by rain or snow, if the air-borne particles encounter a region where precipitation is occurring. Such events may give rise to "hot-spots", ie small areas where a very large amount of radioactivity is deposited; this means, of course, that the fallout would be depleted in other areas. Rain coming down after the fallout may wash away some of the radioactivity.

The fallout pattern is also greatly affected by irregularities of the terrain, as well as by the material of the terrain itself; for example, the particle distribution will vary according to whether the explosion occurs over a city, over fields, or over water. Coupled with the paucity of actual experimental data, all this makes the prediction of the hazard due to early fallout highly unreliable. As an illustration, Figure 10 shows a comparison of (a) an idealized fallout pattern with (b) the pattern that might actually result from variations in local meteorological and surface conditions.

Nevertheless, an idealized picture is still useful in providing an approximate esti-

Table 4. Areas covered by given accumulated doses from fallout

Upper limit of accumulated dose (rads)	Area (km²)	
	1-Mt bomb	10-Mt bomb
1 000	900	11 000
800	1 200	14 000
600	1 700	18 000
400	2 600	27 000
200	5 500	52 000
100	10 500	89 000
50	18 600	148 000
25	32 700	234 000
10	56 000	414 000

31

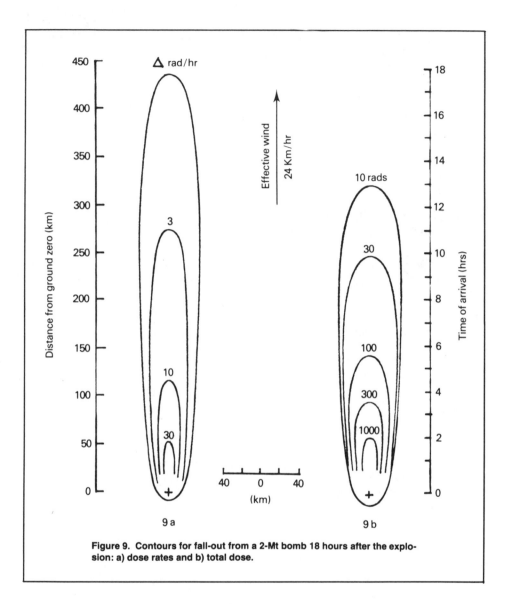

Figure 9. Contours for fall-out from a 2-Mt bomb 18 hours after the explosion: a) dose rates and b) total dose.

mate of the possible radiation hazard from early fallout. Assuming a wind of constant velocity with little directional shear, and no precipitation, the parameters of the fallout pattern for a given reference dose-rate, namely the downwind distance, maximum width, upwind distance, and ground-zero width, can be computed for bombs of different yields exploded at the surface.

Table 4 contains results of such calculations for 1-megaton and 10-megaton thermonuclear bombs with half of the yield due to fission. It gives the areas within which the total accumulated dose could reach the value given in the first column. The areas were calculated down to a value of 10 rads, which is approximately the limit of the dose which populations may accumulate in a lifetime from peace-time activities involving exposure to radiation (about 0.2 rads per year apart from the natural background and medical procedures). It is seen that one 10-megaton bomb could produce a dose near this limit over an area which exceeds the land area of almost every European country.

DELAYED FALLOUT

The division between fallout occurring within 24 hours of the explosion ("early" or "local") and that occurring thereafter ("delayed" or "global") is an arbitrary one for surface or near-surface bursts, since the fine particles will continue to descend after 24 hours. By then the activity has decayed to such an extent that only 20 percent of the total dose is still to be delivered (see Figure 8). Even so, considerable exposures could result from nuclides with medium and long half-lives over distances of some thousands of kilometers in the down-wind direction. The greatest hazard from this fallout arises from iodine-131, which has a half-life of eight days; it would thus take about four weeks for its activity to decrease ten-fold. The main route of iodine-131 into the human body is via milk from cows which grazed on contaminated fields. The route from bomb to atmosphere, to grass, to cow, to milk, to man, is very fast. Milk with a significantly high concentration of radioactive iodine was detected thousands of kilometers from nuclear test explosions. However the main contribution to the delayed fallout comes from explosions which do not produce any early fallout at all, namely bursts at such a height above ground that the fire-ball does not touch the ground. The radioactive products are then taken up to great heights where they may become stabilized in the troposphere, or in the stratosphere.

The initial vertical distribution of the radioactivity within the mushroom cloud depends on the yield of the weapon. The thick and the dotted lines in Figure 11 show, according to one model, the top and base of the cloud as a function of the yield.

The figure also shows the tropopause, which is the border between the troposphere and the overlying stratosphere. The tropopause lies at a height of about 10 kilometers in the polar and temperate zones, and at 17 kilometers in the equatorial zone. As is seen, weapons in the 10 megaton range, exploded at high altitude, inject all their radioactivity into the stratosphere.

The descent of the radioactive particles from the relevant regions constitutes the "tropospheric" and "stratospheric" fallout; together they form the "global" fallout.

The rate of descent and the geographic distribution of the fallout are determined by several events, *ie* the movement within the stratosphere, the transfer from the stratosphere to the troposphere, the movement within the troposphere, and finally deposition on the ground.

The main result of the long delay in the descent of global fallout is that all short-lived nuclides have decayed and the radioactivity, when it does come down, has become so much weaker that the external hazard due to gamma-rays no longer predominates over the internal hazard due to the ingestion of radioactive particles. The main radioactive hazard from the long-delayed fallout is due to strontium-90 and cesium-137. Their half-lives are so long (28 and 30 years) that the delay in deposition decreases their activity very little. These elements are of concern because they may be incorporated in various organs of the body; strontium accumulates in bone, and cesium is taken up by soft tissue. The beta-rays and gamma-rays emitted from them can deliver considerable internal doses. Their incorporation into the human body follows a complicated biological chain from soil to plants, to animals, to man. Strontium-90 reaches man mainly through milk and meat, while cesium-137 enters through fish, vegetables and other plants.

33

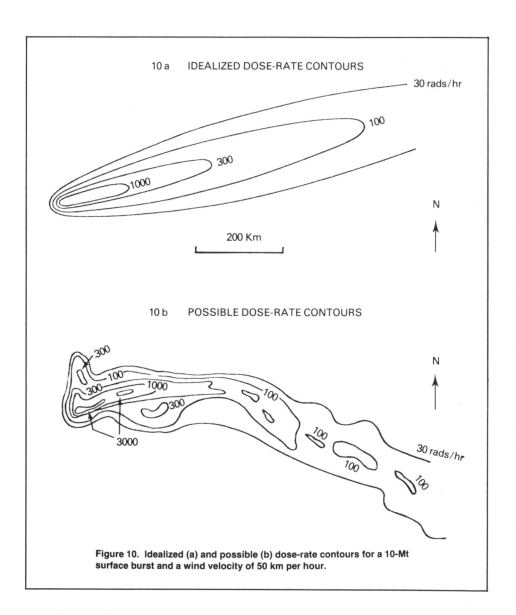

10 a   IDEALIZED DOSE-RATE CONTOURS

30 rads/hr

100

300

1000

200 Km

N

10 b   POSSIBLE DOSE-RATE CONTOURS

300

100

300

1000

300

100

3000

100

100

30 rads/hr

100

100

N

Figure 10. Idealized (a) and possible (b) dose-rate contours for a 10-Mt surface burst and a wind velocity of 50 km per hour.

CONCLUSIONS

It is hard to convey the extent of the damage and suffering which would be caused by even a regional nuclear war. In Western Europe, for example, there are only 145 cities with populations of over 200 000. The destruction of these cities would kill in a short time more than one third of the population of Western Europe.

In a nuclear world war, not only would a fair part of the urban population in the Northern Hemisphere be killed by fire and blast, and most of the survivors by radiation, but much of the rural population would be killed by radiation from fallout. Many millions in the Southern Hemisphere would also be killed by radiation from fallout.

34

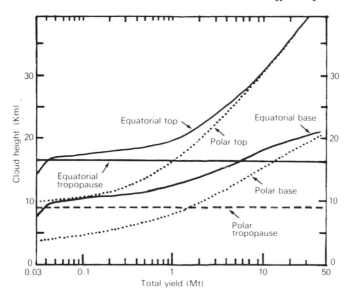

**Figure 11. Top and base
of mushroom cloud as a
function of the yield of the
bomb.**

35

THREE

REFERENCE SCENARIO: HOW A NUCLEAR WAR MIGHT BE FOUGHT

AMBIO ADVISORY GROUP

The purpose of this chapter is to present the assumptions about a nuclear war which provide the basis for the other chapters in this book, in the form of a scenario describing how and where nuclear explosions might occur. This form of presenting the basic assumptions was chosen for two reasons. First, the various environmental effects of a global nuclear war would interact with each other in a number of ways; in order to describe how those interactions might occur, and in order to make the conclusions of each contribution comparable, it is necessary to have a common set of assumptions, which are those contained in this "reference scenario." Second, presentation of the possible dimensions of a nuclear war in the form of a scenario makes the consequences of such a war more accessible, in all their horror, to readers outside the community of professional scientists.

This basic scenario has been designed to generate the major consequences of a global nuclear war, and their interactions with the environment. It does *not* try to describe the most *probable* nuclear war, and it is *not* intended to serve as the basis of a discussion of defense planning. In order to generate the likely environmental effects of a nuclear war, this scenario is more catastrophic than that envisioned by many defense planners.

However it is clear that a nuclear war, even if limited to a relatively small part of the devastation imagined in this scenario, would still be catastrophic enough. For the purposes of this publication, we have assumed that less than half of the total explosive power in the Soviet and American nuclear arsenals will be used— perhaps not the most likely of the nuclear war scenarios, but one chosen as an interesting alternative upon which to base our contributions. Many people believe that any use of nuclear weapons will escalate into a war in which all or most of the weapons in the nuclear arsenals are used, which is why there are scenarios much more catastrophic than this one in the literature.

It is possible that a nuclear conflict would not escalate to the degree shown here, but would be limited, for example, to one city on each side being destroyed. It is also possible that once a nuclear exchange begins, neither side would surrender while a significant portion of its arsenal remains intact. History shows that in the highly emotional atmosphere of war, countries do not surrender under such circumstances —they usually fight on to the bitter end. Since political leadership, command, control and communications centers will be priority targets, some believe that a nuclear war would be virtually impossible to control once it begins. The environmental, social, economic, and health effects of the "limited" scenario presented here are devastating; the effects of an all-out nuclear war would be unimaginably more disastrous.

This scenario assumes that a global nuclear war breaks out at about 11 AM New York time, 6 PM Moscow time, on a weekday in early June, 1985. By this date one side or the other may have developed and deployed sufficiently accurate nuclear weapons and enough first-strike technologies to make its political and military leaders less cautious about using its nuclear forces. Moreover, the superpower rivalry in some areas of the world, like the Persian Gulf, may by then be at an unprecedentedly dangerous level. And a domestic political upheaval may occur at any time in one, or more, countries in say, the Gulf region. The mid-1980s are therefore likely to be a dangerous period for world security.

A nuclear world war is likely to escalate rapidly. A war in a Third World region could spread to Europe. A European war may start with conventional weapons but is likely to escalate to a nuclear war as soon as one side penetrates far into the other's territory. Specifically, nuclear weapons are likely to be used if the weapons themselves are in danger of being overrun by the

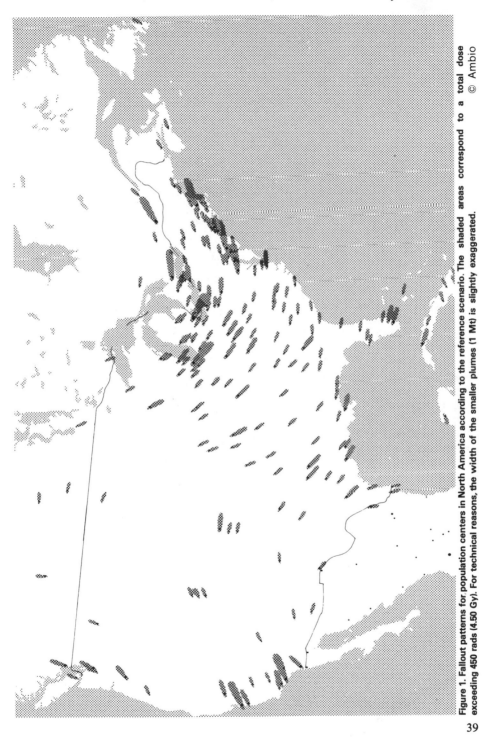

Figure 1. Fallout patterns for population centers in North America according to the reference scenario. The shaded areas correspond to a total dose exceeding 450 rads (4.50 Gy). For technical reasons, the width of the smaller plumes (1 Mt) is slightly exaggerated. © Ambio

enemy. Given that nuclear artillery has a range of less than 20 kilometers, this could happen rather soon after the outbreak of war.

A nuclear war may begin with the use of tactical nuclear weapons, targeted behind the enemy lines and against large targets, like airfields, vehicle storage areas, communication centers, and so on, but is then likely to escalate to a large-scale exchange of strategic nuclear weapons. These escalating steps would probably follow one another over a relatively short period of time—days rather than weeks. Because the consequences of a nuclear world war are unlikely to depend significantly on this time-span, our scenario assumes for simplicity that both sides fire their nuclear weapons in rapid succession.

In 1985 the USA will have a total of about 12 840 strategic nuclear warheads (of which 8175 will be independently targetable), with a total explosive power of about 3510 megatons. The Soviet Union will have about 11 310 strategic nuclear warheads (of which 10 480 will be independently targetable), with an explosive power of 4140 megatons; or if the new Soviet ICBM has a 15 megaton warhead the total megatonnage will be 8641. For our purposes we assume a reasonable figure would be 5000 megatons. The US and Soviet tactical nuclear arsenals each contain roughly 2200 megatons, and the number of tactical nuclear warheads is about 35 000. Thus the total megatonnage in both sides' strategic and tactical arsenals would be *ca* 12 800.

The problem with any scenario of a nuclear world war is to choose a set of targets for fifty to sixty thousand nuclear warheads. There is so much overkill in the arsenals that the exercise becomes overwhelming. It is impossible to find "reasonable" targets for all of these. In our "limited" scenario, we have only targeted 14 737 warheads, comprising less than half the megatonnage in the 1985 arsenals, or about 5750 megatons. According to one strategist, Desmond J Ball, the US

strategic targeting plans include 40 000 designated targets in the USSR for 9000 warheads in the American strategic nuclear arsenal. This allows flexibility in the choice of targets. The targets according to Ball include: 20 000 military targets in the USSR; 15 000 economic-industrial targets; 2000 targets (mostly cities) to kill the Soviet leadership; and 3000 targets associated with the Soviet nuclear forces.

In March 1980, the US Defense Department gave the following examples of targets in each set.

1. **Soviet nuclear forces**
   Intercontinental and intermediate-range ballistic missiles, together with their launch facilities and launch command centers
   Nuclear weapons storage sites
   Airfields supporting nuclear-capable aircraft
   Bases for submarines firing nuclear missiles

2. **Conventional military forces**
   Casernes
   Supply depots
   Marshalling points
   Conventional air fields
   Ammunition storage facilities
   Tank and vehicle storage yards

3. **Military and political leadership**
   Command posts
   Key communications facilities

4. **Economic and industrial targets**
   a. *War-supporting industry*
      Ammunition factories
      Tank and armored personnel carrier factories
      Petroleum refineries
      Railway yards and repair facilities

   b. *Industry contributing to economic recovery*
      Coal
      Basic steel
      Basic aluminum
      Cement
      Electric power

In this reference scenario North America, Europe and the Soviet Union are regarded as the main strategic areas in a nuclear war, although a number of other countries are considered important for strategic and political purposes. The great powers might decide to target some countries to prevent them from dominating international politics following a nuclear war. For example, this scenario includes targets in Latin America, despite the Tlateloco Treaty, which prohibits the placement of nuclear weapons in that area.

The Soviet warheads are targeted mainly on North America, Europe and China, which is a more widespread and complicated pattern of targets than that of the US, whose targets are mainly concentrated in the Soviet Union.

There are three categories of targets in this scenario: population targets, military targets and economic/industrial targets. It should be noted that military and economic/industrial targets are often located in or near cities.

Nuclear explosions at ground level have different effects from weapons exploded in the air. This scenario assumes that bombs detonated at ground level will maximize the number of casualties from local fallout, but will greatly reduce the number of immediate deaths from the effects of blast. The division between ground and air bursts chosen in this scenario differs from that assumed in most other descriptions of nuclear war. The effect is to emphasize in this scenario the immediate environmental impact of the explosions.

Cities in the USA, Canada, Western Europe, Eastern Europe, the USSR, Japan, North and South Korea, Vietnam, Australia, South Africa and Cuba are targeted with the following megatonnages (ground bursts):

a) *Cities with 100 000–1 million people:* 1 megaton (three 300-kiloton warheads, one 100-kiloton warhead)

b) *Cities with 1 million–3 million people:* 3 megatons (three one-megaton warheads)

c) *Cities with 3 million or more people:* 10 megatons (ten 500-kiloton, five one-megaton warheads)

Cities with populations of 500 000 or over in China, South-East Asia (except Vietnam and North and South Korea), India, and Pakistan are targeted with the following megatonnages (ground bursts):

a) *Cities from 500 000–1 million people:* 1 megaton (three 300-kiloton warheads, one 100-kiloton warhead)

b) *Cities with 1 million–3 million people:* 3 megatons (three one-megaton warheads)

c) *Cities with 3 million or more people:* 10 megatons (ten 500-kiloton warheads, five one-megaton warheads)

Cities will use up a total of 4970 warheads and 1941 megatons. Of the strategic warheads, 4845 are targeted on cities in the Northern Hemisphere.

Most industry in the countries directly involved in the nuclear war will be destroyed with the cities. We have targeted —with air bursts—the remaining important industries, energy supplies, and mineral resources in these countries, and in other areas of the Northern and Southern Hemispheres. This uses up another 3136 warheads and 701 megatons.

There are, of course, a very large number of possible military targets. Many of these are in, or close to, cities. In addition to these, we show the airfields and ports in the Northern and Southern Hemispheres likely to be attacked, targeted with ground bursts. This would use up 6620 warheads and 2960 megatons. Twenty-one warheads and 140 megatons were used to close straits.

This brings the total number of warheads used to 14 747, and the total mega-

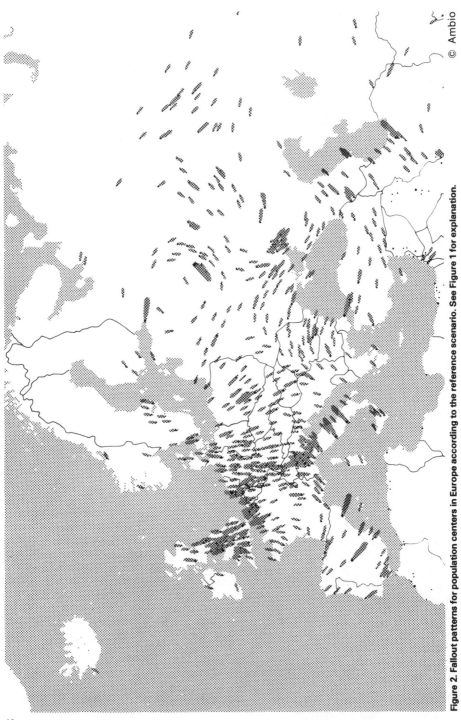

© Ambio

Figure 2. Fallout patterns for population centers in Europe according to the reference scenario. See Figure 1 for explanation.

tonnage used to about 5742 megatons. The Northern Hemisphere receives 5569 megatons, while the Southern Hemisphere receives 173 megatons (Table 1).

In this scenario we have chosen three categories of targets—urban, military and economic. Targets of equal importance in the most strategic areas of the world, the US, the USSR and Europe, have been dealt with on the same "category" basis. For example, all cities with a population of 100 000 or more in these areas are targeted with the same levels of megatonnage. This is also true of military and economic targets, whether they are located in North America, Europe or the USSR. We have not, for example, targeted USSR military bases of lower priority than those targeted in the US or in Europe.

Due to the sheer numbers of targets in the categories outlined above, more goals have been identified for USSR warheads than for US warheads. As a result the USSR expends more of its warheads and megatonnage in this scenario than does the US. If lower-priority targets were to be identified in the USSR than in the other two major areas, then the damages to the USSR would of course be correspondingly greater.

The total megatonnage devoted to different target categories in the scenario (population centers, military targets, economic targets) was calculated in the following way.

1. Megatonnage for all relevant population targets was calculated first.
2. Megatonnage for military targets which did not duplicate population targets was calculated next.
3. Megatonnage for economic targets which did not duplicate population targets or economic targets was then calculated. The resulting figures are shown in Table 1-C.

In preparing the maps showing the distribution of the early fallout from the warheads targeted on population centers we have taken the weather on a particular day — June 10, 1980 — as a starting point. The direction of the individual fallout plumes follows the direction of the wind at an elevation of about 5 kilometers above sea level. Differences in the speed of the wind have been disregarded; an average value of 25 kilometers per hour has been used everywhere. The influence of precipitation on the fallout pattern has not been taken into account. The resulting idealized fallout plume is the one shown in the maps. The plumes are drawn to show areas which would receive at least 450 rad. One half of the people receiving a whole-body dose of about 450 rad (air dose) will die within a month or so. The size of the plume enclosing areas which receive more than 450 rad is approximately 20 by 145 kilometers (13×90 miles) for a 1-megaton bomb. Even though three 300-kiloton warheads and one 100-kiloton warhead are used to reach the 1 megaton figure, for simplicity's sake the plume is drawn as though a 1 megaton warhead was used; this would tend to underestimate the extent of areas which receive 450 rad. Plumes for 3-megaton and 10-megaton targets are drawn on a similar basis.

Since the wind patterns may change very significantly from one day to the next it may seem a rather arbitrary assumption to use the winds of a particular day. However other possible devices, such as using climatological average winds or the most common wind direction and speed for each place, would not have resulted in a fallout pattern more representative than that illustrated here.

Obviously the details of the fallout pattern shown in the maps are very uncertain and might have been very different had the weather of another day been chosen. We believe, however, that the overall picture is fairly realistic. The fact that the plume for each individual target has been drawn independently of the other targets in the neighborhood implies a certain under-

43

Table 1. Warheads and megatonnage, Reference Scenario.

A. Total number of warheads used: 14 747
Total megatonnage used: 5742 Mt

Megatonnage used in Northern Hemisphere: 5569 Mt
Megatonnage used in Southern Hemisphere: 173 Mt

B.

Size of warheads	Number used
100 kt	939
200 kt	2930
300 kt	4410
500 kt	5692
1 Mt	769
10 Mt	7

C. Numbers of warheads used for different target categories,
Megatons used for different target categories:

Military targets:	6620 warheads	2960 Mt
Population (1124 cities:)	4970 warheads	1941 Mt
Industry/Energy	3136 warheads	701 Mt
Closing of straits (14 straits)	21 warheads	140 Mt

D. Warheads used for different target categories:

Military	300 kt	(one 300-kt warhead per target)
	100 kt	(one 100-kt warhead per target)
	200 kt	(one 200-kt warhead per target)
ICBM		(two 500-kt warheads per silo)
Submarine Bases		(one 1-Mt warhead per base)
Population	1 Mt	(three 300-kt + one 100-kt per city)
	3 Mt	(three 1-Mt warheads per city)
	10 Mt	(ten 500-kt + five 1-Mt warheads per city)
Industry	1 Mt	(five 200-kt warheads per site)
Oil fields	1 Mt	(two 500-kt warheads per site)
Closing of straits	10 Mt	(seven 10-Mt + fourteen 500-kt warheads) (this is total for the 14 straits)

E.

Military targets.	Megatonnage per target (average)	
Air bases	300 kt	ground burst
Naval ports	300 kt	ground burst
Army bases	300 kt	ground burst
Command/control/radar	300 kt	ground burst
Early warning systems	100 kt	ground burst
SOSSUS	300 kt	water burst
ICBM	Two 500 kt warheads per silo	ground burst
Energy Resources targets:		
Hydro electric stations	10 kt	airburst
Other energy resources	10 kt	airburst
Oilfields	1 Mt	airburst
Industrial targets: (only large industrial complexes)		
Oil refineries	1 Mt	airburst
Chemical plants (heavy organics, urea/nitric acid, sulfuric acid, ammonia)	1 Mt	airburst
Cement	1 Mt	airburst
Iron ore/steel	1 Mt	airburst

Table 2. Deposit of radioactivity
("delayed fallout") (a) one
month and (b) 10 years after the
war (Reference Scenario). Unit:
Ci/km².

Latitude	(a) After 1 month			(b) After 10 years			Area ×10⁶ km²
	^{90}Sr	^{137}Cs	^{131}I	^{90}Sr	^{137}Cs	^{131}I	
90°–60°N	0.04	0.07	2	0.1	0.1	–	34
60°–40°N	0.7	1.1	60	0.7	1	–	57
40°–20°N	0.2	0.3	15	0.3	0.4	–	77
20°–Equator	0.04	0.05	2	0.1	0.1	–	87
Northern Hemisphere average	**0.25**	**0.4**	**20**	**0.3**	**0.4**	**–**	**255**
Equator–20°S	0.01	0.01	0.5	0.03	0.04	–	87
20°–40°S	0.01	0.01	0.7	0.03	0.04	–	77
40°–60°S	0.02	0.04	1.5	0.04	0.06	–	57
60°–90°S	–	–	–	0.02	0.03		34
Southern Hemisphere average	**0.01**	**0.02**	**0.7**	**0.04**	**0.05**	**–**	**255**
Global average	**0.2**	**0.2**	**10**	**0.2**	**0.2**	**–**	**510**

Notes

Number of bombs of different tonnages/latitude band according to Table 1.
Emission yields:
^{90}Sr : .08 MCi/Mt fission yield
^{137}Cs : .12   ,,
^{131}I : 80   ,,
Reference: *Sources and Effects of Ionizing Radiation: Report of the United Nations Committee on the Effects of Atomic Radiation.* United Nations (New York, 1977). Height of emissions according to Figure 11 Rotblat and Barnaby, pg. 35. Ground bursts assumed to deliver 50 percent of the radioactivity in local fallout (not included in the table). Air bursts give no local fallout.

Tropospheric emissions assumed to be deposited in same latitude belt and within one month. Stratospheric emissions distributed along the latitudes according to observed ^{90}Sr in soils (Ref. M W Meyer, Nature 219:586, 1968). Deposition after one month corresponds to tropospheric emissions only (with due regard to decay of ^{131}I) but without the *local* fallout which is given on Figures 1 and 2. Deposition after 10 years corresponds to the total delayed fallout ie emissions in both troposphere and stratosphere (with due regard to decay).

In reality, the fallout cannot be expected to be distributed evenly within each latitude band. Certain regions, not necessarily in the immediate vicinity of the detonations, may receive a fallout up to ten times higher than the average values given in this table.

It is seen from Table 2 that the delayed fallout is highest in the mid latutudes of the northern hemisphere where most of the detonations take place. After one month the radioactivity is dominated by ^{131}I. Ten years later all the ^{131}I has decayed and the long-lived isotopes ^{90}Sr and ^{137}Cs dominate. Despite their decay, the deposits of ^{90}Sr and ^{137}Cs are higher after ten years than after one month. This is because a substantial fraction of the radioactive material is injected into the stratosphere and remains there several years before it is brought to the ground. For the same reason the fallout after ten years is also more evenly distributed over the globe.

estimation of the areas covered by lethal fallout. A certain location which is not covered by a plume may still receive more than 450 rad if the contributions from two or more nearby targets are added together. This means that for regions which are hit by many bombs the area actually receiving more than 450 rad is appreciably greater than that indicated on the map. The "delayed fallout" remaining after one month and after ten years is given in Table 2.

OTHER POSSIBLE TARGETS

Beyond the targets mentioned in the reference scenario, some authors have chosen to consider targets in three additional categories: nuclear power reactors, nuclear submarines, and explosion of nuclear devices in outer space.

Nuclear Power Reactors

If a nuclear reactor is hit by a nuclear bomb, the radioactivity contained in the reactor will be dispersed together with the radioactivity produced by the bomb itself. Since the reactors contain relatively small amounts of short-lived compounds compared to those produced by the bombs, their contribution to the total dose rate during the first few weeks after the detonation will be only modest. However the amounts of the more long-lived compounds ^{90}Sr and ^{137}Cs contained in nuclear reactors are very substantial, and the long-term radioactivity from the reactors will be very significant compared to that from the bombs.

The difference in decay rates between the total radioactive material produced by a one-megaton thermonuclear bomb and that contained in a one Gigawatt nuclear reactor is illustrated in Figure 3.

Table 3 shows areas for several values of accumulated dose for the same periods as in Figure 4. In Western Europe, where many reactors are in operation and many more are being built or planned, an attack

on them would make practically the whole of these and neighboring countries uninhabitable by ordinary standards of radiation safety for years or decades. The same would be true for North America and Japan. Such an attack would also seriously upset planned civil defense measures.

The contours in the reactor maps (see figures 5 and 6) represent the areas which would receive 100 rads (1 Gy) within a year, starting one month after the detonation of a 1 Mt bomb on each reactor site. A dose of 100 rads is significantly less than the LD_{50} dose used in Figures 1 and 2 (450 rads) but it is still 1000 times the natural background radiation — a high dose by the normal standards of radiation safety.

Should a nuclear weapon be exploded on a reprocessing plant or a storage tank the uninhabitable areas would be even greater, and they would remain so for a longer period because the activity in these plants or tanks is even longer-lived than that in a reactor. As an example, the last column of Table 3 shows the areas covered by doses received in one year, starting one month after the explosion of a 1-Mt bomb on a storage tank of a capacity of about 3000 cubic meters.

The delayed fallout after one month of ^{90}Sr and ^{137}Cs and ^{131}I as illustrated for the reference scenario in Table 2 (column a) would be increased by only 30 to 40 percent even if all the nuclear reactors of the world were hit. However the deposit remaining after ten years would be three to four times higher if the reactors were included in the scenario.

Nuclear Submarines

Developments in anti-submarine warfare are proceeding rapidly, and by 1985 it may be possible to accurately target nuclear submarines. Approximately 45 submarines (30 from the US, 15 from the USSR, or half of the projected 1985 fleets) might be targeted, each with a warhead of 500 kilotons or less. The submarines would probably be attacked in waters of 800 meters depth or more. The blasts would be water-

46

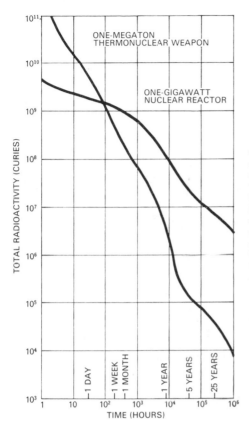

Figure 3. Decay of radioactivity released by the detonation of a nuclear weapon differs from the decay of the radioactivity released by a reactor accident because the two inventories of radioactive nuclei have different proportions of various isotopes. After an hour the radioactivity released by the detonation of a one-megaton thermonuclear weapon is 1000 times greater than the radioactivity that would escape in the worst conceivable peacetime reactor accident. On the other hand, the radioactivity from the reactor takes longer to decay. Source: S A Fetter and K Tsipis, Scientific American 244, 33 (1981).

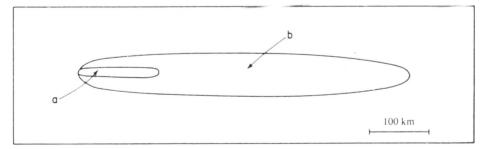

Figure 4. Contours of 100 rads (1 Gy) fallout dose in one year, starting one month after the detonation of a) a 1 Mt bomb, and b) a 1 Mt bomb on a 1 GW(e) nuclear reactor. Source: *Nuclear Radiation in Warfare* by Joseph Rotblat, SIPRI, 1981.

47

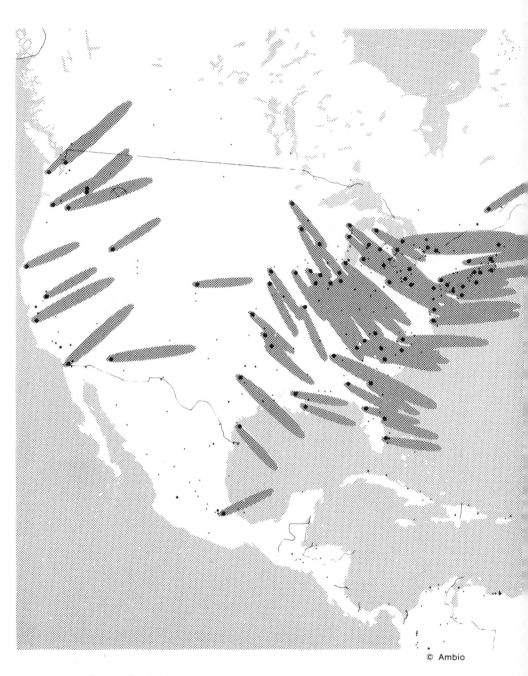

© Ambio

Figures 5 and 6

Local (early) fallout from bombs on nuclear reactors. The shaded areas correspond to a dose of 100 rad (1 Gy) at 1 year starting one month after the detonation. The sites have been divided into 5 categories according to the output of the reactors on the site: from up to 1 GWe to 5 and more GWe. The directions of the plumes have been determined from the direction of the wind at the site. In reality, the plumes would follow the wind and be curved accordingly.

Table 3. Areas affected by detonation of nuclear weapons alone and nuclear power facilities.

Dose* (rads)	Area (km²) 1-Mt bomb	1-Mt bomb on 1 GW(e) reactor	1-Mt bomb on a storage tank
100	2 000	34 000	61 000
50	4 000	46 000	87 000
10	25 000	122 000	164 000

* Dose accumulated in one year starting one month after detonation.
Source: J Rotblat, *Nuclear Radiation in Warfare*, SIPRI, (Taylor and Francis, London, 1981). Dose converted to rads from Greys.

bursts, with practically no global fallout, since most of the radioactive material would fall back into the oceans. Radioactive fog-spray might drift over coastal areas, however.

Radioactive fission products might also be released from the reactors of nuclear-powered submarines and surface vessels. There are about 320 large nuclear-powered submarines and about 10 nuclear-powered surface warships currently in operation. In a nuclear war, the nuclear-powered ships at sea might be sunk with torpedoes, depth charges, or anti-ship missiles equipped with nuclear warheads. It is highly probable that the nuclear reactors of the ships sunk would be ruptured.

A typical nuclear-powered submarine carries a reactor generating about 60 megawatts (thermal) and produces about 40 grams of fission products per day of operation; a nuclear-powered surface warship may have a reactor of about 250 megawatts (thermal), and produces about 160 grams of fission products per day. If its reactor were ruptured, a nuclear submarine which had been at sea for a month before it was sunk would release long-lived

fission products originating from about 1.2 kilograms of original fission products, roughly equivalent to the amount released by a 25-kiloton atomic bomb. A nuclear-powered warship which had been at sea for three months before it was sunk would release roughly the same amount of long-lived fission products as a 300-kiloton fission bomb. (For more details see *Warfare in a Fragile World*, Taylor and Francis/SIPRI, 1978 London).

Outer Space

A number of 1 Mt weapons might be detonated in outer space at an altitude greater than 40 km during the first day of hostilities as a method of disrupting communications. The electromagnetic pulse resulting from the explosions would affect electrical power supplies and electronic equipment, including radio and television. Most military equipment would be shielded against the pulse, but civilian installations would not be, and civil defense programs might be disrupted. There would be no radioactive fallout on the earth as a result of these explosions, and the effect on the ozone layer would also be minimal. (See Crutzen and Birks, Chapter 6).

48

FOUR

EPIDEMIOLOGY: THE FUTURE IS SICKNESS AND DEATH

HUGH MIDDLETON

Of an urban population of nearly 1.3 billion in the Northern Hemisphere, about 750 million would be killed outright and some 340 million seriously injured. Furthermore, of the 200 million initial "survivors" many of them would perish from the latent effects of radiation as well as infectious diseases like cholera, tuberculosis and dysentery. Caring for the vast number of injured would greatly hamper post-war recovery efforts.

A full understanding of the effects of nuclear war requires not only a catalogue of damage to strategic and industrial targets, nor even a description of the peculiarities of injury and disease likely after the discharge of nuclear weapons, but also some appraisal of the overall effect upon human populations. Studies of natural disasters have shown that the response to and recovery from a disaster are as limited by human factors—such as a preoccupation with personal well-being and the care of injured relatives—as they are by the availability of other resources.

Central to the effects of a disaster upon a population of human beings is the extent to which it causes death and injury. An extremely high toll of deaths will lead to a state of social paralysis, due in part to the loss of essential human skills and in part to the ensuing cultural disturbance. Relatively light damage will naturally permit populations to recover, but the intermediate situation—a moderately high death toll, many non-fatal injuries and a limited quantity of medical resources—will have an outcome dependant upon the balance between these forces. The epidemiological study of disasters and in particular the epidemiology of nuclear war is an attempt to understand this balance of forces and if possible make predictions—predictions which hopefully will remain untested.

In terms of its direct effect upon human beings, nuclear war represents a number of related but distinguishable threats. During the "fighting period", when weapons are being discharged, there will be a risk of death or injury from burning, blast, and direct ionizing radiation. For some time immediately afterwards there will be a risk of serious irradiation from immediate fallout. After the exchange of weapons is complete, and immediate fallout has decayed to a level which permits reasonably safe surface activity, the incidence of disease will be altered by the effects of irradiation and impaired sanitation, which will undoubtedly influence the rate of recovery

for the society as a whole. Although in the real situation these effects would undoubtedly interact, for the sake of clarity it is better to consider them separately.

THE IMMEDIATE POST-ATTACK PERIOD

While the nuclear explosions are continuing, the main causes of death and disablement will be injuries caused by blast effects upon buildings and thermal burns. The human body is itself quite resistant to blast damage, being capable of surviving shock waves of a peak overpressure up to some 30 pounds per square inch (psi), but buildings are not so resilient. Large explosions in built-up areas endanger human life by destroying buildings, and it is probably true to say that the fate of human beings under nuclear attack is most closely associated with the fate of the surrounding buildings.

Basing calculations upon measured properties of various building materials, their use in American cities, and the susceptibility of humans to injury within and close to falling buildings, the US Office of Technology Assessment derived a relationship between peak overpressure and the probability of fatal or non-fatal injuries in a North American town or city. This is shown in Table 1. In areas where peak overpressure exceeds 12 pounds per square inch (psi), virtually complete destruction of all buildings would be expected and 98 percent mortality would be likely. Further away from the hypocenter, where peak overpressure is between 5 and 2 psi, much less severe building damage would occur and the number and severity of injuries would consequently be less.

In order to translate these probabilities into actual numbers of casualties it is necessary also to have an estimate of the population at risk. From an epidemiological point of view, the most important of the targets detailed in the reference scenario are the towns and cities. Population densities vary considerably between and within

Table 1. Death and Injury Rates in different Peak Overpressure Zones.

Peak Over-pressure (psi)	Effect
>12	98% dead; 2% injured
5–12	50% dead; 40% injured; 10% safe
2– 5	5% dead; 45% injured; 50% safe

Table 2. Towns and cities of the Reference Scenario and the weapons used against them.

Population Range × 10^3	Average Population × 10^3	Number of cities	Weapons Exploded upon each city
100–300	173	630	300 kt × 3 100 kt × 1
300–1000	550	600	300 kt × 3 100 kt × 1
1000–3000	1730	219	1 Mt × 3
3000–10 000	5500	52	500 kt × 10 1 Mt × 5
>10 000	14 150	13	500 kt × 10 1 Mt × 5

Table 3. The ranges of peak overpressure effects from groundbursts of various sizes (km).

Yield	Peak overpressure effect (psi)			
	12	5	2	1
100 kt.	1.3	1.1	4.2	7.0
300 kt.	1.75	3.1	6.3	7.4
500 kt.	2.25	3.8	7.0	12.0
1 Mt.	2.8	4.2	9.1	14.7

Table 4. Numbers killed, injured and safe from the effects of blast.

Population × 10^3	Killed per city × 10^3	Injured per city × 10^3	Safe from blast × 10^3
173			
@ 4 × 10^3/km^2	147	21	5
@ 8 × 10^3/km^2	163	8	2
550			
@ 4 × 10^3/km^2	303	168	79
@ 8 × 10^3/km^2	414	103	33
1 730			
@ 4 × 10^3/km^2	875	553	302
@ 8 × 10^3/km^2	1140	430	160
5 500			
@ 4 × 10^3/km^2	2700	1800	1000
@8×10^3/km^2	4100	1000	400
14 150			
@ 4 × 10^3/km^2	2000	5000	7350
@ 8 × 10^3/km^2	4000	5150	5000

cities. For example, London has a density of 100 000 per km² in busy parts during the working day, but only 1000–2000 per km² in less densely populated areas of suburbia. In order to make estimates it is therefore necessary to choose representative population densities; 8000 per km² seems reasonable for a more densely populated city and 4000 per km² for a more diffuse urban area.

The Reference Scenario includes 1514 targeted towns and cities, with populations ranging from 100 000 to more than 10 million. The numbers in each category of size and the weapons they receive are given in Table 2. If these cities are thought of as being circular, the area covered by a town of a given size being determined by its population density, then it is possible to estimate the areas subject to different overpressures and, by application of the criteria of Table 1, the numbers expected to be killed, injured or safe. Table 3 gives the extent of 12, 5 and 2 psi overpressures following groundbursts of the weapons used and Figure 1 depicts these effects upon a city of between 1 and 3 million receiving three 1 Mt groundbursts. Where overlaps occur, half of the area involved has been allocated an overpressure of the next highest intensity, in order to take into account the synergistic effects of multiple explosions.

Table 4 gives the rounded estimates of numbers killed, injured and safe in representative cities of each of the types considered, at population densities of either 8000 or 4000 per km². The immediate conclusion that must be drawn from these figures is the huge scale of the damage. In all of the cases apart from the largest, more than half the population would die and in all cases the dead and injured together would greatly outnumber the uninjured. When all of the towns and cities in each category are included, the scenario applies to a total population of some 1290 million, of whom about 750 million would be killed by the effects of blast alone, 340

million seriously injured and 200 million safe, at least initially. Within a few minutes the urban population would be reduced to less than one third; of the survivors, more than half would be injured.

In making these models several important assumptions have been made which have the effect of underestimating the casualties. Clearly it is inaccurate to assume cities to have a uniform population density; the population is unevenly distributed, and there is generally a tendency for it to be concentrated in the centers of cities. As weapons are more likely to be targeted close to the center of such cities, the actual toll of dead and injured is likely to be higher. Furthermore no account has been taken of the effects of heat and fire. All the weapons used against cities in the reference scenario were defined as ground bursts, which reduces thermal effects considerably and increases the extent to which buildings and other structures would provide shade. Nevertheless some will be exposed, and the heat, even from a ground burst, is sufficient to cause third degree burns to the full thickness of the skin among those far enough away to have a reasonable chance of surviving the effects of blast alone.

It is clear that under the conditions postulated in the reference scenario, there would be immense loss of life and enormous numbers of casualties in all of the targeted cities and towns, which means all with more than 100 000 population in the USA, Canada, Western Europe, Eastern Europe, the USSR, Japan, North and South Korea, Viet Nam, Australia, South Africa and Cuba, and all with a population of more than 500 000 in China, India, Pakistan and the rest of South East Asia. In many cases the injured would outnumber the survivors (that is, those escaping the initial effects). There is no conceivable way to prepare for such a large number of casualties. Available medical resources would be totally inadequate; many medical facilities would themselves be destroyed by

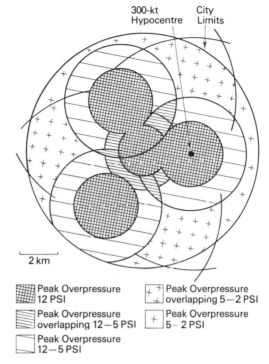

Figure 1. The extent of
different overpressure
effect zones on a
hypothetical city.

300-kt
Hypocentre

City
Limits

2 km

Peak Overpressure
12 PSI

Peak Overpressure
overlapping 12—5 PSI

Peak Overpressure
12—5 PSI

Peak Overpressure
overlapping 5—2 PSI

Peak Overpressure
5—2 PSI

the attack. Treatment of a serious injury, such as an open fracture of the femur or thigh bone, requires specialized facilities, several units of blood for transfusion and trained staff. A fully-equipped, normally-functioning hospital can deal with only four or five such injuries at a time before its resources become stretched.

In battlefield conditions and occasionally in civilian disasters an attempt is made to rationalize the use of medical facilities by the use of a system of casualty sorting that has come to be called "triage." Casualties are sorted into three categories: those whose survival is improbable, those whose survival is possible and those whose survival is probable. Intervention is reserved for the middle category, where the use of scarce resources might be expected to be rewarding. But relief efforts depend on the quantity and quality of resources available, and in fact such classifications have to be based upon some estimate of the available resources. After a nuclear attack, the bal-

ance between available resources and need would be so heavily displaced that the criteria for selection into the "survival possible" category would have to be so precise, in order to identify the small proportion of the total number of injured who could be treated, that the entire system would become impractical.

Considering the vast numbers of casualties likely after a nuclear attack, even if medical facilities were undamaged there would be no future in even attempting to sort casualties. The injured would have to be left to fend for themselves, with whatever help might be available from untrained survivors. Such conditions would undoubtedly have profound effects upon the viability of the population as a whole. Few of the survivors would be able to ignore the demands of the injured and dying; and in conditions where the number of injured would be almost as high as the number of uninjured, much time and effort would be taken in caring for the

53

injured instead of performing other tasks, thus slowing recovery from the disaster.

FALLOUT

In addition to the demands of the injured, organized activity in the early post-attack period would also be compromised by the threat of potentially lethal irradiation from fallout. In the urban areas previously described it would almost certainly be necessary to shelter from fallout for at least 10 days and possibly more; and a second wave of illness due to fallout would further strain medical facilities and impede recovery.

The number of survivors and injured in the scenario considered above means that following the attack there would be between 2500 and 3500 living persons per square kilometer at risk of irradiation from fallout, and in need of shelter. For all the injured and uninjured to be accommodated would require some sort of adequate shelter for 2–3 people every 200–300 meters. In cities provided with specialized shelters or sufficiently large underground tunneling, such as the London Underground, the search for adequate shelter would not be so desperate. But those special circumstances aside, and given the extensive damage to buildings, little cover would be available, and many would unavoidably receive dangerously high levels of ionizing radiation.

The medical effects of ionizing radiation are described elsewhere in this issue, but from an epidemiological point of view there would be two major groups of consequences.

The disease syndromes caused by moderate levels of acute ionizing radiation are both insidious in their onset and initially similar to more benign illnesses. The nausea and diarrhea of the intestinal form is indistinguishable at first from simple infectious gastroenteritis. The malaise and weakness of the bone marrow form is not unlike simple viral infections such as influenza. Given adequate training and simple resources, much can be done to ameliorate the course of the more benign conditions. Without highly-trained personnel and sophisticated resources little can be done to ameliorate the course of acute radiation sickness. Distinguishing the effects of ionizing radiation from simple benign conditions will present considerable difficulties.

The dose/response curve for the effect of acute whole body radiation on humans is steep. Following acute exposure to some 200 rads the probable mortality is very small. But it rises to approximately 99 percent as the dose increases from 200 to 600 rads. In order to effectively establish the extent to which illness could be ascribed to the effect of ionizing radiation, highly accurate measurements of dose have to be made. In the chaos of the post-attack situation it is difficult to see how this could be achieved.

Following the exposure of a considerable proportion of the surviving population to ionizing radiation from fallout, an epidemic of minor disease and disablement, caused partly by relatively benign conditions (exacerbated perhaps by poor nutrition), and partly by the early effects of radiation sickness, would soon develop. The causes would be indistinguishable and the associated uncertainty would lead to a further drain on whatever medical resources there might be, much being wasted upon the attempted and futile treatment of persons suffering what subsequently proved to be quite advanced radiation sickness. As a whole the population would become even further debilitated and concerned with medical rather than reconstructive matters.

In addition to the well-defined disease syndromes caused by moderate levels of acute ionizing radiation, much lower levels can cause a significant impairment of the ability to overcome infection. In the context of the post-attack situation this is likely to be particularly important. The enforced crowding of shelters, serious damage to sewage lines and water supplies, contaminated food and unburied dead are all conditions that encourage the development of easily communicable infections. This would be facilitated by the effects of even relatively low levels of irradiation upon the rapidly dividing cells of the immune system. The spread of such infections would add further to the weight of illness carried by the surviving population.

LONGER TERM

The infectious diseases most likely to cause trouble in the weeks following the decay of fallout would be those now well under control in most parts of the developed world. Diseases caused by poor sanitation, like dysentery, infectious hepatitis, salmonellosis and cholera, would present a particular problem. These are caused by infectious agents that normally gain entry to the body by way of the mouth in the form of contaminated food and drink. Such illnesses were common in Europe before the development of clean water supplies and organized sewage facilities ended the contamination of drinking water by human and animal waste. Avoiding such contamination in most modern cities has been one of the most positive achievements of civil engineering of the past 150 years.

Poor nutrition and overcrowded living conditions would again encourage the infectious diseases of poverty only recently overcome. Meningococcal meningitis, which is considerably enhanced in its spread by crowded sleeping conditions, is now a relative rarity, but was once a major killer. It could be expected to recur. The decline in the incidence of tuberculosis is considered at least in part to be due to a general rise in the material standard of living; it could well become a major determinant of life expectancy again. Without the current levels of protection by vaccination, diphtheria, whooping cough and polio would again be common. More frequently seen infections such as pneumonia

and septicemia or blood poisoning would again become killers, without the antibiotics which are now used to treat them.

The longer-term effects of ionizing radiation upon health have also been discussed elsewhere; in essence they amount to an increased incidence of malignant disease (leukemias and cancer) and a possibly deleterious effect upon the human gene pool. These too would reduce life expectancy, increase the number of sick requiring attention and further debilitate the population.

CONCLUSIONS

Using a simplified model, we have attempted to calculate the likely consequences of the nuclear war described in the opening chapters. Such a model shows that about half of the population of the cities targeted would be killed; about half of the survivors would be injured. Such vast numbers of injured people would totally overwhelm existing or even conceivable medical resources, and the uninjured would be burdened with the task of reconstruction. In non-urban areas not subject to attack the surviving population would also become burdened by the inevitable influx of refugees.

In addition to the burden imposed upon the survivors as a result of the large number of injured from the original attack, there would also be further health problems arising from the early and late effects of ionizing radiation, poor nutrition and an increased incidence of communicable disease. These influences would continue to debilitate the population as a whole for some considerable time. Life expectancy would be reduced and a greater proportion of the population would be disabled; unless there were an undesirable change in attitudes towards the ill, they would represent a large and continuing drain on resources.

The effect of a global nuclear war upon the human population would not simply be to reduce it in size; it would also sicken it, reducing its efficiency and its ability to recover. These effects would be keenly felt, not only in areas intensely targeted like the Eastern United States, Europe and western Russia, but also in areas like India and China. The technically advanced population of the world, those most important in any reconstructive effort, would be the very ones most severely damaged, and the prospects for a speedy recovery are not bright. The declining health of the world's remaining population will contribute significantly to that delay.

Bibliography

1. M F Lechat, The Epidemiology of Disasters, *Proceedings of the Royal Society of Medicine* **69**, 421 (1976).
2. *The Effects of Nuclear War,* US Office of Technology Assessment.
3. *The Effects of Nuclear Weapons,* (Glasstone and Dolan).
4. *United Nations Comprehensive Study on Nuclear Weapons* (UN, New York, NY, September, 1980).
5. H L Abrams, W E von Kaenel, *New England Journal of Medicine*, **305**, 1225 (1981).

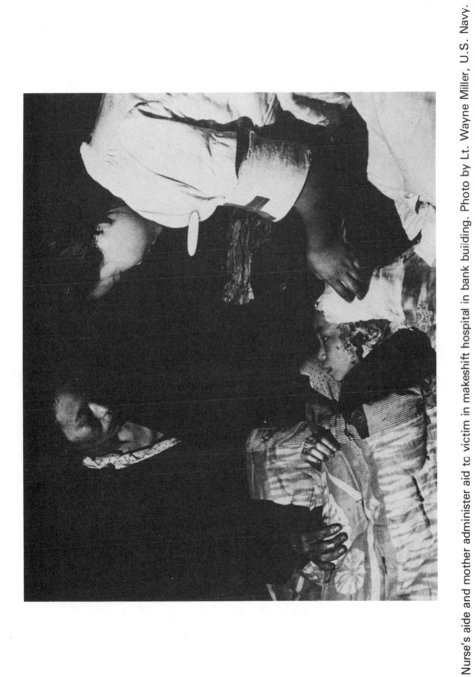

Nurse's aide and mother administer aid to victim in makeshift hospital in bank building. Photo by Lt. Wayne Miller, U.S. Navy. *Photo: National Archives, Washington, D.C.*

Bomb damage in Hiroshima, 14 October 1945.   *Photo: National Archives, Washington, D.C.*

FIVE

MEDICAL CONSEQUENCES OF RADIATION FOLLOWING A GLOBAL NUCLEAR WAR

J. E. COGGLE AND PATRICIA J. LINDOP

By the most conservative estimates the survivors of a nuclear war will suffer from 5.4 to 12.8 million fatal cancers; 17 to 31 million people will be rendered sterile; and 6.4 to 16.3 million children will be born with genetic defects during the subsequent 100 years.

The biological effects of ionizing radiation have been studied throughout this century. However, until 1945 and the US atomic bombing of Japan there was very little information on the sublethal and lethal effects of total body exposure in man. The Japanese experience can be used as a convenient guide when considering the medical consequences of a global nuclear war.

A report of the atomic bomb casualty commission divided the medical effects of the nuclear bombs into four categories (1).

Initial stage (weeks 1–2): the time of greatest number of casualties and deaths, with more than 90 percent of the latter being due to direct or indirect thermal injury and/or blast effects, and about 10 percent to supralethal radiation exposure.

Intermediate stage (weeks 3–8): the main period for deaths from exposure to ionizing radiation in the median lethal range.

Late stage (8–20 weeks): all symptoms in injured survivors tending to show some improvement in this period.

Delayed stage (more than 20 weeks): numerous complications, mostly related to healing of thermal and mechanical injury coupled with infertility, subfertility and blood disorders caused by radiation.

For an authoritative and graphic account of these categories the reader is urged to study the book *Hiroshima and Nagasaki* (2). Besides these "acute" categories, ionizing radiation from fallout causes a range of longterm effects which appear years or even decades later. These include genetic (heritable) effects in future generations; retarded development and abnormalities in children exposed *in utero*; and the induction of cancer, of cataracts, and of late fibrosis and vascular effects in many organs and tissues.

Nuclear weapons kill by blast, heat and ionizing radiation and it is the latter, particularly as fallout, which is the most difficult to quantify. Nevertheless, the local

and global fallout engendered in *Ambio's* scenario will produce a very significant threat to the health and perhaps even to the existence of mankind in the Northern Hemisphere.

In this chapter we shall first briefly describe the acute and longterm effects of ionizing radiation that would occur in a global nuclear war. Then we shall present some quantitative estimates of the early and late effects including deaths from cancer and the hereditary damage that would be likely to follow from the *Ambio* scenario.

THE LETHAL RADIATION SYNDROMES

The three modes of death in Table 1 are called the lethal radiation syndromes and they occur predominantly after total body radiation. The Table gives the principal organs involved, the approximate whole body doses and the likely time of death. The syndromes are called central nervous system (CNS) death, gastrointestinal (GI) death and bone marrow (BM) death, but it must be stressed that all the organs and tissues in the body will be damaged by whole body radiation. As the dose increases the survival time and the proportion of individuals surviving decreases.

Prodromal Syndrome

Following a whole body dose of $\lesssim 1.5$ Gy (150 rads) of gamma radiation no deaths are likely, at least in a physically fit population. But—approximately 50 percent of those so exposed will show signs of gastrointestinal distress with anorexia, nausea, fatigue and possibly diarrhea. The cause of this initial or "prodromal" syndrome is poorly understood. Table 2 gives the radiation dose to produce early symptoms.

Bone Marrow Death

After whole body doses of more than 2 Gy (200 rads) and less than 10 Gy (1000 rads)

60

there is a degeneration of the vascular and cellular architecture of the blood-forming (hemopoietic) tissues of the bone marrow. Radiation also stops the division of the all-important precursor stem cells that are responsible for the production of red and white blood cells and of blood platelets. A dose of 4.5 Gy (450 rads) will kill about 95 percent of the stem cells. The failure of stem cells to divide is rapidly reflected in a life-threatening fall in the number of circulating blood cells. The fall in the number of platelets (responsible for the clotting of blood) causes a proneness to fatal hemorrhage. Such hemorrhages were a prime cause of death in the Japanese victims of the A-bombs (3). The fall in the numbers of circulating white blood cells allows bacteria and other microorganisms into the bloodstream and causes septicemic infections, the other principal cause of death. In contrast, the fall in red blood cells is minimal and causes mild anemia (4).

Within 24 hours of exposure to 4.5 Gy (450 rads) of penetrating gamma rays those exposed will suffer vomiting and diarrhea, which will abate after 6–7 days, only to be followed within 3–4 weeks by a period of extreme illness. Severe, often bloody, diarrhea heralds serious intestinal disorders and will lead to fluid imbalances, which together with extensive internal bleeding and life-threatening septicemic infections, are a major cause of death. The peak incidence of acute BM death corresponds to the 30 day nadir in blood cell numbers; the number of deaths then falls progressively until it reaches zero at 60 days after irradiation.

Figure 1 shows the probability of death from bone marrow failure as a function of X- and gamma ray doses. It can be seen that over the range of 2 to 6 Gy (200 to 600 rads) the probability of death in untreated adults goes from about one percent to about 99 percent. One or two comments are in order. First there is considerable uncertainty attached to the slope of the line in Figure 1 and to its confidence limits. The

$LD_{50/60}$ value (the dose of radiation lethal to 50 percent of a population within 60 days) may be less than 4.5 Gy (450 rads), corresponding to less than 2.5 Gy (250 rads) to the bone marrow (5). Second, the dose/effect relationship in Figure 1 is for healthy adults. In a nuclear war the radiation syndromes are likely to be exacerbated by mechanical and thermal injuries and by the highly infectious, unsanitary conditions pertaining in a society "laid waste by nuclear war". So the whole curve in Figure 1 is likely to be shifted to the left such that exposures of about 1.5–2 Gy (150–200 rads) might cause a few deaths in adult populations. Finally, for a given level of radiation, children will receive larger bone marrow doses. So a 2 Gy (200 rad) dose that may give a healthy adult a reasonable chance of survival is likely to kill a child and almost certainly an infant. All these considerations make the estimation of radiation casualties in nuclear war most uncertain.

CNS Death

Table 1 gives the likely survival time and cause of death in adults from supralethal doses, *ie* the people closest to the center of the explosion. The main cause of death within 24–48 hours among those exposed to more than 50 Gy (5000 rads) will be from damage to the central nervous system (CNS). The symptoms that such heavily irradiated people would show are immediate excitability and the inevitable severe nausea, vomiting and diarrhea. This would be followed by drowsiness, lethargy, tremors, delirium and frequent seizures, and finally convulsions, prostration, coma, respiratory failure and death. The CNS syndrome is medically irreversible.

GI Death

In the intermediate dose range (more than 10 Gy or 1000 rads but less than 50 Gy or 5000 rads) whole-body doses cause damage to the epithelial cells lining the gastrointestinal tract, which together with the

61

Table 1. Acute Radiation Syndrome in Man

Whole Body Dose	Approximate Time of Death	Mode of Death
> 50 Gy (5000 rads)	2 days	CNS Damage, Cerebral Edema, Heart Failure (CNS)
> 10 Gy (1000 rads)	2 weeks	Gastrointestinal Damage, Infection, Hemorrhage and Dehydration (GI)
> 2 Gy* (200 rads)	3–8 weeks	Bone Marrow Damage, Infection, Hemorrhage (BM)
< 2 Gy (200 rads)	–	Prodromal Symptoms – Nausea Vomiting, Diarrhea

* Dose of acute X-or gamma rays which is lethal for 50 percent of population of adults is 4±1.5 Gy (400±150 rads).

Table 2. Radiation doses necessary to produce early symptoms in 10, 50 and 90 % of a human population in Gy (rads)

Symptom	10 %	50 %	90 %
Anorexia	0.4 (40)	1.0 (100)	2.4 (240)
Nausea	0.5 (50)	1.7 (170)	3.2 (320)
Vomiting	0.6 (60)	2.1 (210)	3.8 (380)
Diarrhoea	0.9 (90)	2.4 (240)	3.9 (390)

bone marrow damage is fatal. The signs and symptoms include gastrointestinal pain, anorexia, nausea, vomiting and diarrhea, all of which become increasingly severe, causing exhaustion and emaciation within a few days. Death occurs within 7–14 days from water and electrolyte losses, infection and from starvation due to an inability to assimilate food. Medically, little can be done to alter the inevitable course of the GI syndrome especially after high doses (more than 15 Gy or 1500 rads).

Once again it must be stressed that in the holocaust all these supralethal doses will often be heightened by blast and thermal radiation effects.

OTHER SHORT TERM EFFECTS

Those who do not die within 6–8 weeks from the lethal syndromes mentioned above may nevertheless suffer damage to tissues like the skin, lungs, gonads and eyes.

Victim of atomic bomb blast lies in makeshift hospital in bank building. Photo by Lt. Wayne Miller, U.S. Navy.   *Photo: National Archives, Washington, D.C.*

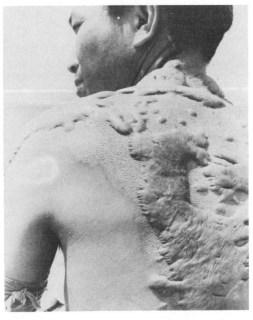

Victim of results of atom bombing.   *Photo: Keystone Press Agency Ltd, London*

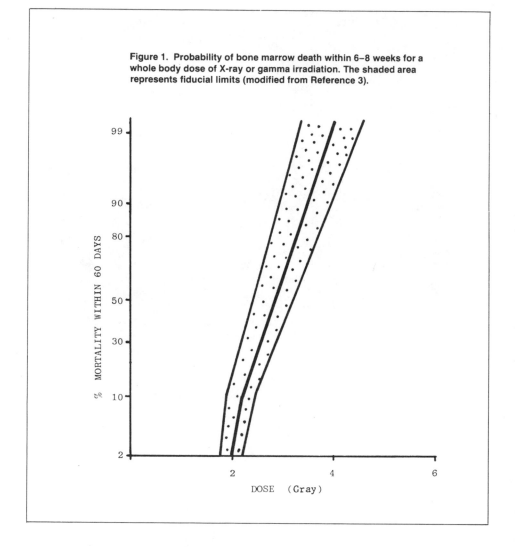

Figure 1. Probability of bone marrow death within 6–8 weeks for a whole body dose of X-ray or gamma irradiation. The shaded area represents fiducial limits (modified from Reference 3).

The Skin

The skin is so accessible to the deposition of beta-emitting radioactive fallout that it is likely to receive relatively high, though localized, doses. The damage is complex and the injuries involve all the layers of the skin. The principal site of damage is the germinal layer but the most rapid response—erythema (reddening)—is due to blood vessel congestion and edema. Erythema lasting about 10 days occurs in approximately 50 percent of people after 5–6 Gy (500–600 rads); flaking and itching of the skin occurs after 10 Gy (1000 rads), and weeping, blistering and ulceration will occur after 10–20 Gy (1000–2000 rads) . In war such lesions may become infected and gangrenous and healing will be protracted. After 2–3 Gy (200–300 rads), hair loss will be temporary, but permanent epilation will follow more than about 7 Gy (700 rads). Months and years after the high localized doses, late injuries to the skin will appear; these include deep fibrosis and contraction of the irradiated area. Such areas will be susceptible to trauma so that heat, cold or bruising will readily cause wounds that do not heal successfully and involve necrosis and ulceration. All such effects have been clinically documented and were seen in the Japanese victims (2).

The Lung

The lung is the most radiosensitive organ of the thorax. It may be irradiated from external gamma rays or internally from inhalation of radioactive fallout particulates. Radiation pneumonitis involves a loss of epithelial cells, edema, inflammation and occlusion of airways, air sacs and blood vessels, and finally fibrosis. All of these effects can cause pulmonary insufficiency and death within a few months of irradiation. Consideration of radiotherapy data suggests the threshold dose for acute lung death is probably 25 Gy (2500 rads) with 100 percent mortality after 50 Gy (5000 rads) to the lung (6), although these doses may be high by a factor of two.

The Ovary and Testis

In the individual, recovery from the acute radiation syndrome in a nuclear war will tend to overshadow many of the other effects of radiation. For example, in heavily-exposed populations both the acute and longterm effects in the testis and ovary may be catastrophic (see also "genetic effects").

The ovary is highly radiosensitive. Single doses of 1–2 Gy (100–200 rads) of gamma radiation will cause temporary sterility and suppress menstruation for periods up to 3 years, and doses of about 4 Gy (400 rads) will cause permanent sterility (7).

The testis is also very radiosensitive. A dose as low as 0.1 Gy (10 rads) produces a low sperm count for up to a year; 2.5 Gy (250 rads) will produce sterility for 2 to 3 years or longer and 4 Gy (400 rads) or more will cause permanent sterility.

LONGTERM EFFECTS

The principal longterm or delayed effects of radiation are genetic damage, cancer induction, cataract induction, late radiation fibrosis and blood vessel damage.

Cataract Induction

Radiation readily causes opacities of the lens of the eye. The threshold dose to produce opacities in a few percent of those exposed is 2 Gy (200 rads) of acute gamma rays, while 6–7 Gy (600–700 rads) would cause opacities in most of those exposed. They would be likely to seriously impair vision and are then called cataracts. The time between irradiation and the appearance of the cataracts is highly variable and may be as short as 6 months or as long as 30 years, with a median time of 2–3 years.

Cancer Induction

The induction of fatal cancer is the most significant longterm risk of radiation. Table 3 shows the major human populations that have been studied to estimate the human radiogenic cancer risk. There are more than a dozen different organs of the body for which there is good epidemiological data (8).

It is widely accepted that for radiogenic cancer a linear no-threshold-dose relationship is not only administratively practical (9, 10, 11) but consistent with much of the epidemiological data (8). A linear response implies that however small the radiation dose there is some increased risk of fatal cancer being induced. Table 4 gives the International Commission on Radiological Protection risk factors for fatal cancer. These factors are a measure of the probability of cancer induction per unit of dose. In the Table the units are sieverts, which for gamma rays can be taken as equivalent to 1 Gy (100 rads).

The risk factors are intended to apply irrespective of age and sex, and since men are not susceptible to breast cancer the

65

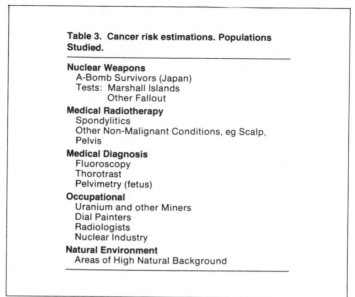

Table 3. Cancer risk estimations. Populations Studied.

Nuclear Weapons
  A-Bomb Survivors (Japan)
  Tests: Marshall Islands
            Other Fallout
Medical Radiotherapy
  Spondylitics
  Other Non-Malignant Conditions, eg Scalp,
  Pelvis
Medical Diagnosis
  Fluoroscopy
  Thorotrast
  Pelvimetry (fetus)
Occupational
  Uranium and other Miners
  Dial Painters
  Radiologists
  Nuclear Industry
Natural Environment
  Areas of High Natural Background

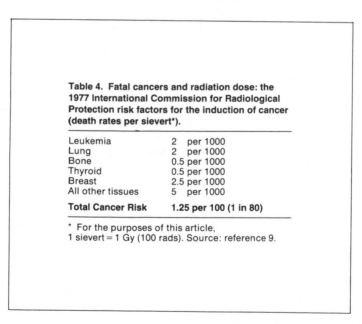

Table 4. Fatal cancers and radiation dose: the 1977 International Commission for Radiological Protection risk factors for the induction of cancer (death rates per sievert*).

Leukemia	2 per 1000
Lung	2 per 1000
Bone	0.5 per 1000
Thyroid	0.5 per 1000
Breast	2.5 per 1000
All other tissues	5 per 1000
Total Cancer Risk	**1.25 per 100 (1 in 80)**

* For the purposes of this article,
1 sievert = 1 Gy (100 rads). Source: reference 9.

factor for females is twice that given in Table 4. The total mortality risk for cancer is 1.2×10^{-2} (1 in 80). This means that on average, for every eighty people exposed to 1 Gy (100 rads), one would subsequently die from radiation-induced cancer. The latent period before the appearance of the cancer will vary with the type of cancer and may be as short as 2 years for leukemia or more than 20 years for skin or lung cancer. The total number of fatal plus non-fatal cancers likely to be induced is probably

Table 5. Probable genetic consequences of exposure to 1 Gy (100 rads) (per 1 million live births).

Disease Category	"Natural" Incidence	Effect of 100 rads per first generation	equilibrium
Autosomal Dominant and X-linked Disease	10 000	2 000	10 000
Recessive Disease	1 100	slight	very slow increase
Chromosomal Disease	4 000	3 800	4 000
Congenital abnormalities, anomalies expressed in later life and constitutional and degenerative disease	90 000	500	4 500
Total	105 100	6 300	18 500
Percentage of Current Incidence		6 %	17 %

Source: reference 8.

Table 6. Dimension of fallout plumes within seven days following surface bursts (in kms).

Bomb size	Radiation dose in Gy (rads)		
	> 1 (100)	> 4.5 (450)	> 6 (600)
1 Mt	30×266	17×129	16×113
3 Mt	60×394	34×177	31×153
10 Mt	114×595	74×274	70×249

Source: reference 16.

more than twice the fatal cancer risk. Despite the apparent precision of these internationally agreed risk factors they are only rough estimates and may be wrong by a factor of 4 or more (12). So once again the magnitude of the late effects of radiation 10, 20 or 30 years after the holocaust is difficult to estimate.

Genetic Effects

Genetic (heritable) effects of radiation have been known for 50 years. Nevertheless few human data are, or are likely to be, available and so all risk estimates have to be derived from experimental studies on mice. It is recognized that some 10 percent of human beings suffer from diseases or defects at some time in their lives which are wholly or partly genetic in origin. Some 90 percent of these defects are "irregularly inherited" congenital conditions such as spina bifida, hydrocephalus, cleft palate, diabetes, myopia and so on.

It is not known what fraction of these spontaneous genetic diseases is attributable to radiation. Nor is it known to what extent the diseases and defects are maintained in a population by mutations. Nevertheless any increase in the mutation rate in humans would be a matter of grave concern. The estimates of the doses to double (*ie* match) the natural mutation frequency in man vary from 0.16 Gy (16 rads) to 2.5 Gy (250 rads) (13, 14). The value of 1 Gy (100 rads) given by the UNSCEAR Genetics Committee (8) will be used in the calculations in this paper. Table 5 gives the likely genetic consequences in a population from 1 Gy (100 rads) of gamma radiation. It must be noted that only about 40 percent of radiation delivered uniformly to a population will be "genetically significant"; 60 percent will be wasted (genetically that is) on people more than 30 years of age who are unlikely to have more children.

IN UTERO EFFECTS

Finally, we must consider the harm likely to be caused to the developing embryo or fetus. These risks are prenatal and perinatal mortality; the birth of malformed children; and the increased frequency of fatal malignant disease in childhood. The natural rate of perinatal mortality in the United Kingdom is 25 per 1000 births; for

67

mental retardation the rate is 4 per 1000 births. Approximately 1 in 4 of perinatal deaths (stillbirths and deaths within 7 days of birth) are caused by congenital abnormalities. The overall risk of the birth of a severely handicapped child in the average pregnancy is approximately 1 in 30 births in the UK (15).

It is estimated that a dose of 1 Gy (100 rads) might cause between zero and 20 extra cases of perinatal mortality per 1000 births and a similar number, 0–20 cases of severe mental subnormality that would be recognized in adolescence (15).

About 1 child in 2000 in the UK is likely to die from cancer before the age of ten. A dose of 0.05 Gy (5 rads) is estimated to increase the expectation of such childhood cancer by tenfold to 5 per 1000. An antenatal dose of 1 Gy (100 rads) in the first trimester of gestation might engender a fatal childhood cancer risk as high as 10 percent. So the carcinogenic risk of antenatal radiation is many times greater than the teratogenic risk (15).

THE ESTIMATED MEDICAL CONSEQUENCES OF RADIOACTIVE FALLOUT IN A GLOBAL NUCLEAR WAR

Using the information given in the previous sections we shall attempt to estimate the health effects from the ionizing radiation associated with the *Ambio* scenario.

It must be stressed that the heat and blast effects will far outweigh those due to ionizing radiation. In the scenario all the major cities in the Northern Hemisphere will be reduced to rubble by blast, and depending upon certain assumptions between 60–90 percent of their populations will be annihilated by blast and thermal radiation (16). These effects are treated elsewhere in this issue.

In calculating the effects of radiation we have assumed that the average population density in the areas directly attacked is 100 persons per km². The actual range is 50–250 persons per km². The calculations therefore do not consider that there are areas of higher density, *ie* cities. According to the UN demographic yearbook the average population densities of the USA and USSR in 1985 will be about 25 and 12 per km² respectively. But the density in the bombed areas will be 50 per km² or more. In 1985 the West European population density will be 170 per km².

Each bomb is assumed to act independently. In reality there would be overlap of the fallout plumes, both with each other and with the areas of blast and thermal radiation. This would produce widespread areas of overkill.

Table 6 gives the dimensions of the elliptical areas likely to receive more than 1 Gy, 4.5 Gy, and 6 Gy (100 rads, 450 rads and 600 rads) of local fallout within seven days of the dropping of 1, 3 and 10 Mt weapons. These dimensions were calculated using data from Glasstone (17). Since about 80 percent of these seven-day doses will be received within 24 hours of the explosion, the dose can be considered to be acute. The main hazard comes from the external whole body gamma ray dose but there will be external beta-irradiation and an internal dose from the inhalation or ingestion of radioactive particles. Besides the fallout those closest to the explosion will receive supralethal doses of initial radiation (gamma rays and neutrons) during the first minute after the explosion. However for megaton weapons the range of this intense radiation is much less than the range of the lethal blast and thermal radiation (16).

Table 7 gives the areas (km²) of Western Europe likely to receive greater than 1 Gy (100 rads), greater than 4.5 Gy (450 rads), and greater than 6 Gy (600 rads), of fallout within seven days after the beginning of the war specified in the scenario. Using the value of 100 persons per km², the Table also gives the likely number of West Europeans who will be so exposed. It is important to emphasize that in our calculations of the populations at risk no allowance has been made for the large number of people that will be killed in the cities by blast and heat. In reality therefore the number of people at risk from fallout would be considerably reduced. Table 7a assumes a protection factor (PF) of one, *ie* that the people remain more or less in the open for the first few days after the explosions. If they stay in their houses all the time a PF of 3 might apply and the adjusted numbers of those exposed to more than 1 Gy (100 rads), 4.5 Gy (450 rads) and 6 Gy (600 rads) given in Table 7b. Similar tables were computed for North America, East, Middle and West Asia, Eastern Europe and for the USSR.

Protection factors greater than 10 may apply if people have stayed in shelters. But evacuation and shelter programs require a knowledge of not only where the fallout is going to go but also how long it is going to last. It might well be unwise for a sheltered population to assume it was safe to emerge at the end of two weeks when the fallout dose rate will have decreased by a factor of 1 000, since if the initial local rate were high the excess radiation levels would be a persistent hazard. This persistence is rec-

ognized by the civil defense authorities (18), and it would mean that even if medical teams were available and coordinated they would not be able to work in fallout areas until several weeks had elapsed, *ie* when it is too late for most of the exposed persons, who will have died slowly of acute radiation sickness.

Table 8 gives the number of radiation deaths that will occur within 6–8 weeks in the areas of the Northern Hemisphere involved in the scenario. The calculations assume that 4.5 Gy (450 rads) or more will kill about 50 percent of an exposed population and 6 Gy (600 rads) or more will kill 100 percent. Table 8 also gives these values assuming people stay indoors (PF = 3). We can see that 19 million North Americans (7.4 percent of the population) will die within weeks after the outbreak of nuclear war. The Table also shows that 62 million (24 percent of the population) will receive doses between 1 Gy (100 rads) and 4.5 Gy (450 rads). Both these figures assume the population remains indoors continuously for at least seven days. Remember also that these deaths are to a large extent additional to those due to blast and thermal radiation.

Table 7. Areas and populations in Western Europe exposed to specific levels of radiation within seven days of a global nuclear war (assuming 100 people/km².).

Number and size of weapons	Dose > 1 Gy (100 rads)	Dose > 4.5 Gy (450 rads)	Dose > 6 Gy (600 rads)
(a) Protection Factor = 1			
284 @ 1 Mt	17.8×10^5	4.9×10^5	4.03×10^5
25 @ 3 Mt	4.6×10^5	1.2×10^5	0.93×10^5
8 @ 10 Mt	4.3×10^5	1.3×10^5	1.1×10^5
Total Area (km²)	26.7×10^4	7.4×10^4	60.6×10^4
Numbers Irradiated (millions)	267	74	61
(b) Protection Factor = 3			
284 @ 1 Mt	6.82×10^5	1.57×10^5	1.25×10^5
25 @ 3 Mt	1.72×10^5	0.4×10^5	0.33×10^5
8 @ 10 Mt	1.79×10^5	0.53×10^5	0.4×10^5
Total Area (km²)	10.33×10^5	2.57×10^5	1.98×10^5
Numbers Irradiated (millions)	103	26	20

69

Table 8. Estimated number of acute radiation deaths from fallout (millions).

Area	N. America		East Asia		Middle S. Asia		Western S. Asia		E. Europe		Europe		USSR	
Protection Factor	1	3	1	3	1	3	1	3	1	3	1	3	1	3
No. of Deaths — Within Days	47	16	56	19	45	15	13	4	13	4	61	20	40	13
Within Weeks	5	3	6	4	5	3	2	1	2	1	7	3	4	2
Total	52	19	62	23	50	18	15	5	15	5	68	23	44	15
%	20.1	7.4	4.9	1.8	4.6	1.7	13.2	4.4	13.2	4.4	18.0	6.1	15.7	5.4
No. Surviving — Total	156	62	187	78	148	60	45	18	45	18	200	80	135	53
% ≥ 1 Gy (100 rads)	60.4	24.0	14.8	6.2	13.7	5.6	39.8	15.9	39.6	15.8	52.8	21.1	48.3	18.9

Table 9. Secondary radiation effects. Number of persons likely to suffer permanent sterility, to die of cancer, or to suffer genetic effects from fallout (in millions).

Area	N. America		East Asia		Middle S. Asia		Western S. Asia		E. Europe		Europe		USSR	
Protection Factor	1	3	1	3	1	3	1	3	1	3	1	3	1	3
Sterility — No.	5	3	6	4	5	3	2	1	2	1	7	3	4	2
Sterility — %	1.9	1.2	0.5	0.3	0.5	0.3	1.8	0.9	1.8	0.9	1.8	0.8	1.4	0.7
Fatal Cancer — No.	2.1	0.9	2.6	1.1	2.1	0.9	0.6	0.3	0.7	0.3	2.8	1.1	1.9	0.7
Fatal Cancer — %	0.8	0.3	0.2	0.09	0.2	0.08	0.5	0.3	0.6	0.3	0.7	0.3	0.7	0.3
Heritable Effects — 1st Generation No.	1	0.4	1.1	0.5	0.9	0.4	0.3	0.1	0.3	0.1	1.2	0.5	0.8	0.3
1st Generation %	0.4	0.2	0.09	0.04	0.08	0.04	0.3	0.09	0.3	0.09	0.3	0.1	0.3	0.1
At Equilibrium No.	2.8	1.1	3.3	1.3	2.6	1.1	0.8	0.3	0.8	0.3	3.6	1.4	2.4	0.9
At Equilibrium %	1.1	0.4	0.3	0.1	0.2	0.1	0.7	0.3	0.7	0.3	0.9	0.4	0.9	0.3

Table 9 gives the estimates of the number of people likely to be sterilized by radiation, *ie* the proportion receiving 4.5–6 Gy (450–600 rads) but who do not die within 6–8 weeks of exposure. It can be seen that between 3 (PF = 3) and 5 (PF = 1) million North Americans are likely to be permanently sterilized by fallout.

The fatal cancer risks given in Table 9 show that 10–20 years after the war, between 5.4 million (PF = 3) and 13 million (PF = 1) people in the Northern Hemisphere will die of a variety of cancers as a result of the fallout exposure. These calculations for fatal cancer and those below for hereditary effects are extremely conservative. All of the people receiving between 1 Gy and 4.5 Gy (100 rads and 450 rads) are assumed to have received 1 Gy (100 rads); similarly, the 50 percent survivors in the 4.5–6 Gy (450–600 rad) group are all assumed to have received 4.5 Gy (450 rads).

Finally, Table 9 gives the likely hereditary consequences of the seven-day fallout doses. It shows that at equilibrium, *ie* within say 100 years of the war, between 6.4 million (PF = 3) and 16.3 million (PF = 1) people in the Northern Hemisphere are likely to suffer some genetic defects attributable to their parents' exposure in 1985.

For the sake of brevity we have confined our calculations to the accumulated seven-day fallout doses; had we chosen, say the 25 year dose, we would have found that the whole of Europe would receive a dose of 1 Gy (100 rads) or more. In peacetime, such a chronic dose would necessitate complete evacuation.

In conclusion, one must again stress the vast uncertainties in all the above calculations and note that similar uncertainties attend attempts to gauge the effectiveness of any medical or civil defense efforts to ameliorate the post-holocaust conditions.

References and Notes

1. A W Oughterson, S Warren, *Medical Effects of the Atomic Bomb in Japan*, 1st Edition, McGraw Hill Book Co. Inc. (1956).
2. *Hiroshima and Nagasaki: the Physical, Medical and Social Effects of the Atomic Bombings*, by the Committee for the Compilation of Materials on Damage Caused by the Atomic Bombs in Hiroshima and Nagasaki, translated by E Ishikawa, D L Swain, Basic Books Inc. (1981).
3. C C Lushbaugh, *Human Radiation Tolerance in Space Radiation Biology and Related Topics*, Edited C A Tobias, P Todd, Academic Press, pp. 475–522 (1974).
4. V P Bond, *Radiation Mortality in Different Mammalian Species in Comparative Cellular and Species Radiosensitivity*, Edited V P Bond, T Sugahara, Igaku Shoin Ltd. Tokyo. pp. 5–16 (1969).
5. C C Lushbaugh, J Auxier, "Reestimation of Human LD_{50} Radiation Levels at Hiroshima and Nagasaki", *Radiation Research* **39**, 526 (1969).
6. H Smith, J W Stather, *Human Exposure to Radiation Following the Release of Radioactivity from a Reactor Accident: A quantitative assessment of the biological consequences*, National Radiobiological Protection Board of UK. NRPB-Report No. 52 (1976).
7. A C Upton, *Effects of Radiation on Man*, in Annual Review of Nuclear Science. **18**, pp. 495–528 (1968).
8. *Report to the General Assembly on Sources and Effects of Ionizing Radiation*, United Nations Scientific Committee on the Effects of Atomic Radiation. UN E.77.IX.1. United Nations, New York. (1977).
9. *Recommendations of the ICRP*, International Commission on Radiological Protection, Publication No. 26 (1977).
10. *Review of the Current State of Radiation Protection Philosophy*, Report No. 43, National Council on Radiation Protection and Measurements, Washington, DC (1975).
11. R Doll. "Radiation Hazards: 25 Years of Collaborative Research", *British Journal of Radiology* **54**, 179 (1981).
12. M W Charles, P J Lindop, "Risk assessment without the bombs", *Journal of the Society for Radiological Protection* **1**, 15 (1981).
13. BEIR I 1972. *The Effects on Populations of Exposure to Low Levels of Ionizing Radiation*. National Research Council, Advisory Committee on the Biological Effects of Ionizing Radiation. National Academy of Sciences, Washington, DC (1972).
14. BEIR III 1980. *The Effects on Populations of Exposure to Low Levels of Ionizing Radiation*, National Research Council, Advisory Committee on the Biological Effects of Ionizing Radiation, National Academy of Sciences, Washington, DC (1980).
15. R H Mole, "Radiation Effects on Pre-Natal Development and Their Radiological Significance", *British Journal of Radiology* **52**, 89 (1979).
16. *The Effects of Nuclear War*, Office of Technology Assessment, Congress of the United States, Washington, DC (1979).
17. S Glasstone, J P Dolan, *The Effects of Nuclear Weapons*, 3rd Edition, US Department of Defense and Department of Energy (1977).
18. *Home Defence Circular* (77) **1**, London, DHHS (1977).

SIX

THE ATMOSPHERE AFTER A NUCLEAR WAR: TWILIGHT AT NOON

PAUL J. CRUTZEN AND JOHN W. BIRKS

As a result of a nuclear war vast areas of forests will go up in smoke—corre-sponding at least to the combined land mass of Denmark, Norway and Sweden. In addition to the tremendous fires that will burn for weeks in cities and industrial centers, fires will also rage across croplands and it is likely that at least 1.5 billion tons of stored fossil fuels (mostly oil and gas) will be destroyed. The fires will produce a thick smoke layer that will drastically reduce the amount of sunlight reaching the earth's surface. This darkness would persist for many weeks, render-ing any agricultural activity in the Northern Hemisphere virtually impossible if the war takes place during the growing season.

The immediate effects of a global nuclear war are so severe that any additional long-term effects might at first thought be regarded as insignificant in comparison. However, our investigation into the state of the atmosphere following a nuclear exchange suggests that other severely damaging effects to human life and the delicate ecosystems to which we belong will occur during the following weeks and months. Many of these effects have not been evaluated before.

Previous investigations of the atmospheric effects following a nuclear war have been concentrated primarily on the expected large depletions of ozone in the stratosphere (1,2). Reduction of the stratospheric ozone shield allows increased levels of harmful ultraviolet (uv) radiation to penetrate to the surface of the earth. Such ozone depletion results from the injection of oxides of nitrogen (NO_x) by large nuclear weapons having yields greater than one megaton. Should the nations having nuclear arsenals choose to use their large warheads in a nuclear war, then the earth's protective ozone layer would be much depleted, and the consequent adverse effects associated with the increased flux of ultraviolet radiation would occur. Our conclusions for such a scenario concur with those found in the 1975 report of the US National Academy of Sciences (1).

As assumed in Ambio's reference scenario, it is now believed that the most likely nuclear war is one in which few weapons having yields greater than 1 Mt are used, with preference given to the detonation of large numbers of smaller yield weapons. For such a nuclear war, very little NO_x would be injected above 15 km into the stratosphere by the nuclear bursts, and thus depletion of the ozone layer would not occur as a direct result of the explosions. Nonetheless, other profound effects on the atmosphere can be expected.

In discussing the state of the atmosphere following a nuclear exchange, we point especially to the effects of the many fires that would be ignited by the thousands of nuclear explosions in cities, forests, agricultural fields, and oil and gas fields. As a result of these fires, the loading of the atmosphere with strongly light absorbing particles in the submicron size range (1 micron = 10^{-6} m) would increase so much that at noon solar radiation at the ground would be reduced by at least a factor of two and possibly a factor of greater than one hundred. In addition, fires inject large quantities of oxides of nitrogen and reactive hydrocarbons, the ingredients of photochemical smog. This creates the potential for photochemical smog throughout much of the Northern Hemisphere which may persist for several months after the particulate matter has been deposited on the ground. Such effects have been largely overlooked or not carefully examined in previous considerations of this problem. They are, therefore, considered in some detail in this study.

NUCLEAR WAR SCENARIOS

The explosion of nuclear weapons produces oxides of nitrogen by heating air to temperatures well above 2000 K. When the major constituents of the air—nitrogen and oxygen—are heated to high temperature, nitric oxide (NO) is formed. The equilibrium between N_2, O_2 and NO is rapidly approached at the temperatures characteristic of the nuclear explosions:

$$N_2 + O_2 \leftrightarrow 2\,NO$$

As the temperature of the heated air falls, the reactions which maintain equilibrium become slow and NO cannot revert to the innocuous oxygen and nitrogen. Consequently, nuclear explosions produce NO in much the same way as it is formed as a pollutant in automobile and aircraft engines. A review of the mechanisms forming NO in nuclear explosions is provided in Appendix I to this chapter. The oxides of nitrogen are important trace atmospheric constituents and play a very important role

74

in atmospheric photochemistry. They are key constituents in the formation of photochemical smog in the troposphere, and the catalytic reaction cycle leading to ozone destruction is the principal means by which ozone concentrations are regulated in the stratosphere. In Appendix I it is estimated that there are 1×10^{32} molecules of NO formed for each megaton of explosion yield. As will be discussed later, large amounts of nitric oxide would also be formed by the many fires that would be started during a nuclear war.

With regard to direct NO_x formation in nuclear explosions, we consider two nuclear war scenarios. Scenario I is Ambio's reference scenario (3). In this scenario bombs having a total yield of 5750 Mt are detonated. The latitudinal and vertical distributions of the 5.7×10^{35} molecules of nitric oxide produced in these explosions are determined by the weapon sizes and targets projected for this scenario. Since most of the weapons have yields less than 1 Mt, most of the NO_x is deposited in the troposphere, and the effect on the chemistry of the stratosphere is much less than if the bomb debris were deposited mainly in the stratosphere. The assumed NO input pattern for the Scenario I war is provided in Table 1.

The Scenario II war is similar to those used in previous studies by investigators using one-dimensional models and is included here mostly for historical reasons. This scenario considers a total yield of 10 000 Mt uniformly distributed between 20° and 60° in the Northern Hemisphere. The vertical distribution of NO is calculated assuming equal yields of 1-Mt and 10-Mt weapons, *ie* 5000 1-Mt weapons and 500 10-Mt weapons are detonated. For this scenario, equal quantities of NO_x are injected above and below 18 km, as seen in Table 2. Thus, the tropospheric effects for the Scenario II war are similar to those for the Scenario I war. However, the Scenario II war also results in an additional large perturbation of the stratospheric ozone layer.

Table 1. Distribution of NO_x produced by nuclear explosions for Scenario I (x 10^{32} molecules).

Alt. (km)	60°S–30°S	30°S–EQ	EQ–20°N	20°N–40°N	40°N–60°N	60°N–NP	Sum
30	–	–	–	0.7	–	–	0.7
29	–	–	–	0.7	1	–	1.7
28	–	–	–	2.3	1	–	3.3
27	–	–	–	2.3	3	–	5.3
26	–	–	–	2.3	3	–	5.3
25	–	–	–	2.3	3	–	5.3
24	–	–	–	3.7	3	–	6.7
23	–	–	–	3.7	5	–	8.7
22	–	–	–	3.7	5	–	8.7
21	–	–	–	3.7	5	–	8.7
20	–	–	–	2.1	5	–	7.1
19	–	–	–	2.1	2.8	–	4.9
18	–	0.3	1.1	0.1	2.8	–	4.3
17	–	1.1	3.5	10.4	0.2	–	15.2
16	0.7	3.5	10.8	30.7	24.5	–	70.2
15	2.3	8.9	27.5	30.7	72.9	–	142.3
14	2.3	8.9	27.5	116.8	72.9	1.1	229.5
13	3.7	13.0	39.7	247.7	121.5	3.5	429.1
12	8.5	12.1	36.7	225.1	276.6	3.5	562.5
11	16.6	6.6	20.4	329.4	533.5	11.9	918.4
10	14.6	0.5	1.5	327.3	470.2	26.4	840.5
9	24.4	–	–	183.2	775.8	25.0	1 008.4
8	24.4	–	–	13.2	775.8	36.7	850.1
7	13.6	–	–	–	434.4	36.5	484.5
6	1.0	–	–	–	21.0	20.4	42.4
5	–	–	–	–	–	1.5	1.5
Sum	**112.1**	**54.9**	**168.7**	**1 544.2**	**3 618.9**	**166.5**	**5 665.3**

Table 2. Distribution of NO_x produced by nuclear explosions for Scenario II (x 10^{32} molecules).

Alt. (km)	20°N–40°N	40°N–60°N	Sum
31	62	62	124
30	62	62	124
29	188	188	376
28	188	188	376
27	188	188	376
26	188	188	376
25	312	312	624
24	312	312	624
23	312	312	624
22	312	312	624
21	175	175	350
20	175	175	350
19	80	80	160
18	54	54	108
17	80	80	160
16	125	125	250
15	375	375	750
14	375	375	750
13	625	625	1 250
12	625	625	1 250
11	350	350	700
10	25	25	50
Sum	5 000	5 000	10 000

FIRES

From an atmospheric point of view, the most serious effects of a nuclear war would most likely result from the many fires which would start in the war and could not be extinguished because of nuclear contaminations and loss of water lines, fire equipment and expert personnel. The devastating effects of such fires in urban areas were indicated by Lewis (4). Here we show that the atmospheric effects would be especially dramatic. Several types of fires may rage. Besides the fires in urban and industrial centers, vast forest fires would start, extensive grasslands and agricultural land would burn, and it is likely that many natural gas and oil wells would be ruptured as a result of the nuclear explosions, releasing huge quantities of oil and natural gas, much of which would catch fire. To give an estimate of the possible effects, we will consider as a working hypothesis that 10^6 km^2 of forests will burn (this corresponds roughly to the combined area of Denmark, Norway and Sweden) and that breaks in gas and oil production wells will release gaseous effluents from the earth corresponding to the current rate of worldwide usage. In our opinion these are underestimates of the real extent of fires that would occur in a major nuclear war (see also footnote).*

Gaseous and Particulate Emissions from Forest Fires

In the US and especially in Canada and the USSR, vast forests are found close to important urban strategic centers, so that it may be expected that many wildfires would start burning during and after the nuclear exchange. Although it is hard to estimate how much forest area might burn, a total of 10^6 km^2, spread around in the Northern Hemisphere, is probably an underestimate, as it is only about 20 times larger than what is now annually consumed by wildfires (5). This amounts to 4 percent of the temperate and boreal forest lands, and is not larger than that of the urban areas combined (6). Furthermore, Ward et al (7) have pointed out that effective fire control and prevention programs have reduced the loss of forests in the US (exclusive of Alaska) from 1.8×10^5 km^2 in the early 1930's to less than 1.6×10^4 km^2 by the mid 1970's. The US Forest Service is quoted as estimating that a nuclear attack on the US of ~ 1500 Mt would burn a land area of $0.4-6 \times 10^6$ km^2 in the US (8). All this information indicates that our assumption of 10^6 km^2 of forest area that could be consumed by fire is not an overestimate.

An area of 10^6 km^2 of forest contains on the average about 2.2×10^{16} g dry matter or about 10^{16} g of carbon phytomass (6) and about 10^{14} g of fixed nitrogen, not counting the material which is contained in soil organic matter. Typically, during forest wildfires about 25 percent of the available phytomass is burned (5), so that 2.5×10^{15} g of carbon would be released to the atmosphere. During wildfires about 75 kg of particulate matter is produced per ton of forest material burned or 450 kg of carbon (7), so that 4×10^{14} g of particulate matter is injected into the atmosphere by the forest fires. Independently, we can use the information by Ward et al (7) to estimate the global biomass and suspended particulate matter expected to be produced by wildfires which would be started by the nuclear war. According to these authors the forest area now burned annually in the US, excluding Alaska, is about 1.8×10^4 km^2, which delivers 3.5×10^{12} g particulate matter to the atmosphere. Accordingly, a total area of 10^6 km^2 would inject 2×10^{14} g particulate matter into the atmosphere, which should come from 3×10^{15} g of burned forest material, or 1.3×10^{15} g C. This is a factor of two less than the earlier derived estimate, so we will use a range of $1.3-2.5 \times 10^{15}$ g of carbon as the global atmospheric gaseous release and $2-4 \times 10^{14}$ g as particulate matter.

In forest fires most of the carbon is released as CO_2 to the atmosphere. The forest fire contribution to the atmospheric CO_2 content, which totals 7×10^{17} g of carbon, is rather insignificant. The repercussions of the forest fires are, however, much

---

*

The attenuations of sunlight at great distances from forest fires have been documented for many years. Phenomena such as "dark days", "dry fog", "Indian summer" and "colored rain" are now attributed to smoke produced by fires in forests, prairies and peat bogs. The great forest fires during October 13-17, 1918 in Minnesota and adjacent sections of Wisconsin produced smoke that had strong optical effects and could even be smelled as far away as the eastern US coast. A report from Cincinnati, Ohio is particularly descriptive (H Lyman, Reference 17): "At 3 PM the smoke and haze became denser, but the sun's light and its disk could be seen until 3:35 PM, at which time the sun was entirely obscured. Objects at this time could not be seen at a distance of 300 feet." More than 100 forest fires in northwestern Alberta and northeastern British Columbia resulted in the "Great Smoke Pall" of September 24-30, 1950 with press reports carrying accounts of smoke being observed as far away as England, France, Portugal, Denmark and Sweden (H Wexler, Reference 17). Most of Canada and the eastern one-third of the continental US were particularly affected. In the eastern US the smoke was confined to the altitude range of about 2.5-4.5 km, so that there was no reduced visibility at the ground. However, the sun was so obscured that it was visible to the naked eye without discomfort and had what was typically described as a violet or lavender color. Measurements in Washington, DC indicated that the solar intensity was reduced by a factor of two on September 25-26 in the absence of clouds.

more important for the contribution of other gases to the atmosphere, *eg* carbon monoxide (CO). With a relative release rate ratio $CO:CO_2$ of about 15 percent (9), the production of CO would amount to $2-4 \times 10^{14}$ g C, which is roughly equal to or two times larger than the present atmospheric CO content (10). Within a short period of time, average concentrations of CO at midlatitudes in the Northern Hemisphere would increase by up to a factor of four, and much larger CO increases may be expected on the continents, especially in regions downwind (generally east of the fires). Accompanying those emissions there will also be significant inputs of tens of Teragrams (1 Teragram = 1 Tg = 10^{12} g) of reactive hydrocarbons to the atmosphere, mostly ethylene (C_2H_4) and propylene (C_3H_6), which are important ingredients in urban, photochemical smog formation. More important, phytomass consists roughly of about 1 percent fixed nitrogen, which is mainly contained in the smaller-sized material such as leaves, bark, twigs and small branches, which are preferentially burned during fires. As a rough estimate, because of the forest fires we may expect an input of 15–30 Tg of nitrogen into the atmosphere (7). Such an emission of NO would be larger than the production in the nuclear fireballs and comparable to the entire annual input of NO_x by industrial processes. Considering the critical role of NO in the production of tropospheric ozone, it is conceivable that a large accumulation of ozone in the troposphere, leading to global photochemical smog conditions, may take place. An increase of ozone due to photochemical processes in forest fire plumes has indeed been observed by several investigators (11, 12).

Particulate Matter from Forest Fires and Screening of Sunlight

The total production of $2-4 \times 10^{14}$ g of particulate matter from the burning of 10^6 km^2 of forests is comparable on a volume basis to the total global production of particulate matter with diameter less than 3 microns (μm) over an entire year (or 200–400 million tons, 13). The physical and chemical nature of this material has been reviewed (14).

The bulk of the mass (>90 percent) of the particulate matter from forest fires consists of particles with diameters of less than 1 μm and a maximum particle number density at a diameter of 0.1 μm. The material has a very high organic matter content (40–75 percent) and much of it is formed from gaseous organic precursors. Its composition is on the average: 55 percent tar, 25 percent soot and 20 percent ash. These particles strongly absorb sunlight and infrared radiation. The light extinction coefficient, b_s (m), is related to the smoke density, d (g/m^3), by the relationship $b_s = ad$, where a is approximately 4–9 m^2/g (14, 15). With most smoke particles in the submicron size range, their average residence time in the atmosphere is about 5–10 days (13). If we assume that the forest fires will last for two months (16), a spread of $2-4 \times 10^{14}$ g of aerosol over half of the Northern Hemisphere will cause an average particle loading such that the integrated vertical column of particles is equal to 0.1–0.5 g/m^2. As a result, the average sunlight penetration to the ground will be reduced by a factor between 2 and 150 at noontime in the summer. This would imply that much of the Northern Hemisphere would be darkened in the daytime for an extended period of time following the nuclear exchange. The large-scale atmospheric effects of massive forest fires have been documented in a number of papers (16, 17). Big forest fires in arctic regions are commonly accompanied by huge fires in peat bogs, which may burn over two meters in depth without any possibility of being extinguished (16). The production of aerosol by such fires has not been included in the above estimates.

Gas, Oil and Urban Fires

In addition to the above mentioned fires there are also the effects of fires in cities and industrial centers, where huge quantities of combustible materials and chemicals are stored. As an example, if the European 95-day energy stockpile is roughly representative for the world (18), about 1.5×10^{15} g C fossil fuel (around 1.5 thousand million tons) is stored globally. Much of this would be destroyed in the event of a nuclear war. Therefore, if the relative emission yields of particulate matter by oil and gas fires are about equal to those of forest fires, similar rates of production of atmospheric aerosol would result. Although it may be enormously important, in this study we will not consider the global environmental impacts of the burning and release of chemicals from urban and industrial fires, as we do not yet have enough information available to discuss this matter in a quantitative manner.

Even more serious atmospheric consequences are possible, due to the many fires which would start when oil and gas production wells are destroyed, being among the principal targets included in the main scenario provided for this study (5). Large quantities of oil and gas which are now contained under high pressure would then flow up to the earth's surface or escape into the atmosphere, accompanied by huge fires. Of course, it is not possible for the nuclear powers to target all of the more than 600 000 gas and oil wells of the world. However, certain regions of the world where production is both large and concentrated in small areas are likely to be prime targets in a nuclear war. Furthermore, the blowout of a natural gas well results in the release of gas at a much greater rate than is allowed when under control and in a production network. For example, one of the more famous blowouts, "The Devil's Cigarette Lighter", occurred at Gassi Touil in the Sahara. This well released 15×10^6 m^3 of gas per day until the 200-meter high flame was finally extinguished by explosives and the well capped (19). Fewer than 300 such blowouts would be required to release natural gas (partly burned) to the atmosphere at a rate equal to present consumption. Descriptions of other blowouts such as the Ekofisk Bravo oil platform in the North Sea (20), a sour gas well (27 percent H_2S) in the province of Alberta, Canada (21) and the Ixtoc I oil well in the Gulf of Mexico (22) may be found in the literature.

As an example of how very few weapons could be used to release large quantities of natural gas, consider the gas fields of the Netherlands. The 1980 production of 7.9×10^{10} m^3 of natural gas in Groningen amounted to 38 percent of that for all of Western Europe and 5 percent of that for the entire world (19). Most of the gas production in the Netherlands is concentrated in a field of about 700 km^2 area. It seems likely that a 300-kt nuclear burst would uncap every gas well within a radius of 1 km either by melting the metal pipes and valves, by snapping the pipes off at the ground by the shock wave, or by breaking the well casings via shock waves propagated in the earth. This is in consideration of the following facts (23): 1) the fireball radius is 0.9 km, 2) for a surface burst the crater formed is approximately 50 m deep and 270 m in diameter, 3) the maximum overpressure at 1 km is 3.1 atmospheres (atm), 4) the maximum dynamic pressure at 1 km is 3.4 atm, and 5) the maximum wind speed at 1 km is 1700 km/h. Considering then that a 300-kt bomb has a cross-section of greater than 3 km^2 for opening gas wells, fewer than 230 such weapons are required to cover the entire 700 km^2 Groningen field of the Netherlands. This amounts to less than 69 Mt of the 5750 Mt available for the Scenario I nuclear war.

Offshore oil and gas platforms might also be targets of a nuclear war. For example, in 1980 the United Kingdom and Norway produced 2.1×10^6 barrels of oil per day from a total of 390 wells (about 40

79

platforms) in the North Sea (19). Considering that a 100-kt weapon would be more than sufficient to destroy an offshore platform, only 4 Mt of explosive yield need be used to uncap these wells, which produce 3.5 percent of the world's petroleum.

One can point out many other regions of the world where gas and oil production is particularly concentrated. Production in the US is considerably more dispersed than in other countries, however. For comparison, in 1980 the US produced an average of 8.6×10^6 barrels of oil per day from about 530 000 wells whereas the USSR production was 12.1×10^6 barrels per day from only 80 000 wells (19). The oil and gas fields of the Soviet Union, particularly the oil producing Volga-Ural region and the gas and oil fields of the Ob region, are highly localized and particularly vulnerable to nuclear attack.

Much of the gas and oil released as a result of nuclear attacks will burn. This is another source of copious amounts of particulate matter in the atmosphere. However, it is also likely that a fraction of the gas would escape unburned to the atmosphere where it would be gradually broken down by photochemical reactions. Much of the escaping oil may likewise burn, but an appreciable portion of it may volatilize as in the Ixtoc I blowout in the Gulf of Mexico, which resulted in the world's largest oilspill. In this case it is estimated that only 1 percent of the oil burned, while 50–70 percent evaporated (22). We next consider the influence of these emissions on the gaseous composition of the atmosphere.

Natural gas consists usually of a mixture of 80–95 percent (by volume) methane (CH_4) and the remaining 5–20 percent heavier hydrocarbons, mainly ethane (C_2H_6) and propane (C_3H_6), and varying amounts of carbon dioxide and nitrogen. Current global consumption of natural gas amounts to about 10^{15} g of carbon per year, which is 20 percent of the total fossil fuel consumption rate (24). The current atmospheric content of ethane is equal to about 6×10^{12} g of carbon, based on observations indicating amounts of 1 ppbv (1 ppbv $= 10^{-9}$ by volume) in the Southern and 2 ppbv in the Northern Hemisphere (25). Consequently the rapid release of C_2H_6 by blow-outs during a nuclear war can increase by many-fold the atmospheric concentrations of this gas, which has an atmospheric residence time of about two months. Similar conclusions can be drawn with regard to the higher hydrocarbons. Although relative increases of methane in the atmosphere will take place at a relatively slower pace—as its present atmospheric abundance is much larger, 3×10^{15} g of carbon—even here the atmospheric concentrations may multiply if a sufficiently large percentage of the gas wells are being destroyed. Once destroyed, it seems unlikely that quick repair can be possible in a chaotic world in which little expert personnel and equipment will be available, while the fields will furthermore be heavily contaminated with radioactivity.

Of course it is impossible to guess how many oil and gas well destructions would result from a nuclear war, how much gas will burn and how much will escape unburned to the atmosphere. As an example to indicate the atmospheric effects, let us assume that quantities of oil and gas will continue to burn corresponding to present usage rates, with 25 percent of the present production gas escaping unburned into the atmosphere. We do not know whether the latter assumption is realistic. If not, the chosen conditions may represent a gross underestimate of the atmospheric emissions which could take place during and after a nuclear war. This is, of course, especially the case when the world's oil and gas production fields are targeted as foreseen in the main scenario of this study. We simulate NO_x emissions from oil and gas field fires with those provided by current industrial rates. This adds 20 Tg of nitrogen to the NO_x source from forest fires.

TROPOSPHERIC PHOTOCHEMISTRY

For the Scenario I nuclear war most of the bomb cloud remains in the troposphere. The sudden input of a large quantity of nitric oxide of 5.7×10^{35} molecules (12 Tg nitrogen) by nuclear explosions and the more gradual input of NO_x from forest fires and gas and oil well fires, mainly in the Northern Hemisphere, will cause important changes in the course of the photochemical reactions taking place. Of course, these reactions should occur only in regions where sufficient sunlight would still penetrate. Alternatively, these reactions begin to occur after an appreciable fraction of the aerosol loading of the atmosphere has diminished because of removal of the particulate matter by rain or dry deposition. The following discussion is, therefore, mainly aimed at illustrating the sort of photochemical effects that may take place. The presence of NO in the troposphere favors chemical processes leading to the production of ozone, *eg* during the oxidation of carbon monoxide (CO) and methane (CH_4), which are present at part per million levels as normal constituents of the troposphere. The production of ozone in these cases takes place with OH, HO_2, NO and NO_2 as catalysts via the cycles of reaction C1 and C2 shown in Box 1. Under present non-war conditions, it appears that a large fraction of the troposphere does not contain enough NO for ozone production to take place. For such conditions the oxidation of CO occurs instead via the reaction cycle C3 of Box 1. In contrast to reaction cycle C1, cycle C3 leads to ozone destruction. From a comparison of reaction cycles C1 and C3, it follows that ozone production takes place as long as the atmospheric concentration of NO exceeds 1/4000 that of O_3, which is the ratio of rate coefficients for the reactions R11 and R3 (26, 27). If enough NO were present everywhere in the troposphere for all atmospheric oxidation of CO and CH_4 to occur via reaction cycles C1 and C2, the

---

BOX 1

Reaction Cycle C1. In the presence of sufficient NO the oxidation of CO to CO_2 results in the formation of ozone as follows:

R1 $CO + OH \rightarrow H + CO_2$
R2 $H + O_2 + M \rightarrow HO_2 + M$
R3 $HO_2 + NO \rightarrow OH + NO_2$
R4 $NO_2 + hv \rightarrow NO + O$
R5 $O + O_2 + M \rightarrow O_3 + M$

C1 $CO + 2\,O_2 \rightarrow CO_2 + O_3$

Reaction Cycle C2. The oxidation of methane in the atmosphere leads to ozone formation as follows:

R6 $CH_4 + OH \rightarrow CH_3 + H_2O$
R7 $CH_3 + O_2 + M \rightarrow CH_3O_2 + M$
R8 $CH_3O_2 + NO \rightarrow CH_3O + NO_2$
R9 $CH_3O + O_2 \rightarrow CH_2O + HO_2$
R3 $HO_2 + NO \rightarrow OH + NO_2$
R4 $NO_2 + hv \rightarrow NO + O$ (Twice)
R5 $O + O_2 + M \rightarrow O_3 + M$ (Twice)
R10 $CH_2O + hv \rightarrow CO + H_2$

C2 $CH_4 + 4\,O_2 \rightarrow CO + H_2 +$
      $H_2O + 2\,O_3$

Reaction Cycle C3. In the absence of sufficient NO in the atmosphere the oxidation of CO leads to ozone destruction as follows:

R1 $CO + OH \rightarrow CO_2 + H$
R2 $H + O_2 + M \rightarrow HO_2 + M$
R11 $HO_2 + O_3 \rightarrow OH + 2\,O_2$

C3 $CO + O_3 \rightarrow CO_2 + O_2$

---

globally averaged, vertical column integrated photochemical production of ozone in the troposphere would be much larger ($\sim 5 \times 10^{11}$ molecules/cm^2/s) than can be balanced by destruction at the earth's surface ($\sim 6 \times 10^{10}$ molecules/cm^2/s) and by photochemical removal via the reactions

$$R12 \quad O_3 + h\nu \rightarrow O(^1D) + O_2$$

$$\textbf{R13} \quad \textbf{O}(^1\textbf{D}) + \textbf{H}_2\textbf{O} \rightarrow \textbf{2 OH}$$

which is estimated at 8×10^{10} molecules/cm^2/s (28, 29). Reactions R12 and R13 constitute the main pathway for the production of hydroxyl radicals (OH), which initiate many oxidation processes in the atmosphere.

The photochemistry of the ethane and higher hydrocarbon oxidation in the atmosphere follows similar reaction paths as for methane, although reactions occur faster because of the higher reactivity of these molecules (27, 30). In the case of ethane, there can be a net production of five ozone molecules per ethane molecule consumed, if sufficient NO is present in the atmosphere. The cycle of reactions, cycle C4, that produces ozone from ethane is shown in Box 2. The compound peroxyacetylnitrate, $CH_3(C=O)O_2NO_2$, which appears in C4 is a strong phytotoxicant and air pollutant, better known by the acronym PAN (31). The compound, CH_2O, is formaldehyde and CH_3CHO is acetaldehyde.

Few observations of NO in the background atmosphere have been made, mainly due to the extreme difficulties which are involved in its measurement at low concentrations (32, 33). The hypothesis that ozone production may take place only in a relatively small fraction of the troposphere is in accordance with present estimations of the sources and sinks of tropospheric NO_x (34). According to this compilation, the tropospheric sources of NO_x are dominated by industrial activities. This could imply that the current concentrations of tropospheric ozone in the Northern Hemisphere are substantially larger than those which prevailed during pre-industrial times.

We have modeled the atmospheric photochemistry following a Scenario I nuclear war under the illustrative assumptions listed above. A description of the

82

BOX 2

Reaction Cycle C4. Atmospheric oxidation of ethane forms ozone as follows. The carbon monoxide (CO) produced may also be oxidized to form additional ozone via cycle C1.

R14 $C_2H_6 + OH \rightarrow C_2H_5 + H_2O$
R15 $C_2H_5 + O_2 + M \rightarrow C_2H_5O_2 + M$
R16 $C_2H_5O_2 + NO \rightarrow C_2H_5O + NO_2$
R17 $C_2H_5O + O_2 \rightarrow CH_3CHO + HO_2$
R18 $CH_3CHO + OH \rightarrow$
        $CH_3(C=O) + H_2O$
R19 $CH_3(C=O) + O_2 + M \rightarrow$
        $CH_3(C=O)O_2 + M$
R20 $CH_3(C=O)O_2 + NO_2 + M \rightarrow$
        $CH_3(C=O)O_2NO_2 + M$
R21 $CH_3(C=O)O_2 + NO \rightarrow$
        $CH_3 + CO_2 + NO_2$
R7 $CH_3 + O_2 + M \rightarrow CH_3O_2 + M$
R8 $CH_3O_2 + NO \rightarrow CH_3O + NO_2$
R9 $CH_3O + O_2 \rightarrow CH_2O + HO_2$
R3 $HO_2 + NO \rightarrow OH + NO_2$
        (2 times)
R4 $NO_2 + h\nu \rightarrow NO + O$ (5 times)
R5 $O + O_2 + M \rightarrow O_3 + M$ (5 times)
R10 $CH_2O + h\nu \rightarrow CO + H_2$
- -
C5 $C_2H_6 + 10 \, O_2 \rightarrow$
        $2 \, H_2O + H_2 + CO_2 + CO + 5 \, O_3$

---

computer model used in this work is provided in Appendix II of this chapter. The mixing ratios of ozone in the present atmosphere as calculated by the unperturbed model for August 1 are provided in Figure 1, and these are in good agreement with the observations (35). The calculated ozone concentrations on August 1, 50 days after the start of the war, are shown in Figure 2. We notice the possibility of severe worldwide smog conditions resulting in high concentrations of ozone. With time, at midlatitudes in the Northern Hemisphere there may be large accumulations of ethane (50-100 ppbv) and PAN (1-10 ppbv).

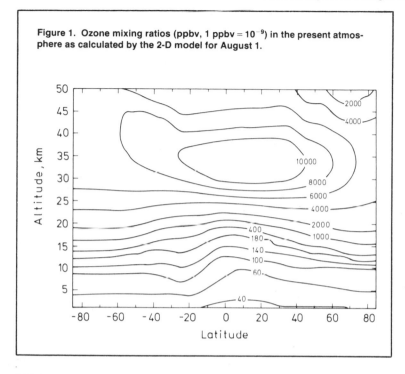

Figure 1. Ozone mixing ratios (ppbv, 1 ppbv = 10⁻⁹) in the present atmosphere as calculated by the 2-D model for August 1.

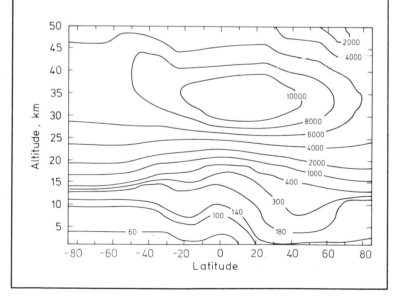

Figure 2. Ozone mixing ratios (ppbv) on August 1, 50 days after the beginning of the Scenario I nuclear war. Inputs from forest fires and oil and gas well fires as described in the text.

EFFECTS OF TROPOSPHERIC COMPOSITION CHANGES

For Ambio's Scenario I type of war the most significant effects in the atmosphere will occur as a result of the wide variety of large fires, which affect especially military, urban and industrial centers, agricultural fields, oil and gas production areas, and forests. In the preceding section, we have considered a scenario of events which, in our opinion, represents probably the minimum of what may occur: wildfires in 10^6 km^2 of forests, and the burning and escape of oil and natural gas at rates comparable to present industrial usage. The estimated atmospheric effects are very large. The fires would create sufficient quantities of airborne particulate matter in the atmosphere to screen out a large fraction of the solar radiation for many weeks, strongly reducing or even eliminating the possibility of growing agricultural crops over large areas of the Northern Hemisphere. Dark aerosol deposits on the vegetation would likewise severely limit plant productivity. In addition, if the war should start during the summer months, as envisaged in the war scenario of this study, much cropland would be destroyed directly by fast-moving fires. Also of special concern are the heavy deposits of air pollutants from the atmosphere which would take place in the months during and following the war. If an appreciable fraction of the NO_x formed in the nuclear explosions and in the resulting fires were to be deposited in rain, the rainwater would be highly acidic with an average pH of less than 4.

If the production of aerosol by fires is large enough to cause reductions in the penetration of sunlight to ground level by a factor of a hundred, which would be quite possible in the event of an all-out nuclear war, most of the phytoplankton and herbivorous zooplankton in more than half of the Northern Hemisphere oceans would die (36). This effect is due to the fast consumption rate of phytoplankton by zooplankton in the oceans. The effects of a darkening of such a magnitude have been discussed recently in connection with the probable occurrence of such an event as a result of the impact of a large extraterrestrial body with the earth (37). This event is believed by many to have caused the widespread and massive extinctions which took place at the Cretacious-Tertiary boundary about 65 million years ago.

For several weeks following the war the physical properties of the Northern Hemispheric troposphere would be fundamentally altered, with most solar energy input being absorbed in the atmosphere instead of at the ground. The normal dynamic and temperature structure of the atmosphere would therefore change considerably over a large fraction of the Northern Hemisphere, which will probably lead to important changes in land surface temperatures and wind systems. The thick, dark aerosol layer would likely give rise to very stable conditions in the troposphere (below 10 km) which would restrict the removal of the many fire-produced and unhealthy pollutants from the atmosphere. Furthermore, fires also produce as many as 6×10^{10} cloud condensation nuclei per gram of wood consumed. The effect of many condensation nuclei is to narrow the cloud droplet size distribution and suppress formation of rain droplets by coalescence, probably leading to a decrease in the efficiency with which clouds can produce rain (38). The influence of large-scale vegetation fires on weather has been recognized by researchers for many years (eg 39). After the settling of most of the particulate matter, ozone concentrations over much of the Northern Hemisphere could approach 160 ppbv for some months following the war. With time, substantial increases in other pollutants such as PAN to several ppbv may also occur. These species are important air pollutants which are normally present in the atmosphere at much lower concentrations ($\sim$30 ppbv for ozone and less than 0.1 ppbv for PAN) (33, 40, 41).

The effects of ozone on public health and plant growth have been studied for several decades, especially in the US in connection with the Los Angeles basin photochemical smog problem. The effects on agricultural plants may be particularly severe. A major EPA report (31), listed several examples of decreases in yields of agricultural crops. For instance: "A 30 percent reduction in the yield of wheat occurred when wheat at antheses [blooming] was exposed to ozone at 200 ppbv, 4 hours a day for 7 days ... Chronic exposures to ozone at 50–150 ppbv for 4–6 hours a day reduced yields in soybeans and corn grown under field conditions. The threshold for measurable effects for ozone appear to be between 50 and 100 ppbv for sensitive plant cultivers ... An ozone concentration of 50 to 70 ppbv for 4 to 6 hours per day for 15 to 133 days can significantly inhibit plant growth and yield of certain species."

As a result of the nuclear holocaust we have indicated the possibility of an increase of average ground level ozone concentration to 160 ppbv with higher values to be expected in areas in the wake of the mix of forest and gas and oil well fires assumed in this study. It follows, therefore, that agricultural crops may become subjected to severe photochemical pollutant stress in addition to the even greater damaging effects due to the large load of aerosol particles in the atmosphere.

We conclude, therefore, that the atmospheric effects of the many fires started by the nuclear war would be severe. For the war scenario adopted in this study, it appears highly unlikely that agricultural crop yield would be sufficient to feed more than a small part of the remaining population, so many of the survivors of the initial effects of the nuclear war would probably die of starvation during the first post-war years. This analysis does not address the additional complicating adverse effects of radioactivity or synergism due to concomitant use of chemical and biological warfare weapons.

The described impacts will be different if a nuclear war starts in the winter months. Forest areas burned may be half as large (7), photochemical reactions would be slower because of less solar radiation and lower temperatures. However, in wintertime, because of the low sun, the darkness caused by the fire-produced aerosol would be much worse.

In this work little discussion could be devoted to the health effects of fire-produced pollutants. They too, no doubt, will be more serious in winter than in summer.

STRATOSPHERIC OZONE DEPLETION

In the stratosphere, molecular oxygen, O_2, absorbs solar radiation of wavelengths shorter than 242 nm and dissociates into two oxygen atoms. These oxygen atoms combine with two oxygen molecules to form two ozone molecules as follows:

R14 $\quad O_2 + h\nu \rightarrow O + O$

R5 $\quad O + O_2 + M \rightarrow O_3 + M$ (Twice)

This formation mechanism is quite different from that described previously for the troposphere and summarized in cycles C1 and C2 of Box 1. Whereas oxides of nitrogen promote ozone formation in the troposphere, in the stratosphere, where the chemical composition and light spectrum are quite different, the effect of oxides of nitrogen is to catalyze ozone destruction via the reactions:

R15 $\quad NO + O_3 \rightarrow NO_2 + O_2$

R16 $\quad O + NO_2 \rightarrow NO + O_2$

R17 $\quad O_3 + h\nu \rightarrow O_2 + O$

Net: $\quad 2\,O_3 \rightarrow 3\,O_2$

It is now recognized that this cycle is the principal means by which ozone is limited in the natural stratosphere (42). Also, whereas ozone is an undesirable pollutant in the troposphere, in the stratosphere ozone performs the necessary function of shielding the earth's surface from biologically damaging ultraviolet radiation.

85

Our model does not predict significant stratospheric ozone depletion for Ambio's reference Scenario I since as seen in Table 1, very little NO_x is deposited in the stratosphere for this scenario. However, for Scenario II (based on previous studies)—which considers the detonation of numerous weapons of large yield—the model predicts very large depletions. For this scenario the quantity of NO_x in the stratosphere of the Nothern Hemisphere is increased by a factor of approximately twenty above the natural level (21). The resulting large ozone depletions would begin in the Northern Hemisphere and eventually spread to the Southern Hemisphere. For purposes of illustration, the Scenario II nuclear war begins on June 11. The resulting ozone depletions on November 1 of the same year are shown in Figure 3. These large ozone depletions are consistent with the one-dimensional model results of Whitten, Borucki and Turco (2) and with the result of Chang as reported by the US National Academy of Sciences (1).

Whitten et al (2) considered total bomb yields in the range of 5000–10 000 Mt. They distributed the weapon yields either equally between 1-Mt and 5-Mt weapons or equally between 1-Mt and 3-Mt weapons. They also considered that the NO_x was either uniformly distributed throughout the Northern Hemisphere or spread uniformly between 30° and 70° N. Maximum depletion of the ozone column occurred two to three months following the NO_x injection and ranged from 35–70 percent. The 35 percent depletion occurred for the 5000 Mt total yield distributed equally between 1-Mt and 3-Mt bombs and spread uniformly over the entire Northern Hemisphere. The maximum of 70 percent depletion occurred for a total bomb yield of 10 000 Mt distributed equally between 1-Mt and 5-Mt explosions and confined to the region 30°–70° N. The time constant (e-folding time) for ozone recovery was approximately three years.

The NAS report (1) reaches similar conclusions. A 10 000 Mt war, confined to the Northern Hemisphere, is projected to result in a 30–70 percent ozone column reduction in the Northern Hemisphere and a 20–40 percent reduction in the Southern Hemisphere. Again, the characteristic recovery time was found to be approximately three years. Within ten years the ozone column depletions were estimated to have

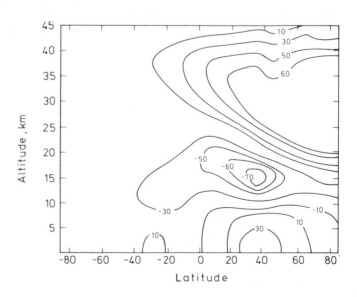

Figure 3. Atmospheric ozone depletion (%) on August 1 of the same year as the Scenario II nuclear war. Negative values indicate ozone increases and show the opposite effects of NO_x injections on ozone in the upper and lower regions of the atmosphere.

decreased to 1–2 percent.

Our two-dimensional model predicts a rather uniform 65 percent depletion of the ozone column spread from 45° N to the North Pole by the 50th day following the war. The depletions become less toward the equator and beyond, being 57, 42, 26, 12 and 1 percent at 35° N, 25° N, 15° N, 5° N and 5° S, respectively. As time progresses, the ozone depletions become less in the Northern Hemisphere, but NO_x is transported to the Southern Hemisphere and causes significant depletion there. Two years following the war in the Northern Hemisphere the ozone column depletions vary uniformly from 15 percent at 5° N to 56 percent at 85° N, with a 39 percent depletion of the ozone column at 45° N. At the same time ozone column depletions range from 12 percent at 5° S to 18 percent at 85° S in the Southern Hemisphere.

An important uncertainty in the model calculations for the stratosphere stems from the perturbations in the heating rates that accompany the large ozone depletions. Reduction of ozone causes a cooling of the stratosphere. By absorbing ultraviolet sunlight, ozone heats the atmosphere and causes the temperature inversion that is responsible for the high degree of resistance to vertical mixing. To a large extent the NO_x is partitioned into NO_2 in the stratosphere, and the absorption of solar radiation by this species also heats the stratosphere. We find that the net effect at midlatitudes in the perturbed stratosphere is heating below about 22 km and cooling above. The net heating below 22 km is due both to greater penetration of solar uv as a result of the reduced ozone column and the added heating in this region due to NO_2. This will undoubtedly affect the dynamics of the stratosphere and the temperature profile in the stratosphere in complex ways which we cannot predict. We can be confident, however, that the perturbation in the ozone column would be quite large for a Scenario II nuclear war.

Finally, we may point out that there is a possibility that even a nuclear war according to Scenario I, in which most NO_x is deposited in the troposphere, may cause ozone depletions in the stratosphere, if the hot fires in the oil and gas production regions become so powerful that the fire plumes penetrate into the stratosphere. Another means of upward transport may occur when the heavy, dark aerosol layer, initially located in the troposphere, is heated by solar radiation and starts to set up convection and wind systems which will transport an appreciable fraction of the fire effluents into the stratosphere. These speculative thoughts may be pursued further with currently available general circulation models of the atmosphere.

Past Nuclear Weapons Tests

In light of this discussion, one might naturally ask whether past nuclear weapon testing in the atmosphere resulted in significant ozone depletion. This topic has been the subject of considerable debate (43–52). That nuclear explosions produce copious quantities of nitric oxide and that multi-megaton bursts deposit this NO in the stratosphere was first recognized by Foley and Ruderman (44). The problem was presented as a possible test of whether NO_x from SST airplane exhaust would actually damage the ozone layer as suggested by Johnston (53) and Crutzen (54). The approximately 300 Mt of total bomb yield in a number of atmospheric tests by the US and USSR in 1961 and 1962 introduced about 3×10^{34} additional molecules of NO to the stratosphere. Using a one-dimensional model, Chang, Duewer and Wuebbles (49) estimated that nuclear weapon testing resulted in a maximum ozone depletion in the Northern Hemisphere of about 4 percent in 1963. Analysis of the ground ozone observational data for the Northern Hemisphere by Johnston, Whitten and Birks (45) revealed a decrease of 2.2 percent for 1960–1962 followed by an increase of 4.4 percent in

1963–1970. These data are consistent with the magnitude of ozone depletion expected, but by no means is a cause-and-effect relationship established. Angell and Korshover attribute these ozone column changes to meteorological factors (47, 48). The ozone increase began before most of the large weapons had been detonated and persisted for too long a period to be totally attributed to recovery from bomb-induced ozone depletion. Considering the large scatter in ozone measurements and our lack of understanding of all of the natural causes of ozone fluctuations, we cannot draw definite conclusions based on ground observations of ozone following the nuclear weapons tests of the late 1950's and early 1960's.

Solar Proton Events

From the previous discussion it is clear that we have no direct experimental evidence for stratospheric ozone depletion as a result of nuclear explosions. However, at least for altitudes above 30 km the sudden input of significant amounts of NO_x has clearly been shown to lead to large ozone destructions. In August 1972 a major solar proton event deposited large amounts of nitrogen oxides in the stratosphere, leading to ozone depletions poleward of about 60° N. The estimated ozone depletions calculated with a photochemical model were confirmed by satellite observations of stratospheric ozone (55).

EFFECTS OF INCREASED UV-B RADIATION

Ozone in the stratosphere serves as a protective shield against the harmful effects of solar radiation in the wavelength region 240–320 nm (10^{-9} meter). The flux of radiation in the wavelength region 290–320 nm ("uv-B" radiation) is particularly sensitive to very small changes in the ozone column (1). This biologically active radiation is also absorbed by the proteins and nucleic acids within living cells, resulting in a large variety of photoreactions and consequent cell damage (56–58).

88

The expected adverse effects of increased levels of uv-B radiation include increased incidence of skin cancer in fair-skinned races, decreased crop yields and a variety of stresses on terrestrial and aquatic ecosystems. Such effects have been considered in the past in connection with possible reduction of the ozone shield by the operation of fleets of SST airplanes (59) and by the continued release of chlorofluoromethanes used as refrigerants and as propellants in aerosol spray cans (60). The information available is insufficient to allow quantification of most of these effects. Epidemiological data were used in the NAS study (1) to estimate that a 50 percent ozone shield reduction lasting three years would lead to an increase of skin carcinoma and melanoma of 3 percent to 30 percent at midlatitudes, with a geometric mean of about 10 percent, that will persist for 40 years. This may be compared with the estimate made in the same study that during the first generation a 10 000 Mt war would increase the spontaneous cancer death rate by about 2 percent as a result of exposure to low levels of ionizing radiation from radioactive fallout.

Effects of increased uv-B radiation on food crops are extremely difficult to predict. The sensitivity of plants to supplemented uv-B has been found to be highly variable from one species to another. For example, whereas peas and onions are sensitive, more important food crops such as soybeans and corn appear to have a higher tolerance (1). Possible climatic changes following a nuclear war further complicate the picture for food crops. Crops are particularly sensitive to temperature, length of growing season and amount of precipitation. The coupling of significant changes in one or all of these factors with a change in the spectrum and intensity of light reaching the earth's surface could be particularly detrimental.

Reduction in stratospheric ozone and the concomitant increase in uv-B radiation would also stress natural ecosystems. As in agriculture, individual species of plants and animals differ considerably in their sensitivities to uv-B radiation. However, in natural ecosystems a direct effect on only one species may be propagated to a large number of species because of complex interdependences. For example, the food chain of the oceans is based on photosynthesis by phytoplankton, and these microscopic, green plants have been demonstrated to be quite sensitive to uv radiation (60). It was estimated from uv-B irradiation experiments that a 16 percent ozone reduction (the degree of ozone depletion projected by the NAS study for continued release of chlorofluoromethanes) could kill up to 50 percent of the anchovies in the top 10 meters of the clearest ocean water or else require them to substantially deepen their usual water depth (60, 61). Avoidance could provide protection for many animals, but it is thought that few species can sense uv-B light.

The "effective" increases in uv-B radiation may be determined by integrating the product of the uv-B radiation flux and the appropriate "action spectrum" over wavelength. We have computed these integrals using the action spectrum for erythema (sunburn). This action spectrum is very similar to the absorption spectrum of DNA, as are most uv-B action spectra, and thus the results apply rather generally to cell damage of all types (62). The relative increases in effective uv-B radiation are shown in Figure 4 for several latitudes as a function of time following the nuclear war. As noted earlier, the uv-B increases are extremely large and persist for several years. The Scenario II nuclear war initially would result in increases in uv-B radiation by a factor greater than 5 throughout most of the Northern Hemisphere and greater than 10 between 55° N and the North Pole. These large increases in uv-B radiation are expected to persist long after the attenuation of light by atmospheric aerosol produced by the nuclear blasts and by the many fires is no longer significant. By comparison, the projected increase in effective uv-B radiation for continued release of chlorofluoromethanes at 1977 levels is 44 percent (60).

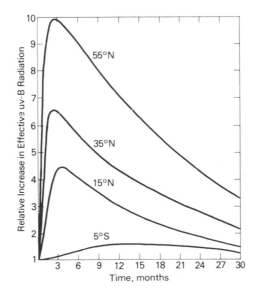

Figure 4. Relative increases in effective uv-B radiation based on the erythema action spectrum for the Scenario II nuclear war.

LONG-TERM EFFECTS

Regarding possible climatic effects, little can be said with confidence. The increase in tropospheric ozone, methane and possibly other pollutant gases may lead to increased temperatures at the earth's surface (63, 64), while the dark aerosol produced by the fires will change the heat and radiative balance and dynamics of the earth and the atmosphere for awhile. Longer lasting effects may be caused by the changes in the reflective properties of the land surfaces because of many fires. In a recent study Hansen et al (65) have been able to trace observed mean global temperatures over the past 100 years with a simple climate model by introducing changes in the atmospheric CO_2 content, volcanic activity and solar variability as the main driving forces. In their model the climate sensitivity was also tested for various global radiation perturbations which are relevant for this study: stratospheric aerosol, tropospheric aerosol (divided into opposite sulfate and soot effects), and atmospheric trace gas content (carbon dioxide, ozone, methane and nitrous oxide). From this study it is conceivable that climate could be sensitive over the short term to the tropospheric and stratospheric aerosol loading. It may be possible to test the impact of a nuclear war on climate with this and similar models, when these are supplied with reasonable estimates of the trace gas and aerosol composition of the earth's atmosphere. Whether the induced perturbation in the climate system could lead to longer lasting climatic changes will, however, be difficult to predict. In fact, it may seem unlikely that it will take place. The Krakatoa volcanic eruption of 1883 injected quantities of aerosol into the atmosphere comparable to those which would be caused by a nuclear war, and global mean temperatures were affected for only a few years (1). Still, we must be cautious with a prediction as the physical characteristics of the aerosol produced by volcanos and fires are different, and much is still unknown

90

about the fundamentals of climatic changes. For instance, we may ask questions such as whether the earth's albedo would be substantially altered after a nuclear war and thus affect the radiation balance or whether the deposition of soot aerosol on arctic snow and ice and on the glaciers of the Northern Hemisphere might not lead to such heavy snow and ice melting as to cause an irreversible change in one or more important climatic parameters.

CONCLUSIONS

In this chapter we have shown that the atmosphere would most likely be highly perturbed by a nuclear war. We especially draw attention to the effects of the large quantities of highly sunlight-absorbing, dark particulate matter which would be produced and spread in the troposphere by the many fires that would start burning in urban and industrial areas, oil and gas producing fields, agricultural lands, and forests. For extended periods of time, maybe months, such fires would strongly restrict the penetration of sunlight to the earth's surface and change the physical properties of the earth's atmosphere. The marine ecosystems are probably particularly sensitive to prolonged periods of darkness. Under such conditions it is likely that agricultural production in the Northern Hemisphere would be almost totally eliminated, so that no food would be available for the survivors of the initial effects of the war. It is also quite possible that severe, worldwide photochemical smog conditions would develop with high levels of tropospheric ozone that would likewise interfere severely with plant productivity. Survival becomes even more difficult if stratospheric ozone depletions also take place. It is, therefore, difficult to see how much more than a small fraction of the initial survivors of a nuclear war in the middle and high latitude regions of the Northern Hemisphere could escape famine and disease during the following year.

We have attempted here to identify the most important changes that would occur in the atmosphere as a result of a nuclear war. The atmospheric effects that we have identified are quite complex and difficult to model. It is hoped, however, that this study will provide an introduction to a more thorough analysis of this important problem.

APPENDIX I

Production and Spatial Distribution of Nitric Oxide From Nuclear Explosions

There have been numerous estimates (43–46, 66) of the yield of nitric oxide per megaton (Mt) of explosion energy, and these have been reviewed by Gilmore (66). Nitric oxide is produced by heating and subsequent cooling of air in the interior of the fireball and in the shock wave.

The spherical shock wave produces nitric oxide by heating air to temperatures above 2200 K. This air is subsequently cooled by rapid expansion and radiative emission, while the shock front moves out to heat more air. At a particular temperature the cooling rate becomes faster than the characteristic time constant for maintaining equilibrium between NO and air. For cooling times of seconds to milliseconds the NO concentration "freezes" at temperatures between 1700 and 2500 K, corresponding to NO concentrations of 0.3–2 percent. Gilmore (66) estimates a yield of 0.8×10^{32} NO molecules per Mt for this mechanism.

The shock wave calculation of NO production does not take into account the fact that air within the fireball center contains approximately one-sixth of the initial explosion energy, having been heated by the radiative growth mechanism described earlier. This air cools on a time scale of several seconds by further radiative emission, entrainment of cold air, and by expansion as it rises to higher altitudes. These mechanisms are sufficiently complex that one can only estimate upper and lower limits to the quantity of NO finally produced.

A lower limit to total amount of NO finally produced may be obtained by assuming that all of the shock-heated air is entrained into the fireball and again heated to a high enough temperature to reach equilibrium. This is possible since the thickness of the shell of shock-heated air containing NO is smaller than the radius of the fireball. To minimize the cooling rate, and thus the temperature at which equilibrium is not re-established rapidly, it is assumed that this air mass cools only by adiabatic expansion as the fireball rises and by using a minimum rise velocity. The resulting lower limit to total NO production is 0.4×10^{32} molecules per Mt (66).

Since the interior of the fireball is much hotter than the surrounding, shock-heated air, it will rise much faster and possibly pierce through the shell of shock-heated air to mix with cold, undisturbed air above it. Thus, an upper limit to NO production may be obtained by assuming that none of the 0.8×10^{32} NO molecules per Mt produced in the shock wave are entrained by the hot fireball interior. Instead, one assumes that the interior is cooled totally by entrainment of cold, undisturbed air to produce additional NO. The upper limit to total NO production is then estimated to be 1.5×10^{32} molecules per Mt (66). Thus, the range of uncertainty for total NO_x formation is $0.4–1.5 \times 10^{32}$ molecules per Mt.

For the purposes of this study we assume a nitric oxide yield of 1.0×10^{32} molecules per Mt. One can make strong arguments against either of the extreme

values. This estimate of NO production applies only to detonations in the lower atmosphere.

In a nuclear war some bombs may be exploded at very high altitudes for the purpose of disrupting radio and radar signals. The ionization of air by gamma rays, X-rays and charged particles creates a phenomenon known as the "electromagnetic pulse" or "EMP" (67). The partitioning of energy between the locally heated fireball, shock wave, and escaping thermal radiation changes dramatically as the altitude of the explosion increases above 30 km. As the altitude increases, the X-rays are able to penetrate to greater distances in the low density air and thus create very large visible fireballs. For explosions above about 80 km, the interaction of the highly ionized weapon debris becomes the dominant mechanism for producing a fireball, and for such explosions the earth's magnetic field will influence the distribution of the late-time fireball. Explosions above 100 km produce no local fireball at all. Because of the very low air density, one-half of the X-rays are lost to space, and the one-half directed toward the earth deposits its energy in the so-called "X-ray pancake" region as they are absorbed by air of increasing density. The X-ray pancake is more like the frustum of a cone pointing upward, with a thickness of about 10 km and a mean altitude of 80 km. The mean vertical position is essentially independent of the explosion altitude for bursts well above 80 km (67).

The absorption of X-rays by air results in the formation of pairs of electrons and positively charged ions. One ion pair is formed for each 35 eV of energy absorbed (68), and in the subsequent reactions approximately 1.3 molecules of NO are produced for each ion pair (69). A 1-Mt explosion corresponds to 2.6×10^{34} eV of total energy. Thus, considering that only half of the X-rays enter the earth's atmosphere, the yield of NO is calculated to be 4.6×10^{32} molecules per Mt (ie this mechanism is about five times more effective at producing NO than the thermal mechanism described above).

In the course of a nuclear war up to one hundred 1-Mt bombs might be detonated in the upper atmosphere for the purpose of creating radio wave disturbances. The injection of NO would therefore be 4.8×10^{34} molecules or 1.1 Tg of nitrogen. Natural production of NO in the thermosphere due to the absorption of EUV radiation depends on solar activity and is in the range 200–400 Tg of nitrogen per year (34). Thus the amount of NO injected by such high altitude explosions is about equal to the amount of NO produced naturally in one day and falls within the daily variability. In addition, the X-ray pancake is positioned at an altitude where nitrogen and oxygen species are maintained in photochemical equilibrium. Excess nitric oxide is rapidly destroyed by a sequence of reactions involving nitrogen and oxygen atoms as follows:

R22 $NO + h\nu \rightarrow N + O$
R23 $N + NO \rightarrow N_2 + O$

Net: $2 NO \rightarrow N_2 + O + O \rightarrow N_2 + O_2$

For these reasons, we expect that high altitude explosions of such magnitudes will have no significant global effect on the chemistry of the stratosphere and below.

Results of past tests of nuclear explosions show that nuclear clouds rise in the atmosphere and finally stabilize at altitudes that scale approximately as the 0.2 power of bomb yield. An empirical fit to observed cloud geometries at midlatitudes gives the following expressions for the heights of the cloud tops and cloud bottoms, respectively (44):

$$H_T = 22Y^{0.2}$$
$$H_B = 13Y^{0.2}$$

where H is in kilometers and Y has units of megatons. Thus, bomb clouds from weapons having yields greater than about 1 Mt completely penetrate the tropopause at midlatitudes. For such explosions all of the NO_x produced in the fireball, and perhaps a significant fraction of that produced in the shock wave but not entrained by the bomb cloud, is deposited in the stratosphere. Oxides of nitrogen formed in nuclear explosions having yields less than 1 Mt have little effect on stratospheric ozone since: 1) only a minor fraction of the NO_x formed is deposited above the tropopause, 2) the residence time in the stratosphere increases with altitude of injection, and 3) the NO_x-catalytic cycle for ozone destruction is most effective at higher altitudes. In fact, below about 20 km NO_x additions to the atmosphere tend to result in ozone concentration increases (70, 71).

The stabilized nuclear bomb clouds have diameters ranging from 50 to 500 km depending on bomb yield. They are sheared by horizontal winds at constant latitude, and within a few weeks may be uniformly distributed around the earth at a constant latitude (72).

APPENDIX II

Model Description

The computer model used in this study is a two-dimensional model of coupled photochemistry and dynamics. It treats transport in both the vertical and latitudinal directions by parameterization of these motions by means of eddy diffusion coefficients and mean motions. The model covers altitudes between the ground and 55 km and latitudes between the South Pole and North Pole, and it attempts to simulate the longitudinally averaged, meridional distributions of trace gases. Therefore, the main assumption is that composition variations in the zonal (East–West) directions are much smaller than those in the vertical and latitudinal directions. Although the 2-D model is a step forward from 1-D models, which take into account only variations in the vertical direction, the neglect of longitudinal variations in air composition will clearly introduce substantial deviations from reality, especially at lower altitudes, where the influence of chemical and biological processes at the earth's surface are large. One should keep these limitations of the 2-D model in mind especially when interpreting the results obtained for the troposphere.

The model photochemistry considers the occurrence of nearly one hundred reactions, which are now thought to be important in global air chemistry. It takes into account the reactions of ozone and atomic oxygen, and the reactive oxides of nitrogen, hydrogen and chlorine, which are derived from the oxidation of nitrous oxide (N_2O), water vapor (H_2O), methane (CH_4) and organic chlorine compounds. In the troposphere, the photochemistry of simple reactions leading to ozone formation in the presence of NO_x, carbon monoxide (CO), methane and ethane (C_2H_6) are taken into account. The influence of industrial processes is an important consideration of the model. A more detailed description of the model may be found elsewhere (71, 72). Detailed descriptions of atmospheric photochemistry are given in a number of review articles (34, 73–75).

References and Notes

1. National Academy of Sciences, *Long Term Worldwide Effects of Multiple Nuclear-Weapon Detonations*, Washington, DC (1975).
2. R C Whitten, W J Borucki and R P Turco, *Nature* **257**, 38 (1975).
3. *Ambio* Advisory Group, Chapter 3.
4. K N Lewis, *Scientific American* **241**, 35 (1979).
5. W Seiler and P J Crutzen, *Climate Change* **2**, 207 (1980).
6. *The Global Carbon Cycle*, SCOPE 13; B Bolin, E T Degens, S Kempe and P Ketner, Editors (Wiley, New York), 491 p (1979).
7. D E Ward, E K McMahon and R W Johansen, Paper 76-2.2, 69th Annual Meeting of the Air Pollution Control Association, Portland, Oregon, June 27–July 1, 15 p (1976).
8. FAS, Effects of Nuclear War, *Journal of the Federation of American Scientists* **34**, 3 (1981).
9. P J Crutzen, L E Heidt, J P Krasnec, W H Pollock and W Seiler, *Nature* **282**, 253 (1979).
10. W Seiler, *Tellus* **26**, 116 (1974).
11. L F Evans, I A Weeks, A J Eccleston and D R Packham, *Environmental Science and Technology* **11**, 896 (1977).
12. L F Radke, J L Stith, D A Hegg and P V Hobbs, *Journal of the Air Pollution Control Association* **28**, 30 (1978).
13. R Jaenicke, in *Climatic Variations and Variability: Facts and Theories*, A Berger, Ed (D Reidel, Dordrecht, Holland), pp 577–597 (1981).
14. C K McMahon and P W Ryan, Paper 76-2.3, 69th Annual Meeting of the Air Pollution Control Association, Portland, Oregon, June 27–July 1, 21 p (1976). See also: R G Vines, I Gibson, A B Hatch, N K King, D A McArthur, D R Packham and R J Taylor, CSIRO Division of Applied Chemistry, Technical Paper No 1, 32 p (1971).
15. P Chylek, V Ramaswamy, R Cheng and R G Pinnick, *Applied Optics* **20**, 2980 (1981); A D Waggoner, R E Weiss, N C Ahlquist, D S Covert, S Will, and R J Charlson, *Atmospheric Environment* **15**, 1891 (1981).
16. V B Shostakovitch, *Journal of Forestry* **23**, 365 (1925).
17. F G Plummer, *Forest Fires*, US Department of Agriculture Forest Service Bulletin 117, pp 15–22 (1912); H Lyman, *Monthly Weather Review* **46**, 506 (1919); H Wexler, *Weatherwise*, December 3, 1950; C D Smith, Jr., *Monthly Weather Review* **77**, 180 (1950).
18. Kommission der Europäischen Gemeinschaften, 26 p (1981).
19. *International Petroleum Encyclopedia*, Vol. 14 (PennWell Publishing Co, Tulsa, Oklahoma, 1981).
20. Y Gotaas, *Journal of the Air Pollution Control Association* **30**, 789 (1980).
21. D M Leahey, G L Brown and R L Findlay, *Journal of the Air Pollution Control Association* **30**, 787 (1980).
22. A Jernelöv and O Linden, *Ambio* **10**, 299 (1981).
23. Nuclear Bomb Effects Computer, Revised Edition, 1977, Lovelace Biomedical and Environmental Research Institute, Inc.
24. International Institute for Applied Systems Analysis, *Energy in a Finite World: Paths to a Sustainable Future* (1981).
25. H B Singh and P L Hanst, *Geophysical Research Letters* **8**, 941 (1981); also J Rudolph and D H Ehhalt, *Journal of Geophysical Research* **81**, 11959 (1981).
26. C J Howard and K M Evenson, *Geophysical Research Letters* **4**, 437 (1977).
27. M Zahniser and C J Howard, *Journal of Chemical Physics* **73**, 1620 (1979).
28. J Fishman and P J Crutzen, *Nature* **274**, 855 (1978).
29. P Fabian and C E Junge, *Archiv Für Meteorologie, Geophysik und Bioklimatologie* **A19**, 161 (1970).
30. K L Demerjian, J A Kerr and J G Calvert, *Advances in Environmental Science and Technology* **4**, 1 (1974).
31. *Air Quality Criteria for Ozone and Other Photochemical Oxidants*, EPA-600/8-78-004, US Environmental Protection Agency, Washington, DC (1978)
32. J F Noxon, *Journal of Geophysical Research* **83**, 3051 (1978).
33. M McFarland, D Kley, J W Drummond, A L Schmeltekopf and R H Winkler, *Geophysical Research Letters* **6**, 605 (1979).
34. P J Crutzen, *Annual Review of Earth and Planetary Science* **7**, 443 (1979).
35. H V Dütsch, *Canadian Journal of Chemistry* **52**, 1491 (1974).
36. D H Milne and C P McKay, Response of Marine Plankton Communities to Global Atmospheric Darkening, Proceedings of the Conference on Large Body Impacts, Special Paper, Geological Society of America (in press).
37. L Alvarez, W Alvarez, F Asaro and H Michel, *Science* **208**, 1095 (1980).
38. R C Eagan, P V Hobbs and L F Radke, *Journal of Applied Meteorology* **13**, 553 (1974).
39. W Knoche, *Meteorologische Zeitschrift* **54**, 243 (1937).
40. W A Lonneman, J J Bufalini and R L Seila, *Environmental Science and Technology* **10**, 374 (1976).
41. H Nieboer and J van Ham, *Atmospheric Environment* **10**, 115 (1976).
42. P J Crutzen, *Quarterly Journal of the Royal Meteorological Society* **96**, 320 (1970).
43. Y Zel-dovich and Y Raizer, *Physics of Shock Waves and High Temperature Phenomena*, p 565 (Academic Press, New York, 1967).
44. H M Foley and M A Ruderman, *Journal of Geophysical Research* **78**, 4441 (1973).
45. H S Johnston, G Whitten and J W Birks, *Journal of Geophysical Research* **78**, 6107 (1973).
46. P Goldsmith, A F Tuck, J S Foot, E L Simmons and R L Newson, *Nature* **244**, 545 (1973).
47. J K Angell and J Korshover, *Monthly Weather Review* **101**, 426 (1973).
48. J K Angell and J Korshover, *Monthly Weather Review* **104**, 63 (1973).
49. J S Chang, W H Duewer and D J Wuebbles, *Journal of Geophysical Research* **84**, 1755 (1979).
50. A D Christie, *Journal of Geophysical Research* **81**, 2583 (1976).
51. H S Johnston, *Journal of Geophysical Research* **82**, 3119 (1977).
52. E Bauer and F R Gilmore, *Reviews of Geophysics and Space Physics* **13**, 451 (1975).
53. H S Johnston, *Science* **173**, 517 (1971).
54. P J Crutzen, *Journal of Geophysical Research* **76**, 7311 (1971).

55. D F Heath, A J Krueger and P J Crutzen, *Science* **197**, 886 (1977).
56. A Wacker, *Progress in Nucleic Acid Research* **1**, 369 (1963).
57. K C Smith, in *Photophysiology*, A C Giese, Ed, Vol. 2 p 329 (Academic Press, New York, 1964).
58. J K Setlow, in *Current Topics in Radiation Research*, M Ebert and A Howard, Eds, Vol. 2, p 195 (North-Holland, Amsterdam, 1966).
59. CIAP Monograph 5, *Impacts of Climatic Change on the Biosphere*, Part 1, *Ultraviolet Radiation Effects*, D F Nachtway, M M Caldwell, and R H Biggs, eds DOT-TST–75-55 (US Department of Transportation, Washington, DC, 1975).
60. National Academy of Sciences, *Protection Against Depletion of Stratospheric Ozone by Chlorofluorocarbons*, Washington, DC (1975).
61. J R Hunter, J H Taylor and H G Moser, *Photochemistry and Photobiology* **29**, 325 (1979).
62. D Benger, D F Robertson and R E Davies, in CIAP Monograph 5, *Impacts of Climatic Change on the Biosphere*, Part 1, *Ultraviolet Radiation Effects*, D F Nachtway, M M Caldwell, and R H Biggs, Eds, DOT-TST-75-55, pp 2-235 to 2-264 (US Department of Transportation, Washington, DC, 1975).
63. W C Wang, T L Yung, A A Lacis, T Mo and J E Hansen, *Science* **194**, 685 (1976).
64. J Fishman, V Ramanathan, P J Crutzen and S C Liu, *Nature* **282**, 818 (1979).
65. J Hansen, D Johnson, A Lacis, S Lebedeff, P Lee, D Rind and G Russell, *Science* **213**, 957 (1981).
66. F R Gilmore, *Journal of Geophysical Research* **80**, 4553 (1975).
67. S Glasstone and P J Dolan, *The Effects of Nuclear Weapons*, 3rd ed (US Government Printing Office, Washington, DC, 1977).
68. P M Banks and G Kockarts, *Aeronomy*, Part A (Academic Press, New York, 1973).
69. D W Rusch, J-C Gerárd, S Solomon, P J Crutzen and R C Reid, *Planetary and Space Science* **7**, 767 (1981).
70. W H Duewer, D J Wuebbles, H W Ellsaesser and J S Chang, *Journal of Geophysical Research* **82**, 935 (1977).
71. H Hidalgo and P J Crutzen, *Journal of Geophysical Research* **82**, 5833 (1977).
72. P J Crutzen, in Fourth Conference on CIAP, US Department of Transportation, Cambridge, p 276 (1975).
73. H Levy II, *Advances in Photochemistry* **9**, 5325 (1974).
74. P J Crutzen, *Pure and Applied Geophysics* **106–108**, 1385 (1973).
75. J A Logan, M J Prather, S C Wofsy and M B McElroy, *Philosophical Transactions of the Royal Society of London* **290**, 187 (1978).
76. The authors are especially thankful to the following scientists for critically reading earlier versions of this chapter and providing us with advice in their various fields of expertise: Robert Charlson, Tony Delany, Jost Heintzenberg, Rupert Jaenicke, Harold Johnston, Chris Junge, Jeffrey Kiehl, Carl Kisslinger, James Lovelock, V Ramanathan, V Ramaswami, Henning Rodhe, Steven Schneider, Wolfgang Seiler, Robert Sievers, Darold Ward, Ellen Winchester, Jack Winchester and Pat Zimmerman.

SEVEN

EFFECTS ON GLOBAL SUPPLIES OF FRESHWATER

KLAUS GUENTHER WETZEL

The fission products from a nuclear war would cause widespread contamination of freshwater reservoirs, and that contamination would persist for a number of years. Rainwater would be a deadly poison in the period immediately following the war, and genetic damage to large numbers of survivors would be unavoidable.

This chapter attempts to estimate the radioactive contamination of freshwater reservoirs following a global nuclear war, and to consider the consequences for domestic, industrial and agricultural uses of freshwater. The discussion will not consider those coastal regions where freshwater is supplied by desalination of ocean water, since that is more properly part of the discussion of the effects of a nuclear war on ocean systems, and it will not touch on the effects of the destruction of the means of supplying freshwater to human populations, although it should be emphasized that in the regions directly exposed to nuclear explosions that destruction would cause severe problems.

A number of assumptions have been made for the purposes of this presentation. Early fallout was assumed to be evenly distributed on all areas directly exposed to nuclear explosions, and the half-residence time of early fallout in the atmosphere was taken to be two days, *ie* half of this fallout was assumed to be deposited after two

days. For global fallout, the half residence time for both the northern and southern hemispheres was assumed to be two years.

In keeping with the reference scenario for this book, we assumed the following yields from nuclear explosions:

^{89}Sr	11.1 MCi per Mt
^{90}Sr	0.08 ,,
^{137}Cs	0.13 ,,
^{106}Ru	1.92 ,,
^{131}I	80.0 ,,

Our calculations deal only with ^{89}Sr, ^{90}Sr, ^{137}Cs and ^{106}Ru, which were chosen because of their long half-lives, their abundance in fallout from nuclear explosions, and their high toxicity; ^{235}U, ^{238}U and ^{239}Pu are not included in our calculations because they are preferentially deposited in insoluble form, and would probably not contaminate freshwater systems to any substantial extent. Our calculations of the way fission products enter freshwater reservoirs are based on the model of the freshwater cycle described in Figure 1. The

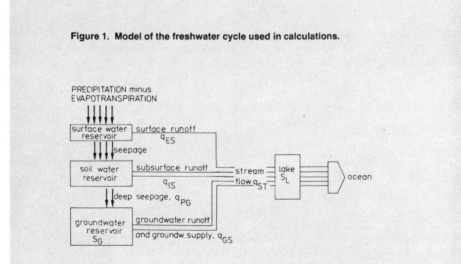

Figure 1. Model of the freshwater cycle used in calculations.

specific activities of the dissolved radionuclides were assumed to be the same both in areas directly exposed to nuclear explosions and in areas remote from explosions.

For simplicity we have ignored the existence of two or even more aquifers separated from each other by impermeable or nearly inpermeable horizons, a condition which exists in wide areas of each of the continents. However distinctions must be made, first, between regions directly exposed to nuclear explosions and regions remote from explosions, and second, between regions of different climatic, hydrologic and soil conditions—for example, between arid and humid regions, or between humid regions with more-or-less continuous precipitation and humid regions with alternating rainy and dry periods. In our calculations we have used the hydrologic characteristics of a typical low-land area in a temperate climate, as shown in Table 1.

It should also be noted that the freshwater supply in developed countries—and especially the supply for the major cities —is frequently based on aquifers of outstanding depth, often covered by clay or other more-or-less impermeable layers. As a result, the inhabitants of these cities could be supplied with drinking water almost free of radioactive contamination, assuming they survived the other consequ

ences of a nuclear war. However, it is also worth noting that those cities would be the preferential targets for nuclear weapons.

FORMATION AND TRANSPORT OF RADIONUCLIDES

The radionuclides formed by nuclear explosions would enter freshwater systems through three main routes: surface run-off, leaching of fission products from contaminated soil by sub-surface run-off, and discharge of contaminated groundwater into streams. Direct deposition of fallout on the surface of freshwater reservoirs would be relatively minor and can be safely ignored.

For a rough calculation of the transport of fallout into streams via surface run-off we assumed precipitation yielding 15 mm every seven days, which would carry the fallout into streams and mix it with streamwater within three days. Following the results of experimental investigations (1) we assumed that the rate of leaching of ^{89}Sr and ^{90}Sr from the soil is on the order of 1.5 percent per year, and that the rate for ^{137}Cs was 0.5 percent annually. Leaching from the soil of ^{106}Ru and ^{131}I would probably not be significant, since ^{106}Ru would probably form an anion which is not absorbed in the soil, and ^{131}I, in addition to its relatively short half-life, is strongly absorbed by humic matter. Dis-

---

Table 1. Hydrologic characteristics used for calculations

q_{PG}	= Proportion of precipitation infiltrated to groundwater (recharge of groundwater)	80×10^6 l/km^2/y
q_{GS}	= Groundwater runoff to the streams	67×10^6 l/km^2/y
q_{IS}	= Subsurface runoff averaged over the year	80×10^6 l/km^2/y
q_{ES}	= Surface runoff averaged over the year	40×10^6 l/km^2/y
d_{ES}	= Surface runoff owing to one event of rainfall (15 mm), assumed to flow off within 3 days	0.75×10^6 l/km^2
q_{ST}	= Average flow of stream water divided by the catchment area	200×10^6 l/km^2/y
q_{SB}	= Average base flow of stream water divided by the catchment area	160×10^6 l/km^2/y
s_G	= Renewable groundwater stores	1.2×10^{10} l/km^2
s_L	= Water storage in a representative lake divided by the catchment area of its river system	1×10^8 l/km^2

charge of contaminated groundwater into surface water would be a significant factor only for ^{106}Ru.

The formation of radionuclides as a result of the reaction of soil constituents with particles and gamma quanta released by nuclear explosions, and the formation of tritium by neutron activation of deuterium would not make any substantial contribution to contamination of freshwater supplies. About 2000 Ci/km^2 of ^{45}Ca would be formed in soils of average chemical composition in areas directly exposed to nuclear explosions. In normal soils this ^{45}Ca is strongly absorbed by ion exchange, and is thus prevented from entering freshwater systems before radioactive decay. Soils with a low ion exchange capacity usually have low Ca contents, and are therefore less contaminated by ^{45}Ca. The only exception should be karstic regions where the freshwater supply would probably be severely contaminated by ^{45}Ca.

Given these assumptions, Figures 2a and b show the results of our calculations on the contamination of stream water by ^{89}Sr, ^{90}Sr, and ^{137}Cs in a region directly exposed

to nuclear explosions. Figure 2c shows the contamination of stream water by ^{131}I and ^{106}Ru in a region directly attacked by nuclear weapons. The corresponding curves for stream water contamination in regions of the Northern Hemisphere not directly attacked by nuclear weapons are shown in Figures 3a, b, and c.

Figure 4 shows the contamination of groundwater by ^{106}Ru in a region directly attacked by nuclear weapons and in a region in the Northern Hemisphere exposed to global fallout only. In our calculations of groundwater contamination we ignored ^{89}Sr, ^{90}Sr, ^{137}Cs and ^{131}I, which are strongly absorbed in the seepage area, and we assumed no retention of ^{106}Ru and complete mixing with the groundwater reservoir.

As mentioned above, these calculations are based on the hydrologic characteristics of a typical low-land area in a temperate climate. In regions with a moist and rainy climate marked by frequent rainfalls—the tropical regions of South America for example—exceptionally high amounts of run-off occur. In those regions the surface,

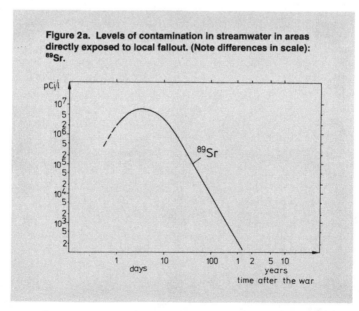

Figure 2a. Levels of contamination in streamwater in areas directly exposed to local fallout. (Note differences in scale): ^{89}Sr.

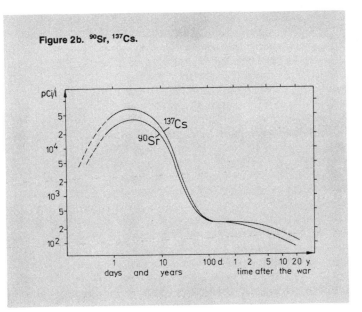

Figure 2b. ^{90}Sr, ^{137}Cs.

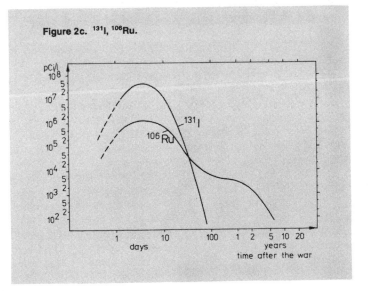

Figure 2c. ^{131}I, ^{106}Ru.

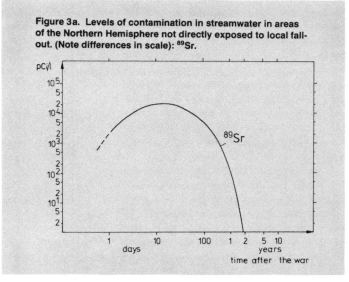

Figure 3a. Levels of contamination in streamwater in areas of the Northern Hemisphere not directly exposed to local fallout. (Note differences in scale): ^{89}Sr.

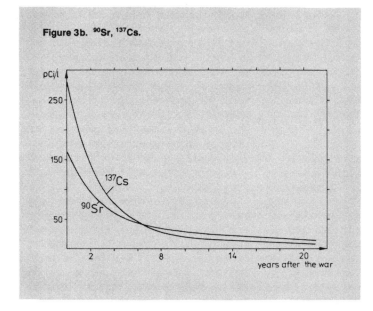

Figure 3b. ^{90}Sr, ^{137}Cs.

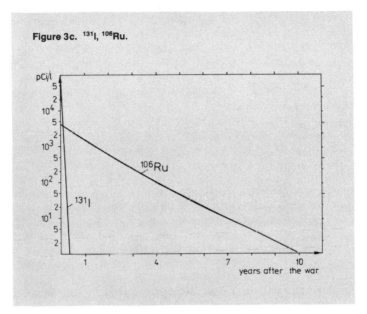

Figure 3c. ^{131}I, ^{106}Ru.

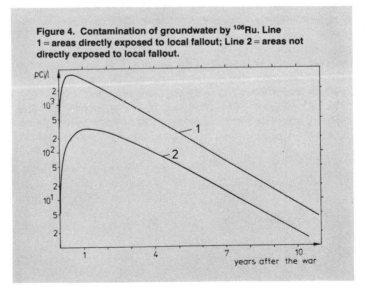

Figure 4. Contamination of groundwater by ^{106}Ru. Line 1 = areas directly exposed to local fallout; Line 2 = areas not directly exposed to local fallout.

subsurface and groundwater run-off would be increased by a factor of three, and the contamination of freshwater would be diluted by about the same factor, although this dilution effect would be moderated to some extent by increased local fallout due to heavy rains, and by accelerated leaching of fission products from the contaminated soil.

However the effect would not necessarily be the same in all regions with high run-off. For example, in regions of mountainous morphology in the vicinity of a coast line, surface run-off can be expected to reach some 100 mm per year, assuming a slightly increased precipitation rate. As a result, a great part of the fallout enters the freshwater immediately, and the concentration of fission products would increase two or three fold over the averages we have calculated.

Lakes act as buffering volumes, reducing the short-term increase in contamination of stream water. Figure 5 shows the ^{90}Sr contamination of a lake with a water residence time of five years, assuming the streamwater in Figure 2b runs through it. The calculation is based on the formula given in Reference 2.

The longer the residence time in a well-mixed lake, the greater its effect in diluting a substance which enters via the stream flow. For lakes with longer residence times than that used in the calculations for Figure 5—ie residence times of 30 to 75 years —we calculate that the maximum specific activity of ^{90}Sr would be about 100 pCi/l in regions directly exposed to nuclear explosions, and about 20 pCi/l in areas exposed to global fallout only, although it must be noted that levels of contamination will be higher in portions of the water if the lake is not well mixed.

A rough check of the validity of these calculations can be made by comparing them with the results of experimental investigations of freshwater contamination by global fallout from above-ground tests of nuclear weapons in the years up to about 1964 (3). The weapons used in these tests amounted to about 250 Mt (4, 5), which is about five percent of that assumed in the reference scenario for this book. In the case of ^{90}Sr and ^{137}Cs, these experiments show good agreement with our calculations.

The highest concentrations of radionuclides due to fallout are found in precipita-

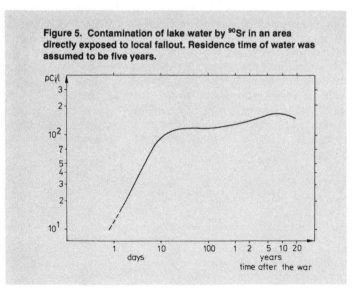

Figure 5. Contamination of lake water by ^{90}Sr in an area directly exposed to local fallout. Residence time of water was assumed to be five years.

tion. In 1963, shortly following tests of nuclear weapons, rainwater in central Europe was tested and found to contain 500 pCi/l of residual beta activity. At the same time stream water was found to contain about 30 pCi/l (6). It would therefore seem that beta activity in rainwater is greater than beta activity in streamwater by a factor of 100 to 200 for a certain period after nuclear explosions, and that a rough calculation of the concentration of fission products in rainwater could be reached by multiplying the values given in Figures 2a–2c by a factor of about 100.

CONCLUSIONS

The most severe radioactive contamination of freshwater systems following a nuclear war would be due to ^{131}I, ^{89}Sr, ^{90}Sr, and [106]Ru in regions exposed to local fallout, and to ^{131}I in regions exposed only to global fallout. Groundwater reservoirs would be least seriously affected by this contamination, followed by lakes, then by rivers, and finally by rainwater, which would be the most seriously contaminated.

In regions directly exposed to local fallout, rainwater would be a deadly poison, at least with respect to its contamination by [131]I. In these regions the rainwater would not only be unsuitable as drinking water but would be dangerous to human health through contact with the skin. If we assume a layer of contaminated rainwater 1 mm thick over the entire body, the maximum permissible radiation dose of 15 rads for skin would be reached in three hours during the period when contamination by ^{131}I is greatest. After 60 hours a dose of 300 rads would be reached, the point at which visible changes to the skin would begin to appear. Clothing permeable to water would offer no protection, and in fact would increase the damage from contaminated rain. Given the wholesale destruction of housing which is to be expected in a nuclear war, it is reasonable to assume that large numbers of people would be exposed to radioactive rain, and

while the whole body irradiation from contaminated rainwater would be small in comparison with that from fallout deposited on the ground, it would still cause a significant number of casualties.

In addition, rainfall would have the effect of concentrating radioactive fallout in some localities, thus producing levels of contamination far higher than the averages we have calculated. Within regions directly exposed to nuclear explosions, freshwater contamination in some localities would be enhanced by a factor of from 10 to 100 over the average levels we have calculated; for regions exposed only to global fallout, local enhancement of freshwater contamination by a factor of up to 10 is to be expected.

Streamwater in regions directly exposed to nuclear explosions would be contaminated by ^{131}I, ^{89}Sr, ^{90}Sr and [106]Ru to levels far above the International Atomic Energy Agency's recommendations for maximum concentrations in drinking water for radiation workers. This situation would last for a period of about four weeks. The most dangerous contamination would be due to ^{131}I and ^{89}Sr, which would exceed the recommended maximum concentrations by a factor of 10^3 and 10^2 respectively. In regions of the Northern Hemisphere exposed to global fallout only, streamwater would be contaminated by concentrations of ^{131}I higher than the recommended maximum for a period of about two weeks.

It should be emphasized that these maximum permissible concentrations of radionuclides in drinking water imply some health risks, particularly with respect to genetic damage, and of course those risks are increased greatly when these maximums are exceeded. Limits for general populations, while they vary from one nation to another, are generally lower than the standards for radiation workers by one or two orders of magnitude.

Groundwater would not be as severely contaminated as other freshwater reservoirs. The strong absorbtion of the most dangerous fission products by most types of soil tends to protect groundwater reservoirs from contamination, although it also causes severe and long-lasting contamination of the food chain. In general, contamination of groundwater would be tolerable, with certain exceptions. In aquifers with a water residence time of only a few years or less, and in aquifers covered either by grails (or any other sediment with low ion exchange capacity) or by a soil layer of less than one meter, the radioactive contamination of the groundwater would be comparable to or higher than that of the surface freshwater. That contamination might include not only ^{106}Ru but the other fission products as well. In general, in regions not directly exposed to nuclear explosions contamination of shallow groundwater is in the same range as that of streamwater; in regions directly exposed to explosions, values are about one tenth those in streamwater, which would still exceed the IAEA recommended maximum for ^{131}I and reach it for ^{89}Sr.

Regional Fluctuations

The levels of contamination indicated in Figures 2–5 are valid averages for low-land regions of temperate climate whose hydrologic situation is similar to that described in Table 1. Other conditions would change those levels. Exceptionally high contaminations of surface freshwater would occur in montiform, karstic, permafrost, desert ard marshland regions, and include ^{90}Sr and ^{137}Cs contaminations lasting many years. Even if those regions received global fallout only, the maximum recommended concentrations would be exceeded by a considerable margin.

In semi-arid regions the collection of rainwater in cisterns is a very common method of compensating for the shortage of fresh water. In the aftermath of a nuclear war the rainfall would be highly contaminated and unsuitable for drinking. The groundwater horizons in these regions tend to be deep and are therefore well

106

protected from contamination, but that also makes groundwater reservoirs difficult to reach, and therefore of minor importance as a source of freshwater. During the periods of higher precipitation there is some stream flow in semi-arid zones, but with little or no groundwater discharge. The result is substantially increased leaching of fission products from contaminated soil which would result in remarkably high concentrations of radionuclides in the streamwater.

In contrast with semi-arid zones, tropical regions are characterized by shallow groundwater and by soils which have little capacity to retain radioactive substances, both of which tend to increase the contamination of groundwater. But the heavy rainfall tends to dilute the contamination of streamwater, and tropical streamwater would contain lower concentrations of contaminants than that of semi-arid regions.

In tropical regions with spring and autumn rainy periods, ^{131}I would undergo radioactive decay before the autumn rainfall (assuming the nuclear explosions were detonated during June, as postulated in the reference scenario) and would therefore not enter the freshwater systems, apart from the small amounts deposited directly on surface freshwater; ^{137}Cs, ^{89}Sr, ^{90}Sr and ^{106}Ru accumulated in catchment areas would be delayed about three months in entering the freshwater systems. Global fallout in the tropical regions would be about half that of the temperate regions.

Finally, freshwater in the Southern Hemisphere would be less contaminated from global fallout by a factor of 0.03, assuming hydrologic characteristics similar to those described in Table 1.

CONSEQUENCES FOR HUMAN ACTIVITIES

The danger of ionizing radiation from the contamination of freshwater systems is relatively small in comparison with the hazards posed by the radiation released by the initial nuclear explosion or by the induction of fission products into the food chain via fallout deposited on the soil. Despite this, the number of people killed or severely sickened by drinking contaminated freshwater (other than rain) would be substantial, although small in comparison with the number of casualties from the other effects of a nuclear war. The deaths due to contaminated water, however, will occur among those who survived the first effects of the nuclear explosions, and who might otherwise have escaped.

Supplies of freshwater would be severely restricted following a nuclear war. It would be difficult to draw freshwater from groundwater reservoirs, which would be the source best protected from contamination, or from lakes and rivers in areas directly attacked by nuclear weapons. In addition, many millions of people would be left without shelter, and thus exposed to radioactive rainfall. The genetic damage arising from the contamination of freshwater supplies would be substantial, although still less than that resulting from the initial release of radiation from nuclear explosions or from the radioactive contamination of the food chain.

The industrial uses of freshwater would not be severely restricted by radioactive contamination, even in regions directly exposed to explosions, with one important exception: for several years it would be impossible to produce, package or use photographic films, plates, emulsions or papers anywhere in the Northern Hemisphere, or in regions of the Southern Hemisphere exposed to local fallout, without first decontaminating the water or using water from extremely deep and well-protected groundwater reservoirs. Such photographic products are extremely important for medical care.

Agriculture would not be greatly affected by the radioactive contamination of freshwater supplies. It would be possible to decrease slightly the contamination of

plants by using groundwater from protected sources for irrigation, but the effect is very slight, except in the case of ^{106}Ru, which would be effectively removed from the food chain. However the use of synthetic fertilizers, especially those containing calcium, potassium or ammonium, would increase the contamination of freshwater —including groundwater—by a considerable amount, because these ions effectively displace ^{89}Sr, ^{90}Sr and ^{137}Cs from the soil (7, 8). Because some fission products are long lasting, this would be the case for many years.

References and Notes

1. Y Miyake. Estimation of the direct contribution of meteoric water to river waters by means of fallout of radiocaesium and radiostrontium. Radioisotopes in Hydrology, IAEA publication STI/PUB/71. (Vienna, 1963), 425–431.
2. The concentration over time, c_L, of a given radionuclide in a lake is given by the formula:

$$c_L(t) = c_S + (^{\circ}c_L - c_S) \cdot e - \frac{q_{SL}}{s_L} \cdot t$$

where s_L is the water storage of the lake, q_{SL} is the portion of stream flow being completely mixed with the lake water, and $^{\circ}c_L$ and c_S are the initial concentrations in the lake and the constant concentrations in the stream, respectively, and the ratio represents $\frac{s_L}{q_{SL}}$ resents the residence time of water in the lake which may be assumed to be in the range of 1 to 30 years. The direct fallout on the surface of a lake gives a contribution of less than 20 pCi per liter and can therefore be neglected.
3. *Effects of Ionizing Radiation on Aquatic Organisms and Ecosystems*, International Atomic Energy Agency. Technical report series 172. IAEA, (Vienna, 1976).
4. A Aarkrog. *Environmental studies on radioecological sensitivity and variability with special emphasis on the fallout nuclides ^{90}Sr and ^{137}Cs*. Danish Atomic Energy Commission. Risk report 437 (1979).
5. *Sources and Effects of Ionizing Radiation: Report of the United Nations Scientific Committee on the Effects of Atomic Radiation*. United Nations (New York, 1977).
6. J Kunert *et al. Ergebnisse der Strahlenschutzüberwachung des Territoriums der Deutschen Demokratischen Republik auf Fallout radioaktivität.* Staatliches Amt für Atomsicherheit und Strahlschutz, report SAAS-235 (Berlin, 1978).
7. J Benes. *Radioaktive Kontamination der Biosphäre.* VEB Gustav Fisher Verlag Jena (1981).
8. W Ratschinski. *Isotope und Strahlenquellen in der Landwirtschaft.* VEB Deutscher Landwirtschaftsverlag Berlin (1979).

EIGHT

THE IMPACT ON OCEAN ECOSYSTEMS

ALLYN H. SEYMOUR

A nuclear war would have less impact on ocean ecosystems than on terrestrial systems. But damage to coastal regions and estuaries might be substantial.

This chapter discusses the distribution, effects, and hazards of fallout radionuclides in the ocean, and attempts to assess the impact on ocean ecosystems of dust particles in the atmosphere, ozone depletion, and temperature change following a nuclear war. This information offers some insight into the impact of a nuclear war, but does not provide definitive predictions.

DISTRIBUTION OF FALLOUT RADIONUCLIDES

The distribution of radionuclides in the atmosphere has been discussed elsewhere in this book. However it should be noted that the radionuclides—either fission products, neutron-activated nuclides, or unfissioned uranium or plutonium—arrive at the ocean's surface either as fallout particles or gases. Fallout of heavy particles occurs near the detonation site and if a rain storm is encountered, as much as 75 percent of the fallout may be brought to the earth's surface in 30 minutes and produce a "hot spot" (1). Delayed fallout both from the troposphere and stratosphere is deposited in broad latitudinal bands and its arrival time at the surface varies from days to several years.

The vertical and lateral distributions of radionuclides in ocean waters and bottom sediments are governed by physical, chemical and biological processes. Radionuclides enter the ocean either as solutes, colloids, or particulates. If they remain as solutes or colloids they will be incorporated into and transported laterally by advective forces of the water into which they fall, and will also be slowly transferred to deep water by mixing and diffusion processes. At a later time, some of the solutes and colloids may become associated with particulates by biological or physiochemical activities. On the other hand, insoluble particulates with densities greater than seawater will sink relatively rapidly by gravitational forces at rates which can be

110

approximated by use of Stoke's Law for particles of known sizes and densities.

Fallout radionuclides move downward at a relatively fast rate in the surface layer but at a slow rate in deep water. Mixing throughout the surface layer (50–200 m) may occur as rapidly as a few days or weeks for some of the fallout radionuclides, but the pycnocline, the surface–deep water boundary, is a temporary barrier to downward movement, especially for the solutes and colloids. The effectiveness of the pycnocline as a barrier is indicated by the half-residence time—3.5 years—for ^{3}H in surface water. Below the pycnocline the downward movement of soluble radionuclides is even slower; the time required for the cycle to reach the bottom (mean depth, 3800 m) and back is of the order of decades to hundreds of years. Residence times for deep ocean waters are a relative measure of water exchange, and values of 100–400 years for Atlantic Antarctic Intermediate Water, 600 years for North Atlantic Deep Water and 1000–1300 years for Pacific and Indian Ocean Deep Water have been reported (2).

In addition to mass water transport by advection and diffusion processes, there are other ways in which radionuclides are transported vertically: by upwelling, sinking of surface water, diurnal plankton migrations, or sinking of fecal pellets. In areas of upwelling, radionuclides in water of moderate depths (approximately 300 m) may be brought to the surface. At one location off the California coast, the upward rate was estimated to be 20 m per month. Cold surface water at high latitudes will sink and at the same time move toward the equator, carrying with it surface fallout radionuclides. Hence the sources of fallout radionuclides in deep water at mid and low latitudes can be either the overlying or the high-latitude surface waters or both. Plankton accumulate radionuclides from water by sorption and the diurnal migration by some species from deep water through the pycnocline to the surface layer, and back, provides a vehicle for both upward and downward movement of radionuclides. Fecal pellets of organisms living in the surface layer can also be a means for the rapid transport of radionuclides to the ocean's floor. Evidence has been presented that ^{144}Ce–^{144}Pr and ^{95}Zr–^{95}Nb were transported to a depth of 2800 m in 7 to 12 days in this manner (3), a depth that normally would not be reached by soluble radionuclides for many decades.

Direct observations on the horizontal movement of soluble radionuclides were made of the "footprint" of radioactivity that was placed in the North Equatorial Current System by the 15 Mt detonation at Bikini Atoll on March 1, 1954. The "footprint" was found within the North Equatorial Current System in May–June 1954, again in March–April 1955, and finally in August–September 1955. During this period the maximum observed ^{90}Sr value in water decreased from 194 to 3.9 to 0.5 pCi per liter. From these data the horizontal eddy diffusion coefficient was derived and the lateral rates of advance were calculated to be 14.8 and 7.7 km per day at two months and one year respectively (4). By comparison, vertical transport is about 5 m per year in deep ocean water of the Pacific (2).

Although there is limited observational data on the oceanic distribution of fallout radionuclides, the behavior of ^{90}Sr and ^{137}Cs in the North Atlantic Ocean 10 or more years after fallout has been exceptionally well documented (5). These data provide a model for reliable predictions of the depth and latitudinal distribution of soluble fallout radionuclides. Some of these data have been converted to percentages of total inventory for presentation in Table 1. After 10 years, 73 percent remained above 1000 m, 25 percent was below 1000 m and the remainder, 2 percent, was in either the sediments or shelf water. It should also be noted that from about 1969 on the annual addition of ^{90}Sr to North Atlantic surface water has been 1 to 1.5 percent and this has been sufficient to maintain a uniform mean ^{90}Sr concentration. Two other observations are pertinent: the ^{137}Cs/^{90}Sr ratio (1.45) was practically constant for all samples; and the latitudinal distributions of ^{90}Sr on land and in the ocean closely parallel each other, but a difference of about 25 percent suggests that either fallout on land has been underestimated or fallout into the ocean is greater than on land (5).

The distribution of ^{137}Cs in the Pacific Ocean is not as well known, but the pattern appears to be more complicated. Also

Table 1. 1972 Latitudinal and depth distributions of ^{137}Cs in the North Atlantic Ocean as percentages of the total inventory.*

Latitudinal Band	Shelf Water	Off Shore Water			Total		Total: Water + Sediments
		0 to 1 000 m	1 000 to 2 000 m	2 000 m to bottom	Water Column	Sediments	
0–10°	0.04	2.4	0.3	0.4	3.1	0.18	3.3
10–20°	< 0.01	5.3	0.9	0.0	6.1	0.28	6.4
20–30°	< 0.01	20.4	1.6	1.3	23.3	0.15	23.5
30–40°	< 0.01	21.5	4.6	0.5	26.8	0.37	27.2
40–50°	0.13	11.7	4.4	3.4	19.6	0.58	20.2
50–60°	0.06	8.6	3.9	2.8	15.2	0.15	15.4
60–66°	0.02	2.7	0.8	0.4	3.9	0.09	4.0
							100.0 %
TOTAL	0.3	72.6	16.6	8.8	98.2	1.8	
							3 272 kCi**

* Calculated from Table 3 (5); small errors in the total values are due to rounding off.
** The combined statistical and systematic uncertainty is +84, −344.

the ratio of inventory to input (calculated from land fallout) is 2.2, compared to 1.25 for the North Atlantic. A part of this difference is assigned to close-in fallout from nuclear detonations at the Pacific Test Site (6). The distributions of ^{137}Cs and ^{3}H were compared and found to be broadly similar.

The observed distribution of a "non-soluble" radionuclide, Pu, in the central and north Pacific Ocean was a surprise. Truly non-soluble nuclides would be expected to be found near bottom, or in transit, but Pu was found in two layers, one a shallow subsurface layer (450 m) and the other near bottom where the concentration of Pu was less. The shallow layer was present throughout the area and the mean maximum ^{239,240}Pu value was 0.68 disintegrations per minute (dpm) per 100 kg seawater (6). The principal explanation for the presence of the shallow layer was resolubilization of Pu from sinking particles.

For Pu that has already reached the ocean floor in near-shore areas, the observed concentrations in bottom sediments have been explained by postulating that Pu was transported on a mixed population of particles for which the annual rates of descent were 70 m for 30 percent, 140 m for 40 percent, and 392 m for the remaining 30 percent (7).

The bottom sediment will ultimately be the resting place for all the long-lived radionuclides, just as it is for all chemical elements that enter the ocean. The transport times will be relatively short for the nonsoluble particulates and very long for the radionuclides that remain as solutes. Sediments have a great capacity for the sorption of some radionuclides and the extent of this interaction appears to be controlled by the physiochemical state of both the sediment and the radionuclide (8). Radionuclides in bottom sediments may be mixed and moved by bioturbation, or interstitial water, or be released for recycling. The bottom sediments could be a sink for those radionuclides that arrive on the ocean's floor in a relatively short period of time and have long radioactive half-lives. The fallout radionuclides most likely to play this role are the transuranic nuclides and they would be a potential hazard if significant quantities were transferred to man via the food chain.

EFFECTS

Ionizing radiation may affect the exposed individual (somatic effects) and/or the progeny of the exposed individual (genetic effects). The effects range from the most obvious, death, to those that are very subtle and difficult to identify with ionizing radiation. The results of experiments to determine lethal doses demonstrate a general relationship between the phylogeny and ontogeny of an organism and its sensitivity to ionizing radiation. Primitive organisms are less sensitive than more complex forms of life, so that bacteria < protozoa < algae < mollusca < crustacea < fish < man. Hence marine organisms as a group are considered to be less sensitive to ionizing radiation than man. Although the radiation sensitivity of bacteria is 10^3 or more lower than for man, the range of radiation sensitivity values within a phylogenetic group may be as great as 10^2. Also, there are other factors, perhaps not obvious, that affect laboratory radiation sensitivity experiments. For example, one research group reported a significant increase in the number of abnormal fish larvae reared at ^{90}Sr-^{90}Y concentrations of 10^{-10}Ci/liter whereas researchers elsewhere did not observe similar effects until the concentration was increased to 10^{-4}Ci/liter (9).

The impact of both somatic and genetic effects is greater upon man than the creatures of the sea for reasons other than radiation sensitivity. One is an ethical consideration: the loss of one man is regarded as important while the loss of one fish is not. The loss of fish is not considered important until it threatens the reduction or extinction of the population. So far as

112

genetic effects are concerned, the impact upon marine organisms is considered to be relatively less because their reproductive rate is high, and genetic damage at the population level can be repaired by natural selection (9).

Other effects may result from a drastic reduction in the incidence of solar light at the earth's surface or a significant increase in the flux of ultraviolet light following a nuclear war. Both factors have the potential to produce devastating effects upon marine populations at the bottom of the food chain. Crutzen and Birks (10) state, "If the production of aerosol by fires is large enough to cause reductions in the penetration of sunlight to ground level by a factor of a hundred, which would be quite possible in the event of an all-out nuclear war, most of the phytoplankton and herbivorous zooplankton in more than half of the Northern Hemisphere oceans would die . . . This effect is due to the fast consumption rate of phytoplankton by zooplankton in the oceans."

The increase in the flux of ultraviolet (uv) light at the earth's surface is associated with the introduction of nitrous oxide (NO_x) into the stratosphere, which would reduce the ozone reservoir and permit uv penetration. Bacteria and yeasts in the surface film of the ocean would receive the greatest exposure, but their vulnerability to injury may be tempered by their long history of exposure to natural uv. However, other marine organisms appear to have little reserve tolerance to uv, and the effectiveness of uv-B in killing bacteria and other microorganisms is well established (11).

Long-term changes in water temperature resulting from either or both of these factors are not expected to exceed $\pm 1°C$, a change which marine organisms can accept.

HAZARD EVALUATION

The principal hazards from radioactive contaminants in the ocean are the survival of marine organisms, the impact on marine ecosystems and the transfer of radionuclides from the ocean to man.

The survival of marine organisms is determined by the dose received from radionuclides in the water and absorbed onto outer body surfaces (external dose), the dose from ingested foods or other matter (internal dose), and their sensitivity to ionizing radiation. Generally, marine organisms will have a much better chance for survival than man.

The impact on a marine ecosystem will be determined by the ability of each system component to withstand the combined stresses from all sources. There is some information about the effects of ionizing radiation on marine species, but no data about the impact on entire marine ecosystems. The marine environment is characterized by its constancy of composition; as a result, marine biota have less ability to accommodate change than biota elsewhere. However, one reason for stability is the complexity of the food web, which to some degree can moderate the effects of minor insults and stresses. The fact that marine environments are characterized by greater species diversity, longer food chains and perhaps greater species dependence than those of land or fresh water may also be of significance in evaluating the impact on marine ecosystems (12).

Of the many fallout radionuclides in the ocean, those considered significant are those that are either produced in abundance by nuclear detonations, or are concentrated to a high degree by plants or animals, or have a long radioactive half-life. The list of significant radionuclides will change with time as the short-lived radionuclides disappear and the longer-lived radionuclides advance in rank. For a scenario that called for four detonations (total 4 Mt) in an ocean reef environment, the 20 most significant radionuclides immediately following detonation were predicted to be:

^{64}Cu, ^{103}Ru, ^{99}Tc, ^{127}Te, ^{106}Ru, ^{185}W, ^{140}La, ^{32}P, ^{140}Ba, ^{131}I, ^{58}Co, ^{141}Ce, ^{181}W, ^{54}Mn, ^{144}Ce, ^{95}Zr, ^{55}Fe, ^{59}Fe, ^{14}C and ^{57}Co (13).

The listings are in approximate order of greatest to least hazard as determined by the ratio of predicted radionuclide concentrations in the ocean to radionuclide MPCC values (maximum permissible seawater concentration; to be defined in the following section). In another theoretical exercise, the 11 significant radionuclides in seawater 20 years after multiple nuclear detonations totalling 10^4 Mt were predicted to be the following, listed in order of their mass numbers:

^3H, ^{14}C, ^{55}Fe, ^{60}Co, ^{85}Kr, ^{90}Sr, ^{129}I, ^{137}Cs, $^{238,239}Pu$, ^{241}Am (11).

When the two lists are compared, it should be noted that 18 of the 20 radionuclides on the first list would have decayed away in 20 years, and that the kinds and amounts of neutron-activated radionuclides produced are related to the types of materials near the detonation points and therefore their presence in fallout is neither consistent nor constant. It should also be noted that the definitions of "significance" were different.

Table 2 lists the radionuclides of significance 20 years after detonation, exclusive of the neutron-induced radionuclides, and the characteristics that qualify them for the classification of "significant". The list of significant radionuclides at 10 years would be the same. Also presented in Table 2, as an aid to understanding the concentration values for the marine biota, is information about the water concentration, concentration category and the primary dissolved species for the chemical element to which the radioisotope belongs.

Additional comments about the radionuclides of Table 2 will further explain their fate in the marine ecosystem. Although ^3H is produced in great abundance by thermonuclear detonations, it is present mostly as an atom in the water molecule

and hence its concentration in marine biota is about that of ^3H in ambient water. Carbon-14 (^{14}C) produced by nuclear detonations is diluted by the large reservoir of natural ^{14}C, and exists in the atmosphere as CO_2 where it is a part of the carbon geochemical cycle. The concentration of ^{14}C in marine plants and animals does not exceed environmental ^{14}C levels. Both ^{90}Sr and ^{137}Cs remain soluble in seawater but a small fraction may become attached to fine particles. Strontium is chemically similar to calcium and hence ^{90}Sr is concentrated in bone, shell, fish scales, *etc.* Cesium is chemically similar to potassium and hence ^{137}Cs is concentrated in the soft tissues, including muscle. Because ^{90}Sr is mostly deposited in non-edible tissues of seafoods and its concentration in seawater is less, ^{137}Cs is the greater hazard to man. Iodine-129 is unique in that it will essentially remain in the ocean forever, because of its extremely long half-life. However, it is produced in small quantities, is significantly diluted by stable iodine in the ocean and decays by emission of low energy radiation. The other three radionuclides are transuranic elements—^{238}Pu, ^{239}Pu, ^{239}Am—which are mostly insoluble, and are transported relatively rapidly to the bottom sediments, although it appears that a fraction of the Pu on sinking particles can be resolubilized. These radionuclides are most available to the organisms living in and on the bottom sediment, and to animals that feed on the bottom-living organisms.

One quantitative measure of the hazard to man is the internal radiation dose from the consumption of seafood. To calculate the internal dose rate the following information is required: seawater radionuclide concentration values; transfer rates from water to biota; concentration factors for organisms in the food web; man's seafood consumption rate; transfer rates for seafood to man; concentration factors for man; and factors for the conversion of body burden to dose rate. Models and

Table 2. Characteristics of the significant long-term fallout radionuclides and the chemical elements to which they belong in the ocean 20 years after detonation.*

| RADIONUCLIDES | | | CHEMICAL ELEMENTS | | | | | | | | |
Species	Abundance M Ci**	Half-life, years	Species	Water Characteristics concentration category	Water Characteristics concentration µg/liter	dissolved species	Concentration in Biota fish	crustacea	mollusks	plants
^{3}H	20 000	12.3	H	A	1.1×10^{8}	H_2O	1	1	1	1
^{14}C	1 300	5 400	C	A	28 000	HCO_3^{-1}; H_2CO_3; CO_3^{-2}	1	1	1	1
^{90}Sr	2 900	28.9	Sr	A	8 000	Sr^{+2} $SrSO_4$	1	1	1	20
^{129}I	48	1.6×10^{7}	I	A	60	IO_3^{-1}	20	100	100	10 000
^{137}Cs	4 300	30.2	Cs	A	0.4	Cs^{+1}	30	50	10	10
^{238}Pu	0.1	87.4	Pu	B	–	$Pu(OH)_2^{+2}$	3	200	200	1 000
^{239}Pu	5.8	24 000			–	PuO_2				
^{241}Am	2.3	433	Am	B	–	$Am(OH)_2^{+1}$ Am_2O_3	25	1 000	1 000	5 000

* Radionuclides, exclusive of those produced by neutron activation, relatively abundant, long half-lives, and biologically important; data from reference 11.
** Initial approximate values from detonations yielding 5750 Mt; scenario values (11) × 0.575.
*** A, conservative elements, concentration directly proportional to salinity; B, concentration variable and governed by biochemical and geochemical processes.

115

computer programs are now available that make use of these kinds of information to predict the dose to man from known concentrations of radionuclides in seawater. However, the error in the predicted dose can be expected to be large, since many of the parameters used in the model are not well known.

After the dose rate prediction has been completed the degree of hazard is usually determined by comparing the predicted value with the maximum permissible dose rate for the civilian population, which is 0.5 rem per year or 5.0 rem per 30 years. An alternate method stops at the point of predicting the seawater radionuclide concentration value and then compares this value with an MPCC (maximum permissible seawater concentration) value which, with minor corrections, is the specific activity—for example, ^{90}Sr/total Sr, for the critical organ (man). This concept recognizes the presence of stable isotopes in seawater that reduce the biological uptake

of the introduced radioisotopes, but it has some inherent errors which limit its usefulness.

PREDICTIONS

A crude prediction of the impact of ionizing radiation upon marine organisms—fish, crustacea, mollusks, plants—has been made by estimating the radiation dose they would receive according to the Reference Scenario. Data for calculating the concentration of ^{90}Sr and ^{137}Cs in seawater at one month and 10 years were taken from Table 2 of the Reference Scenario. The relationship between exposure to ^{90}Sr and ^{137}Cs in seawater and radiation dose is taken from reference 11. Both sets of data are presented in Table 3. Although the data are not entirely comparable, the predicted concentrations for ^{90}Sr and ^{137}Cs in seawater are of the same order for both sets of data and therefore it is reasonable to assume that the radiation doses will also be of the same order. Other radionuclides

Table 3. Calculated seawater radionuclide concentration values at one month and ten years for Reference Scenario and predicted radiation doses to marine organisms from exposure to given concentrations of radionuclides in seawater for the NAS scenario given in reference 11.

	Reference Scenario					
Area	Northern Hemisphere					
Time	1 month			10 years		
	^{90}Sr	^{131}I	^{137}Cs	^{90}Sr	^{131}I	^{137}Cs
Concentration (pCi/liter*)						
average all latitudes	2.5	200	4	0.2	–	0.3
60–40°N, only	7.0	600	11	0.5	–	0.8

	NAS Scenario		
Area	Northern Hemisphere		
Time	20 years		
	^{90}Sr	^{129}I	^{137}Cs
Concentration (pCi/liter**)			
average 80°–equator; surface	1.0	0.3	1.5

Dose m rad/year***	internal	external	total
fish	0.8	0.01	0.8
crustacea	2	70	70
molluscs	2	70	70
plants	10	0.04	10

* Calculated from surface fallout values from Table 2 of Reference Scenario assuming that 100 % of soluble fallout radionuclides are above 100 m at one month and 75 % above 1000 m at 10 years (5).
** From Table 4.11 of (11).
*** From Table 4.15 of (11).

could make a significant contribution to the total dose at one month, but not at 10 years or later. Conclusion: the radiation dose to marine organisms from ^{90}Sr and ^{137}Cs would be insignificant.

Relevant predictive information is also available from three other sources. One is the prediction of the radiation dose to residents of Eniwetok Atoll, a former nuclear test site, a prediction based on strong observational data; a second is the theoretical exercise to predict the impact of radioactive contamination in the ocean immediately following nuclear detonations of 4 Mt in an ocean-reef environment given in reference 13; and the third, the theoretical exercise to predict the impact, 10–20 years later, of a global nuclear war in which devices totalling 10^4 Mt were detonated, as described in reference 11.

The best available sources of empirical data on the biological impact of nuclear detonations in an oceanic environment are the reports from the Pacific Test Site. There were numerous detonations at Bikini and Eniwetok Atolls between 1946 and 1952, and measurements of environmental contamination and biological accumulation of radionuclides were made on numerous occasions. However the complicated fallout pictures that developed during and after each series of detonations drastically limited the value of these data in answering specific questions. Some incidental observations at the Pacific Test Site during and following nuclear test series are as follows: generally (but with exceptions) the predominant radionuclides in marine organisms from the lagoons were neutron-activated radionuclides such as ^{65}Zn, ^{60}Co and ^{54}Mn, whereas the predominant radionuclides in the terrestrial forms were ^{137}Cs, ^{90}Sr and other fission products; exceptionally large fish kills were not observed but the removal rate of injured or dead fish by predators was not known; there was extensive destruction of habitat in some areas from the deposition of sediment.

Studies 10 or more years after the discontinuation of the testing program have produced a clear picture of the distributions of long-lived fallout radionuclides at Bikini and Eniwetok Atolls and have provided reliable data for the calculation of the present and future radiation dose to those who may live there.

Robison, *et al* (14) summarize part of their recent studies at Eniwetok Atoll as follows:

"The terrestrial food chain is the most significant exposure pathway—it contributes more than 50 percent of the total dose—and external gamma exposure is the second most significant pathway. Other pathways evaluated are the marine food chain, drinking water, and inhalation.

Cesium-137 produces more than 65 percent of the predicted doses; ^{90}Sr is the second most significant radionuclide; ^{60}Co contributes to the external gamma exposure in varying degrees, but is a small part of the total predicted dose; the transuranic radionuclides contribute a small portion of the total predicted lung and bone doses but do present a long-term source of exposure."

In that study the maximum concentration values (in pCi/g, wet weight) for seven groups of marine species were as follows: ^{137}Cs, 1.7 (crabs); ^{90}Sr, 0.43 (crabs); ^{239,240}Pu, 0.044 (clams); and ^{241}Am, 0.0095 (clams). Since concentrations of this order would result in less than one percent of the permissible continuous daily intake for man, the hazard from the seafood pathway is considered insignificant. The dose to marine organisms would also be insignificant.

In 1974 Isaacs and Hendricks (13) calculated the radionuclide concentrations in seawater a few days after four detonations over open ocean or a coral reef, and compared the predicted values for 20 significant radionuclides to MPCC values. Since the major fallout was over the ocean, the

117

principal concern was the direct impact on the fishery resources and indirectly on man. They concluded that the radionuclide concentrations in some of the contaminated water would exceed the MPCC values for a period of from a few days to eight weeks for the 170 and 420 kt detonations, and from seven to eight months for the 1.5 Mt detonation. If fish lived in water contaminated to that extent for their entire lifetimes, there is a possibility that the amount of the radionuclide eventually concentrated in man as a result of eating those fish would exceed the allowable radionuclide burden for the critical organ or tissue. Because the water/radionuclide concentration decreases rapidly by dilution and radioactive decay, and because it is very unlikely that fish will remain in the contaminated water for their lifetimes, a reasonable interpretation of the results from the use of MPCC values is that they provide a warning but not an absolute limit.

The third source of information is the NAS-NRC report (11). One section of this report provides predictions for the radiation doses to marine organisms and to man from predicted concentrations of ^{90}Sr, ^{129}I and ^{137}Cs in seawater 20 years after a nuclear war. The mathematical model used for the calculation was developed by Battelle Pacific Northwest Laboratories and made use of ICRP dosimetry equations and parameters. The predicted doses to marine organisms are given in Table 3 and are discussed above. The seafood pathway does not transfer significant amounts of radionuclides from seawater to man 20 years after the nuclear war of this scenario, since the maximum predicted dose to man from seafoods was 2 mrem/year to the thyroid.

Most of the discussion about the impact of a nuclear war has concentrated on open ocean or atoll environments. But the areas where the greatest impact could be expected are the estuary, inshore, and coastal regions. The reasons are many: productiv-ity, since these are the most productive seafood areas of the ocean; loss of habitat, since many warheads are targeted for coastal sites, and so major losses can be expected in coastal regions from the physical forces of the detonation and from deposition of sediments; photosynthesis, since solar energy transmission drastically reduced by particles in the atmosphere will be further reduced by suspended sediments in the water; feeding, since heavy loads of sediments in water present special problems to filter and detritus feeders; ultraviolet light, since the impact would be greater here than elsewhere in the ocean; immediate post-detonation impact, since the ecosystems in these areas are more exposed to prompt radiation, heat, and pressure than ecosystems elsewhere in the marine environment; and runoff, since land runoff may significantly increase radionuclide concentrations in water of estuaries.

SUMMARY

The distribution of radionuclides in the ocean is governed by the physical and chemical properties of the fallout particles as well as the advection and diffusion processes within the ocean. Mixing within the surface layer (0 to 50–100 m) may occur as rapidly as a few days or weeks for some fallout radionuclides. In deeper water, the heavy, insoluble particles will descend relatively rapidly to the ocean floor (mean depth, 3800 m) but the solutes and colloids will require from decades to hundreds of years to make this journey. Solutes may remain in surface or near-surface water for several years; their rate of advance in these waters has been observed to be about 14 km per day two months after detonation. In the North Atlantic, ten years after the 1962 series of nuclear detonations, three fourths of the ^{90}Sr and ^{137}Cs inventories remained above 1000 m.

The ranking of the significant radionuclides—according to abundance, half-life, biological importance—changes rapidly

118

with time. Many of the fission products of biological importance have short half-lives, *eg* eight days for ^{131}I. After a few weeks, the radionuclides with intermediate half-lives move up in rank. In this group and of special importance to marine biota are the neutron-activated radionuclides such as ^{55}Fe, ^{60}Co and ^{65}Zn. After five years or more ^{90}Sr and ^{137}Cs head the list, followed by the transuranic elements, Pu and Am. Both ^{3}H and ^{14}C are present but are not concentrated in organisms above environmental levels; ^{129}I is of interest only because of its half-life, 10^7 years. The two fission products, ^{90}Sr and ^{137}Cs, occur in water mostly as solutes; the transuranic elements occur mostly as insoluble particulates in bottom sediments, although some Pu is present in near surface water of the Pacific Ocean.

The impact of ionizing radiation upon marine organisms is expected to be relatively less than upon terrestrial organisms including man for the following reasons: marine organisms except in shallow water are better protected from the immediate impact of prompt radiation, heat, and pressure; greater mixing and dilution of radionuclides in the ocean; generally, a relatively lesser biological concentration of radionuclides due to dilution by stable isotopes or nuclides; and marine organisms are less sensitive than man. Although precise predictions about radiation doses to marine organisms and man cannot be made because of imprecise data on radionuclide concentrations in sea water, transfer coefficients, and concentration factors, the dose predictions that have been made support this conclusion. However predictions have not been made of the short term impact of ionizing radiation in estuaries and coastal regions, the most valuable areas of the ocean.

Two other consequences of nuclear war, however, do have the potential for devastating effects upon marine ecosystems. It has been predicted (10) that a 100-fold reduction in solar light intensity at the earth's surface due to particles in the atmosphere is possible; this would result in death to most of the phytoplankton and herbivorous zooplankton in more than half of the oceans of the Northern Hemisphere. And under some circumstances, the depletion of ozone in the stratosphere by NO_x could increase uv radiation at the earth's surface, and the magnitude of the change would be sufficient to seriously reduce the populations of organisms at the base of the food web (11). Temperature changes would be of little consequence.

Although the impact of ionizing radiation on ocean systems may be less than elsewhere, nothing that has been said here should be interpreted as an argument lending credence to or justifying a nuclear war.

References and Notes

1. S Glasstone, P J Dolan, *The Effects of Nuclear Weapons*, US Department of Defense—US Department of Energy, Third Edition (1977).
2. D W Pritchard, R O Reid, A Okubo, H H Carter, *Radioactivity in the Marine Environment*, National Academy of Science, Washington D C (1971).
3. F G Lowman, R Rice, F A Richards, in *Radioactivity in the Marine Environment, op cit*, (1971).
4. Y Miyake, K Saruhashi, in *Disposal of Radioactive Wastes*, Proceedings of Conference, IAEA (Vienna, 1960).
5. S L Kupferman, H D Livingston, V T Bowen, *Journal of Marine Research* 37, 1 (1979).
6. V T Bowen, V E Noshkin, H D Livingston, H L Volchok, *Earth and Planetary Science Letters* 49, 411 (1980).
7. V E Noshkin, V T Bowen, in *Interaction of Radioactive Contaminants with the Constituents of the Marine Environment*, IAEA Symposium (1973).
8. E K Duursma, M G Gross, in *Radioactivity in the Marine Environment, op cit*, (1971).
9. W L Templeton, R E Nakatani, E E Held, in *Radioactivity in the Marine Environment, op cit*, (1971).
10. P J Crutzen, J W Birks—see Ch.6
11. *Long-Term Worldwide Effects of Multiple Nuclear Weapon Detonations*, Committee Report, National Research Council, National Academy of Science Washington, D C (1975).
12. V T Bowen, J S Olsen, C L Osterberg, J Ravera, in *Radioactivity in the Marine Environment, op cit*, (1971).
13. J D Isaacs, T Hendricks, personal communication (1974).
14. W L Robison, W A Phillips, M E Mount, B R Clegg, C L Conrado, UCRL-53066 UC-11, National Technical Information Service (Springfield, Virginia, USA, 1980).

A tall column of smoke billows 20,000 feet above Hiroshima after the first atomic bomb strike by the American Air Force on 6 August 1945. A cloud of smoke 10,000 feet in diameter covers a part of the city at the base of the column. This picture was taken after the bomb was released from an altitude of between 20,000 and 30,000 feet.

Photo: National Archives, Washington, D.C.

NINE

EFFECTS ON AGRICULTURE

ERNEST A. BONDIETTI

Radioactive contamination of croplands would be widespread in the Northern Hemisphere. And delayed fallout, in areas not directly involved in the war, would raise radioactivity levels in food and human tissues to 20 times the levels reported during the weapons' testing period of the 1960s. Agriculture would revert to a non-mechanized age and many Third World countries, dependent on enormous imports of food from the developed countries, would be severely affected.

A global nuclear war will affect the world's agriculture in many diverse ways. Among the impacts of major concern will be:

1) High levels of radionuclides in food, especially in the Northern Hemisphere;
2) Destruction of the industrial infrastructure upon which mechanized agriculture depends;
3) Decreases in crop yields because of disruptions in pest control, plant breeding, and other productivity management techniques;
4) Failure of national and international food distribution/processing systems;
5) Decreases in crop yields because of large scale changes in atmospheric composition and climate.

The immediate effects on human beings of the June 1985 attacks described by the Reference Scenario (1), upon which this article is based, will be so catastrophic that in many ways all subsequent effects become trivial. Nevertheless, everyone not killed by blast, thermal, or early radiation exposure will be immediately faced with a drastically altered social and physical environment. Shelter, food, and medical needs will be of paramount concern. This article, however, will consider only the short- and long-term agricultural situation, especially the contamination of food with radioactivity.

For a large portion of the population living in the downwind areas blanketed by nonlethal levels of fallout from targets, the external radiation dose received during the first month or so will dominate the dose accumulated over their lifetimes from the eventual global deposit of radioactivity from the war. Most of the discussion of this globally dispersed radioactivity will concern dietary contamination although external radiation exposure will result in doses comparable to those derived from the diet (2, 3).

In order to illustrate the short-term and long-term role of diet in radiation expo-

sure, the contamination of the Northern Hemisphere will be discussed from two perspectives. First, the local effect of a radioactive deposit downwind from the detonation of 1 megaton (total) is discussed; second, the effect of the fission product deposit on the Northern Hemisphere originating from that fraction of the total megatonnage used in the war which would be injected into the stratosphere. Since dietary habits following the war are hard to predict, the anticipated contamination of humans by their diet is based on present patterns of food consumption.

EARLY RADIOACTIVE FALLOUT

When a nuclear weapon is detonated at ground level, large amounts of surface materials are pulled up into the ascending fireball. Most of this debris immediately begins to fall back to earth. Those particles (and associated radioactivity) larger than about 20 microns in diameter which will be deposited in about one day are considered early or local fallout. Particles smaller than this will tend to stay in the troposphere for longer periods of time and may actually be injected into the stratosphere. For this article it is assumed that 50 percent of the fission yield (fission yield is assumed to be 50 percent of total megatonnage) will be deposited as early fallout; the remainder enters the stratosphere where its mean residence time is one year (2). This latter radioactivity constitutes the global fallout resulting from high-yield nuclear explosions.

Figure 1 represents an idealized early fallout pattern for strontium-90 deposition, in units of curies $(Ci)/km^2$, within about 500 km of ground zero. For this example, an area in central France was chosen to provide a perspective of the area contaminated by a surface detonation. Similar deposits could occur downwind from other targets. The isopleths of strontium-90 deposition were estimated by converting dose rates (R/hr) to deposit con-

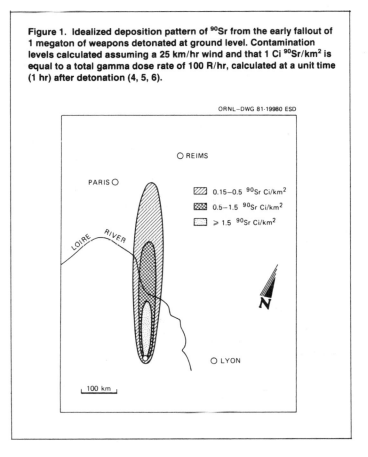

Figure 1. Idealized deposition pattern of ⁹⁰Sr from the early fallout of 1 megaton of weapons detonated at ground level. Contamination levels calculated assuming a 25 km/hr wind and that 1 Ci ⁹⁰Sr/km² is equal to a total gamma dose rate of 100 R/hr, calculated at a unit time (1 hr) after detonation (4, 5, 6).

centrations for a 1 megaton detonation (4, 5, 6). Up to about 150 km, the strontium-90 deposit could be ≥1.5 Ci/km², while at more than 400 km the deposit would be about 0.15 Ci/km². This deposition pattern was constructed in terms of strontium-90 for comparison to the global deposit of strontium-90. Shorter-lived radioisotope levels would be much greater; for example iodine-131 would be 1700 times higher at the time of detonation (4), assuming no fractionation of the radioactivity.

The 150 km distance delineated by the 1.5 Ci/km² isopleth in Figure 1 will be the region where absorbed doses (greater than 450 rads) accumulated over the first 24 hours after detonation could be fatal to humans and livestock. In this high dose region, crop yield reductions might also be expected. For example, maize is very sensitive to radiation during the first two months of growth, with almost complete loss of yield from a 2500 rad (gamma) exposure delivered over 8 hours (7). At the same dose rate, soybean yields were reduced between 10 and 50 percent, depending on exposure date, during the first two months of growth (7). The doses delivered by beta radiation to fallout-contaminated vegetation can be higher by a factor of 10 over the gamma dose because of the relatively short range of beta particles (8). Beta radiation will also cause skin lesions to develop on livestock contaminated with

123

sub-lethal amounts of fallout and may cause injury to the gastrointestinal tract when contaminated foliage is eaten (9). These lesions would cause additional mortalities because of the higher bacterial infection rates which are a direct result of the marked reduction in the immune response capability of radiation-exposed mammals.

The early fallout, because of its large size (≥20 μm), is much less available to organisms than the finer-sized global deposit (3). Also, the early fallout does not tend to remain on plant surfaces because of its coarse size, further reducing its entry into food chains (3). Despite this relatively low biological availability, the deposition of early fallout onto pastures can pose an important hazard because of the contamination of milk with iodine-131 and other fission products. Figure 2 illustrates the 30 day behavior (hypothetical) of ^{131}I, ^{89}Sr, and ^{137}Cs radionuclide contamination in milk along the 0.5 Ci/km^2 ^{90}Sr isopleth of Figure 1. The milk concentrations were estimated using calculations in reference 10, and assuming that 2.5 percent of the local deposit remained on pasture plants and was available for biological absorption by grazing cows. Iodine-131 (8 day half-life) is by far the most important nuclide because of its high fission yield, rapid entry into milk, and accumulation in the human thyroid gland. During the first week after deposition, ingestion of one liter of this

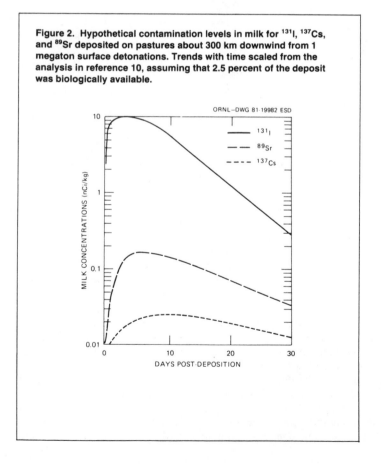

Figure 2. Hypothetical contamination levels in milk for ^{131}I, ^{137}Cs, and ^{89}Sr deposited on pastures about 300 km downwind from 1 megaton surface detonations. Trends with time scaled from the analysis in reference 10, assuming that 2.5 percent of the deposit was biologically available.

milk could result in an infant thyroid dose of about 200 rem (2). This dose greatly exceeds the 1.5 rem non-occupational maximum recommended by the International Commission on Radiological Protection (10). It is comparable to the reference dose used by the US Nuclear Regulatory Commission during site licensing to establish the population exclusion boundary for a design basis nuclear reactor accident (11).

The external dose to farm workers at this location will be high, initially dominated by ^{140}Ba, ^{131}I, ^{131}Ce, ^{95}Zr as well as activation products like ^{239}Np and ^{237}U. The resulting whole body dose (greater than 200 rem in the first year) would be greatly in excess of current international standards for occupational exposure.

Strontium-90 and cesium-137 will be the most important dietary nuclides after about one year because most other radionuclides decay more quickly and are generally not as biologically available to plants from soil (2,5). The radiological importance of other fission products in the diet during the immediate post war period is not enough to warrant discussion here.

GLOBAL OR LATE RADIOACTIVE FALLOUT

On the average about 0.3 Ci/km^2 (^{90}Sr) and 0.4 Ci/km^2 (^{137}Cs) will eventually be deposited on the Northern Hemisphere. This will result from the tropospheric and stratospheric injection of these two radionuclides corresponding to about 1600 megatons of fission yield from air bursts (100 percent injected) and ground bursts (50 percent injected). This quantity is about 23 times the stratospheric inventory present at the beginning of 1963 following the Test Ban Treaty (2). Extensive monitoring through 1968, the year of the next atmospheric test, allows a direct scaling of dietary contamination data obtained from this period to the post-war period. The inventory of the stratosphere will deplete at a rate of about 50 percent per year,

taking about 7 years for 99 percent of the fission products to be deposited on the Northern Hemisphere. Most of the ^{90}Sr and ^{137}Cs in the diet during the first half of this period will result from direct deposition of the fine global fallout particles on vegetation surfaces—pastures (milk, meat), cereals and vegetables. Only after about three years will the uptake of radionuclides through plant roots begin to dominate the contamination of food (2, 6, 12). During the immediate post-war period, much of the area significantly contaminated by the local fallout deposits may actually produce food whose primary source of contamination is the annual global deposit. For the idealized local ^{90}Sr deposit illustrated in Figure 1 as an example, the annual total global deposit would probably dominate food contamination at least in all of the area outside the 1.5 Ci/km^2 isopleth, and probably more of the inside area. This dominance of food contamination is due to the longer period of direct deposition and the higher solubility of the global deposit (2,6). Therefore, areas contaminated by local fallout may not necessarily have to be restricted from producing food, although the higher levels of external gamma radiation would increase the radiation hazards to cultivators. The magnitude of the global fallout relative to the local fallout may seem incongruous; however it is a direct result of the intense targeting of population and military targets in the Northern Hemisphere.

Dietary Components

Food chain contamination from global fallout can be illustrated by scaling (upward) measured 1963–1973 levels in foodstuffs (2, 12, 13) by a factor of 23, with approximate corrections for post-1968 atmospheric test inputs. Examples of this scaling for milk, wheat, and beef are illustrated in Figure 3, an 11-year representation of possible foodstuff levels following the war. Concentrations of radiostrontium and radiocesium will be highest in the first year and

125

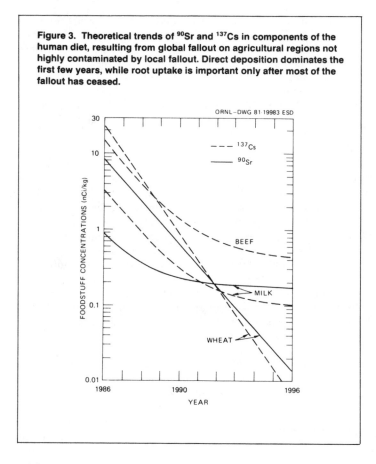

Figure 3. Theoretical trends of ^{90}Sr and ^{137}Cs in components of the human diet, resulting from global fallout on agricultural regions not highly contaminated by local fallout. Direct deposition dominates the first few years, while root uptake is important only after most of the fallout has ceased.

decline thereafter. The rapid decline during the first few years represents the corresponding depletion of the stratospheric inventory; the stabilizing levels in beef and milk after this period reflect the increasing influence of root uptake over direct foliage contamination as the cumulative deposit increases. Radiocesium will behave differently than radiostrontium with time because in most temperate zone soils, illitic clay minerals immobilize cesium, reducing plant availability (14). The result is that the cumulative deposit in soil becomes a significant dietary contributor of ^{90}Sr sooner than for ^{137}Cs as the annual global deposition rate from global fallout declines. This is illustrated in Figure 3 for milk and wheat. Until about 1991, ^{137}Cs will dominate ^{90}Sr (as a result of its higher abundance in fallout); after this period the lower soil availability of ^{137}Cs makes ^{90}Sr the more abundant nuclide in the foodstuffs. A discussion of the reasons for the differences in radionuclide behavior between tilled soils (wheat) and pastures (beef, milk) is available elsewhere (3, 13, 15). It is also evident from Figure 3 that cultural dietary habits will influence ^{90}Sr and ^{137}Cs intakes. However, worldwide studies generally show remarkably similiar annual intakes except in unusual cases (2).

Diet and Body Burdens

Figure 4 represents the observed behavior of ^{137}Cs and ^{90}Sr in adults and their diet (2, 12) scaled to the post-war period. The diet is typical of "western" cultures; that is, high in milk and milk products. The whole body calculations were based on an adult containing 1050 g of calcium (Ca) and 140 g of potassium (K) since most fallout measurements are given as ^{90}Sr/g(Ca) and ^{137}Cs/g(K) in biological tissues (2). It is apparent that ^{137}Cs in the body (mostly in muscle tissue) follows the diet quite closely. This is because the biological half-life of most of the cesium in humans is only a few months (2). Based on Figure 4 and Northern Hemisphere fallout data (2), the total

^{137}Cs body burden will be about 100 times that of the daily diet. In contrast to ^{137}Cs, radiostrontium has a much longer turnover time in adults (about 30 percent per year) because it deposits mostly in bone tissue (2). Younger children can accumulate about twice as much ^{90}Sr (on a unit calcium basis) as adults because of new bone growth. However, this ^{90}Sr is also eliminated faster because of a faster bone turnover rate (2). The trends illustrated in Figure 4 are for high milk and milk product diets; high meat diets would have more ^{137}Cs and lower ^{90}Sr.

There can be notable exceptions to these patterns arising when dietary habits or soil properties differ significantly from the typ-

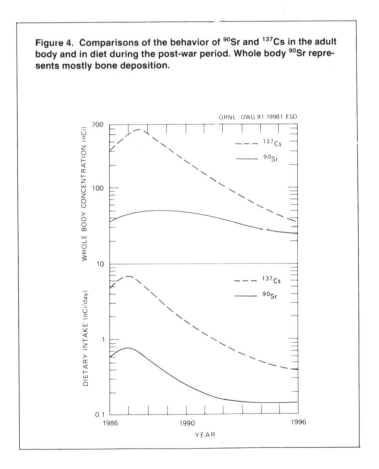

Figure 4. Comparisons of the behavior of ^{90}Sr and ^{137}Cs in the adult body and in diet during the post-war period. Whole body ^{90}Sr represents mostly bone deposition.

127

ical temperate zone case. The lichen-rein-deer-man food chain of arctic and subarctic regions will result in ^{137}Cs burdens about two orders of magnitude above the middle latitude estimates of Figure 4 (2, 16). In contrast to the changing ^{137}Cs to ^{90}Sr relationship in milk illustrated by Figure 3, certain soil properties (acidic, low illitic clay content) can allow much higher ^{137}Cs levels to occur in milk or meat, resulting in high ^{137}Cs body burdens. This pattern was identified both in the Faeroe Islands (13) and the Ukrainian Polessye region of the Soviet Union (17) and accounted for a 10 to 100 fold increase in ^{137}Cs body burdens over expected middle latitude levels. Elevated dietary levels of ^{137}Cs have also been noted in southern Florida, the tropics, and in regions of Norway because of poor soil fixation of cesium (2, 17).

The transuranium elements, tritium, ^{129}I, and ^{14}C will also enter the food chain. However compared to ^{137}Cs and ^{90}Sr, their dose contribution is small (2).

The preceding discussion of radioactivity in the diet was presented to illustrate the levels and modes of contamination occurring after the global nuclear war. The overall dose commitment to the survivors is discussed in a separate article (18). However, it can be estimated that diet will contribute about half the lifetime bone exposure resulting from global fallout, and that the lifetime dose commitment from dietary intake will be about 50 percent of the average lifetime background dose before the war, using the weapons'-testing fallout studies for calibration (2).

NON-RADIOLOGICAL CONSEQUENCES

Although most of this chapter has been concerned with radioactive contamination of the world's food supply, there are other effects which, in the short term, will impact the survivors far more severely. A June war will find grain stocks at low levels since the 1985 crop will have been planted

only about one month earlier. Transportation disruptions will cause major imbalances in the population-food supply relationship and will force urban migration to rural areas. The social and physical consequences of this massive food supply imbalance are hard to evaluate, although the minimal result will be a large population dispersal. This dispersal, when coupled with heavy population losses in urban centers, would compensate for the reduced productivity (output per farmer) which would occur because of fuel, fertilizer, and pesticide shortages. Much of the 1985 grain harvest may have to be done by hand rather than by machine.

Loss of visible light caused by the large amounts of fine particles injected into the atmosphere by surface detonations would seriously affect agricultural productivity (see Crutzen and Birks, chapter 6). If a nuclear war depletes the ozone layer, the increased ultraviolet radiation would also affect crop yields and genetic mutation rates (19).

Effects on the Third World

As a result of the war food-importing countries not severely impacted by the war will suffer an almost complete cut-off of food from the major exporting nations. North America, for example, which supplies the majority of food aid to the Third World (20), would be unable to harvest and ship the 1985 crop. The length of this food cut-off would depend on the recovery of fuel refinery, rail, and port facilities. Thus a grain surplus (possibly unharvested) would exist in the US during 1985, but not thereafter. The effects of this cut-off on the Third World will vary, but if it occurred at the same time as a major natural catastrophe (eg, drought or insect plague) then the consequences could be enormous. The dependence of many Third World countries on agricultural technology from the industrialized North will create problems when the industrial nations are devastated. For example, hybrid seed-stocks have become extremely important throughout the world for reasons related to disease resistance and higher yield per hectare. Any disruption in the capacity to produce these seeds will have enormous short-term repercussions for food production. Likewise, the control of insect plagues like the desert locust has become heavily dependent on chemicals produced in the industrial countries. The true magnitude of the effect of a cutoff in the support that advanced agricultural nations give to food-deficient nations is hard to evaluate but it could be catastrophic in some cases. Thus it is entirely possible that the disruption in trade may overwhelm the direct impact of radioactive contamination (see chapter 11, "Economic Effects: Back to the Dark Ages").

CONCLUSION

In the period immediately following the nuclear war, the inventory of growing food may be greater than the ability of the post-attack harvest and distribution systems to deliver it. Surviving populations may have to relocate closer to sources of production. Meat, milk, and green vegetables would be a prime source of food for several years, as the agricultural economy reverts to a less specialized scale. For both industrial and aid-dependent Third World countries, the food struggle will involve shortages and readjustments in cultural practices. Faced with shortages, radioactivity levels in the diet will not be a factor governing food allocations, especially since the global fall-out insures that most of the production is uniformly contaminated. In fact, the increased radiation doses received by survivors may be the least detrimental aspect of the post-war existence, although considerable space was devoted to the levels of radioactivity in diet because of their predictability. It is certain, however, that millions may eventually suffer premature

deaths caused by malnutrition, diseases, and chronic radiation exposure, and that many of these people will be in countries not involved in the ideological struggle which precipitated the war.

References and Notes

1. Reference Scenario. Chapter 3.
2. *Ionizing Radiation: Levels and Effects*, (United Nations, New York, 1977).
3. R Scott Russell, *Radioactivity and Human Diet*, (Pergamon Press, 1966), (Chapter 5).
4. Y C Ng, H A Tewes, in *Proceedings of a Symposium on the Survival of Food Crops and Livestock in the Event of Nuclear War*, (CONF-700909, National Technical Information Service, Springfield, Virginia, USA, December 1971, pp 131-172.
5. S Glasstone, *The Effects of Nuclear Weapons* (US Atomic Energy Agency, 1962).
6. R Scott Russell, B O Bartlett, R S Bruce, in *Proceedings of a Symposium on the Survival of Food Crops and Livestock in the Event of Nuclear War*, (CONF-700909, National Technical Information Service, Springfield, Virginia, USA, December, 1971), pp 548–565.
7. A H Sparrow, S S Schwemmer, P J Bottino, in *Proceedings of a Symposium on the Survival of Food Crops and Livestock in the Event of Nuclear War*, (CONF-700909, National Technical Information Service, Springfield, Virginia, USA, December, 1971, pp 670–711.
8. W A Rhoads, H L Ragsdale, R B Platt, E M Romney, In *Symposium on the Survival of Food Crops and Livestock in the Event of Nuclear War*, (CONF-700909, National Technical Information Service, Arlington, Virginia, USA, December 1971), pp 352–369.
9. M C Bell, in *Proceedings of a Symposium on the Survival of Food Crops and Livestock in the Event of Nuclear War*, (CONF-700909, National Technical Information Service, Springfield, Virginia. USA, December, 1971), pp 656–669.
10. International Commission on Radiological Protection. *Recommendations of the ICRP, ICRP Publication 9*. (Pergamon Press, Oxford, 1969).
11. US Nuclear Regulatory Commission, *Seismic and Geologic Siting Criteria for Nuclear Power Plants*, 10 CFR Part 100 (1973).
12. A Aarkrog, *Health Physics* **20**, No. 3, 297 (March, 1971).
13. A H Booth, E R Samuels, in *Proceedings of a Seminar on Environmental Contamination by Radioactive Materials* (International Atomic Energy Agency, Vienna, Austria, 1969), pp 393–401.
14. L Fredriksson, R J Garner, R Scott Russell, in *Radioactivity and Human Diet*, R Scott Russell, Ed (Pergamon Press, 1966) Chapter 15.
15. J D Barton, R J Garner, and R Scott Russell, in *Radioactivity and Human Diet*, R Scott Russell, Ed (Pergamon Press, 1966) Chapter 20.

16. M N Troitskaya, P V Ramzaev, A A Moiseev, A I Nizhnikov, D I Bel'tser, M S Ibatullin, B Ya Litver, I M Dmitriev, in *Radioecology*, V M Klechkovskii, G G Polikarpov, R M Aleksakhin, Eds (John Wiley and Sons, New York, 1971) Chapter 13.
17. A N Marci, R M Barkhudarov, N J Novikora, E V Petukhova, L D Dubova, V M Briganina, *Health Physics* **22**, 9 (January, 1972).
18. J E Coggle, P J Lindop — see chapter 5.
19. L R Brown, *Science* **214** 995 (November 27, 1981).
20. This chapter was supported by The Office of Health and Environmental Research, US Department of Energy, under contract W-7405-eng-26 with Union Carbide Corporation. Publication No. 1965, Environmental Sciences Division, Oak Ridge National Laboratory.

TEN

THE BIOTIC EFFECTS OF
IONIZING RADIATION

G. M. WOODWELL

Exposure to high levels of ionizing radiation will devastate the natural plant and animal communities of the earth, especially forests, leaving an impoverished residual vegetation of hardy successional species. The circumstances likely to prevail following a nuclear war favor small-bodied, rapidly reproducing organisms that are often identified as pests.

The effects of the widespread destruction of biotic resources that would occur in a nuclear war are well beyond experience and almost beyond imagination. My purpose is to draw on experience as carefully as possible to appraise the most important biotic transitions. I do this recognizing that the range of possibilities inherent in a nuclear war includes the release of sufficient ionizing radiation to kill all humans in the Northern Hemisphere, an event which would render this type of analysis quite beside the point.

I shall emphasize the biotic effects of gamma exposures (similar to X-rays) from fallout in the period from a few hours to a few weeks after an exchange of nuclear weapons. In such an exchange there would also be exposures from alpha and beta particles, not discussed here. I shall also omit detailed discussion of the acute exposures from gamma radiation and from neutrons from the fireball itself, as well as discussion of the much longer term exposures from long-lived radionuclides incorporated into living systems.

Any exchange of nuclear weapons in war will produce not only areas of destruction due to blast, heat and ionizing radiation from the fireballs themselves, but also extensive areas downwind from each of the points of detonation where radioactive dust produced in the fireballs will accumulate. Many factors affect the location, area, and intensity of these fallout fields. Experience with bombtests shows that the fallout field may extend a hundred miles or more and provide cumulative exposures over hundreds of square miles in excess of several thousand roentgens (1). Such exposures are many times greater than the mean lethal exposures for man, all other mammals, and most higher plants. One of the best known tests of nuclear weapons, BRAVO, was held at Bikini Atoll on March 1, 1954. The fallout from this test was carried east instead of west by upper altitude winds to Rongelap Atoll about 100 miles away. Parts of the atoll received

more than 1000 roentgens (R) over the course of the next few days. The approximate pattern of the field is shown in Figure 1, constructed from fragmentary data. In such fields exposure rates from gamma radiation as high as 10 000 R per hour one hour after the detonation can be expected. What are the biotic effects of such massive exposures to ionizing radiation?

Interest focuses, quite naturally, on man. The mean lethal exposure for man is usually considered to be 450–500 R, if the total exposure is delivered in less than a day. At lower rates of exposure (the same total dose delivered over a longer period of time) the mean lethal exposure is increased. But a fallout field that is hundreds of miles or more long, 25 or more miles wide, and which contains areas where acute exposures can be expected to be in the range of tens of thousands of R will have effects on many organisms in addition to man. What will these effects be? What are the ecological implications, apart from direct effects on man, of the exposures from the fallout fields associated with a nuclear war or other extensive radioactive contamination?

These questions arose during the late 1950's and early 1960's and became the topic of a program of research in the US which embodied extensive studies of the effects of ionizing radiation on plants, animals, and on whole ecosystems. Dr John N Wolfe, at that time an ecologist on the staff of the US Atomic Energy Commission, recognized the need to develop groups of ecologists acquainted with nuclear energy, especially the biotic effects of ionizing radiation. With the support of others in the AEC he succeeded in establishing a series of programs of basic research in ecology at the US National Laboratories and at several universities.

At Brookhaven National Laboratory a group of ecologists was asked to design an experiment to investigate the potential effects on natural communities of exposure to high levels of ionizing radiation. The

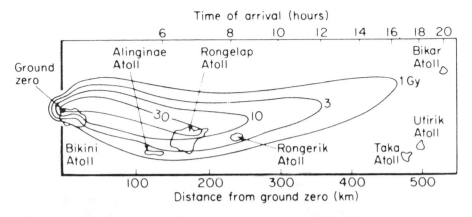

Figure 1. Fallout pattern from nuclear weapon tests on Bikini Atoll, March 1954.

question was made the more urgent by the discovery by A H Sparrow and his colleagues at Brookhaven that certain plants, especially the native pine of Long Island, *Pinus rigida*, have mean lethal exposures in the same range as that of man, 450–500 R, when the duration of exposure is a few hours or less. After much discussion it was decided to examine the effects of a long-term exposure on a natural forest stand. A natural community was chosen to take advantage of the richness of successional and evolutionary relationships found in such a community, as opposed to a plantation or an agricultural field.

A large (9500 curie ^{137}Cs) source of gamma radiation was placed in the center of a stand of oak-pine forest. The source of radiation was arranged in such a way that it could be lowered from the top of a 15 foot tower into a lead cask heavy enough to contain all of the radiation. The source provided exposures to gamma radiation that varied from more than 1000 R/day within 10 meters to 1 R/day at about 125 m. Such a field of radiation was expected to produce striking changes in the forest in a few weeks. While the pattern of exposures was chronic as opposed to the acute exposure expected from fallout, the results of this experiment after six months provide a reasonable estimate of the pattern of effects and the doses that caused them.

The design of the experiment offered two types of comparisons with unaffected forests (controls): first, the forest was studied in detail prior to irradiation and these data were available for comparison in subsequent years; second, the gradient of intensity of exposure assured that segments of the forest that were either not exposed or had no visible effects could be used for comparison in subsequent years. The experiment was maintained for 15 years.

The source was operated for the first time on November 22, 1961 and was exposed daily thereafter for 20 hours. It was shielded for four hours daily to allow work in the forest. By the spring of 1962 the pattern of damage had been established. Subsequent irradiation only enlarged this pattern, which became accentuated as hardy species invaded or expanded their populations while susceptible species declined and disappeared.

PATTERN OF EFFECTS

By the spring of 1962, six months after the start of the irradiation, a circle of radiation damage was conspicuous around the source. The effects ranged from a zone of virtual sterilization at total exposures in excess of 63,000 R over 6 months through a series of zones of progressive biotic complexity with greater distance and lower exposure. In the first year the forest showed

133

no obvious effect at an exposure level of 1 R/day (180 R total), although in subsequent years effects could be detected at a few tenths of a roentgen per day.

There were six well-defined zones. The inner zone, exposed chronically to from hundreds to thousands of R/day, supported no higher plants (six months exposure = 63 000 R). Within this zone, but at its outer perimeter, was the second, where certain populations of lichens survived; ultimately, after several years, this zone expanded outward and was marked by dense populations of *Cladonia cristatella*. Crustose forms were more resistant than foliose or fruticose forms. The third zone was marked by a vigorous population of a sedge, *Carex pensylvanica*, indigenous in small tufts in the intact forest. Here the sedge expanded in abundance to cover virtually the entire ground surface in areas that received more than 27 000 R but less than 63 000 R in six months. Outside the sedge zone the indigenous shrubs of the forest survived, with the shorter-statured shrubs commonly the more resistant: *Vaccinium angustifolium*, *Vaccinium heterophyllum*, and *Q. ilicifolia* (11 000 R in six months). At greater distance and lower exposure (3600 R in 6 months) the oaks, both white and scarlet (*Q alba* and *Q coccinea*) joined the more resistant species to provide a vegetative cover that resembled the original forest without pine. An experienced botanist might well have considered this segment of the forest well within the "normal" variability of the oak-pine forest of eastern North America and might have attached no significance to the absence of *Pinus rigida*. In this instance, however, standing pines were dead. Twenty meters farther down the radiation gradient (180 R in six months) the oak-pine forest was intact.

The zonation became more conspicuous in ensuing years as effects accumulated and the circle of damage expanded. In appearance it was as though the forest had been dissected layer by layer, the trees removed, then the shrubs, then all the higher plants, to leave a residual but vigorous community of hardy lichens. But the effect was more complicated: the trees differed in sensitivity, the pines being more sensitive than the oaks, and within the lichen community certain populations of low-growing, crustose lichens were the most resistant of all. The patterns were complicated still further by more or less continuous invasions of the disturbed zone by plants normally found on disturbed sites. At least two species of blackberries (*Rubus spp*), the sweetfern, (*Myrica asplenifolia*), the pokeweed (*Phytolacca*) and a hybrid poplar joined the sedge zone over the first five years. So did several other herbs such as the fireweed (*Erechtites*). All proved capable of surviving chronic irradiation at rates that killed most of the woody plants of the forest.

In addition to this study of a late successional forest various other studies of biotic effects of ionizing radiation were carried out over more than a decade. These included carefully designed experiments in an old field at Brookhaven, a native grassland near Fort Collins, Colorado, and various experiments using cultivated plants exposed to irradiation from sources established in cultivated land.

PECULIARITIES OF FALLOUT FIELDS

The radiation fields in these studies were substantially different from that of fallout from a bomb. The difference is important because the biotic response depends on the rate of exposure as well as on the total dose. A fallout field produces a very high rate of exposure initially, but the rate drops off rapidly with time depending on the mixture of radionuclides in the fallout. According to one estimate (2) the rate of decay of the mixture common in fallout fields is such that at 100 hours after the detonation the intensity of ionizing radiation drops to 1.0–0.1 percent of the intensity at one hour after detonation. This relationship means that the exposures are "acute" as opposed to "chronic"; that is, they are administered in a short time and can therefore be expected to have greater biotic effects per unit of exposure than the same total exposure administered over a longer time.

The system used to irradiate the forest at Brookhaven was designed to administer a chronic exposure to a natural community. It was not designed to mimic the complex exposure to be expected from fallout from a bomb. The chronic exposures at which effects become conspicuous in the forest are difficult to transform into the exposures from fallout required to produce similar effects. Nonetheless, the patterns of changes in the vegetation observed in the forest under chronic irradiation are the patterns that can be expected in the short term from any gradient of ionizing radiation from any source, including fallout, if the intensity is high enough.

The damage observed in the irradiated forest after six months was probably caused by exposures early in the period, because the symptoms require time to develop. In an earlier analysis (3) I estimated that the difference between the six month cumulative exposure and the fallout exposure required to produce the same effect was a factor of two. Additional experience suggests that it may be 2–3. That is, acute exposure from a fallout field would produce the same effects with an exposure one third to one half of that accumulated over six months in the irradiated forest. In the ensuing discussion I have used a factor of two to estimate the fallout exposure from the cumulative exposure over 6 months.

DATA FROM EXPERIMENTAL STUDIES OF PLANTS

A second source of information on the effects of ionizing radiation is the extensive body of data accumulated by A H Sparrow and his co-workers on the sensitivity of plants to gamma radiation. Sparrow and his colleagues, working over more than two decades, showed that sensitivity to

ionizing radiation is correlated with the volume of the cell nucleus and with the number of chromosomes. The larger the nucleus and the smaller the number of chromosomes, the more sensitive the plant. Various other factors also affect responses, of course, such as the time in the life cycle at which irradiation occurs as well as the length of time over which the irradiation is applied.

The relationship was used by Woodwell and Sparrow (3) to estimate the range of sensitivity of the dominant plants of major North American ecosystems (Table 1). The tabulation emphasizes the sharp difference in sensitivity between Gymnosperms and Angiosperms, between the coniferous forests and deciduous forests. Most conifers have mean lethal exposures in the range of a few hundred to 1000 R. The Angiosperms have smaller nuclei, smaller chromosomes, and greater resistance to ionizing radiation. Mean lethal exposures for the Angiosperms that dominate deciduous forests range generally between 3500 and 10 000 R, administered acutely (Table 1).

EFFECTS ON FORESTS

The experience with the Brookhaven Irradiated Forest suggests that in that forest the trees are most sensitive and the entire canopy would be eliminated by an exposure from fallout of 5000–6000 R. The tall shrub stratum would succumb to exposures of 13 000–14 000 R and the ground cover would survive up to as much as 30 000 R. The plant communities that normally occur on disturbed sites are more resistant, with certain plant populations, such as crabgrass (*Digitaria spp*) surviving six-month exposures in excess of 100 000–200 000 R, and therefore probably capable of surviving fallout exposures well in excess of 50 000 R.

These estimates are inherently crude, and errors of a factor of two are probably common. However such errors diminish in importance when we recognize the ex-

135

Table 1: Estimated acute exposures required to affect dominants of major North American vegetations. Estimates are based on correlations between radiosensitivity and interphase chromosome volume. Variability introduced into the estimates by the measurements of nuclear volumes alone is about ±30 % of the means listed. Other uncontrolled intrinsic and environmental factors increase the potential errors greatly. Source: reference 3.

Species	Somatic chromosome number	Interphase chromosome volume (μ^9) = S E	Sensitivity range (slight inhibition of growth to mortality, r)
FORESTS			
Boreal			
Picea glauca	24	39.7 ± 1.6	220– 590
Abies balsamea	24	33.4 ± 2.2	270– 700
Subalpine (Rocky Mountains)			
Picea engelmannii	24	26.8 ± 1.6	330– 880
Abies lasciocarpa	24*	33.5 ± 1.7	270– 700
Montane (Rocky Mountains)			
Pseudotsuga menziesii	26	28.5 ± 1.1	310– 820
Pinus ponderosa	24	36.7 ± 2.8	240– 640
Montane (Sierra-Cascades)			
Abies cuncolor	24	23.3 ± 0 9	380– 1 010
Pinus lambertiana	24	57.8 ± 3.1	150– 410
P. jeffreyi	24	48.1 ± 1.9	190– 490
P. ponderosa	24	36.7 ± 2.8	240– 640
Pseudotsuga menziesii	26	28.5 ± 1.1	310– 820
Pacific Conifer			
Tsuga heterophylla	24*	23.7 ± 0.9	377– 990
Thuja plicata	22	8.6 ± 0.4	1 040– 2 730
Abies grandis	24	33.2 ± 1.1	270– 710
Eastern Deciduous			
Mixed Mesophytic			
Fagus grandifolia	24	2.3 ± 0.1	3 810–10 000
Magnolia acuminata	76	4.8 ± 0.2	1 850– 4 840
Tilia americana	82	2.5 ± 0.1	3 520– 9 230
Liriodendron tulipifera	38	6.4 ± 0.5	1 400– 3 680
Acer saccharum	26	3 2 ± 0.2	2 800– 7 360
Quercus alba	24	6.6 ± 0.3	1 350– 3 550
Tsuga canadensis	24	21.3 ± 0.8	420– 1 100
Beech-Maple & Maple-Basswood			
Fagus grandifolia	24	2.3 ± 0.1	3 810–10 000
Acer saccharum	26	3.2 ± 0.2	2 800– 7 360
Tilia americana	82	2.5 ± 0.1	3 520– 9 230
Hemlock-Hardwoods			
Tsuga canadensis	24	21.3 ± 0.8	420– 1 100
Betula lutea	84	2.2 ± 0.1	3 860–10 120
Pinus strobus	24	46.5 ± 2.8	190– 500
P. resinosa	24	43.2 ± 3.5	210– 540
Acer saccharum	26	3.2 ± 0.2	2 800– 7 360
Oak-Chestnut			
Castanea deniata	24	4.7 ± 0.3	1 900– 5 000
Quercus coccinea	24	3.6 ± 0.3	2 490– 6 530
Q. prinus	24	6.1 ± 0.3	1 470– 3 870
Pinus rigida	24	48.3 ± 2.8	190– 490
Oak-Hickory			
Quercus alba	24	6.6 ± 0.3	1 350– 3 550
Q. rubra	24	5.5 ± 0.3	1 620– 4 250
Q. velutina	24	3.2 ± 0.2	2 830– 7 430
Q. stellata	24	4.4 ± 0.2	2 040– 5 350
Q. marilandica	24	3.3 ± 0.2	2 690– 7 060
Carya ovata	32	2.5 ± 0.2	3 560– 9 340
C. cordiformis	32	1.8 ± 0.1	5 090–13 370
C. tomentosa	64	1.8 ± 0.5	5 080–13 350
C. laciniosa	32	2.6 ± 0.1	3 470– 9 110
Pinus tarda	24	52.6 ± 4.1	170– 450
GRASSLANDS			
Andropogon scoparius	40	6.4 ± 0.4	2 330– 9 200
AGRICULTURE			
Zea mays HV Golden Bantam	20	14.0 ± 0.6	1 060– 4 200
Tetraploid	40	10.8 ± 0.6	1 370– 5 410
Triticum aestivum	42	14.6 ± 1.1	1 020– 4 020

* Probable chromosome number.

traordinary range of the sensitivity of different groups of organisms, a range that extends through three, possibly four, orders of magnitude within the plant kingdom. Second, the ecological effects of exposure follow a predictable pattern. The sensitivity of populations of plants in a natural community is correlated with stature: the tree canopy is in all instances the most vulnerable part of the forest; the tall shrubs, next; the low shrubs next; and among the higher plants, the ground cover last. But more resistant yet are certain populations of mosses, lichens and organisms of decay. Among the higher plants the most resistant appear to be the plants of impoverished and disturbed sites, the species of roadsides, abandoned land, the weeds of lawn and garden (Table 2).

Table 2. Exposures from fallout radiation required to cause mortality of dominants of various strata in plant communities of major ecosystems. Ranges are based on six-month exposure of the oak-pine forest of central Long Island and a parallel exposure of the plant communities of old fields. (Adapted from reference 3).

Coniferous Forests	Range of Exposure (roentgens)
Tree Canopy	500– 1 800
Shrub Canopy	1 800–13 000
Ground Cover	5 000–30 000
Deciduous Forests	
Tree Canopy	1 000– 5 000
Shrub Canopy	1 800–13 000
Ground Cover	5 000–30 000
Communities of Disturbed Sites	
Sensitive Successional Species	
Trifolium spp.	5 000–10 000
Resistant Successional Species	
Digitaria spp.	50 000–75 000
Senecio spp	75 000–>1 000 000

The information used in this study is valid for interpreting effects of ionizing radiation on temperate zone ecosystems of low diversity; it does not apply to tropical forests.

The radiation exposures required to transform a forested zone into an impoverished landscape are well within the range of contemporary war, a few hundred to many thousands of roentgens. The areas affected might be large, tens to hundreds of square miles per bomb. Enough bombs are available that minor military and civilian centers, universities, colleges, small industrial or scientific centers, even individual laboratories, can all be individually favored with nuclear attention, providing overlapping zones affected by blast, heat and ionizing radiation from the fireballs. The fallout fields will also overlap, and cover hundreds of thousands of square miles.

The biotic effects of such transitions are beyond human experience. The uncertainties of weather would cause anomalies in the distribution of fallout, sparing some areas, depositing heavier doses elsewhere. The result would probably be a mottled necrosis of the landscape, with whole valleys escaping virtually untouched by fallout, others scorched by radiation and subsequently by fires feeding on the devastation.

The process started by irradiation from fallout would proceed variously in different places. Certain areas of the tropics serve as a model for impoverishment: once the tree canopy has been destroyed, the soils made vulnerable to erosion, and the stock of nutrients lost, the potential for recovery to forest is lost indefinitely. In other areas recovery is rapid, soils are not lost, fires do not compound the damage and the site becomes revegetated with forest in a decade or so. Between these extremes lie a full range of intermediate possibilities, all of which involve varying degrees of biotic impoverishment. (However, an increased frequency of the small-bodied, rapidly-reproducing organisms that we so often find in competition with man and label "pests" can be expected. A corollary of the disturbance is the stimulation of indigenous pests that thrive on weakened plants. For instance *Ips*, a bark-beetle, destroyed weakened pines in the Brookhaven Irradiated Forest, and extraordinarily high populations of aphids and other insects occurred on radiation-

137

weakened trees). The impoverishment includes the loss of both forest products for man and the loss of the array of services the biota normally performs in maintaining an environment suitable for man.

I have emphasized effects on forests because forests dominate the natural vegetation in most of the habitable sections of the globe. Forests, moreover, have an extraordinarily large influence on the rest of the biosphere. They have the capacity for fixing and releasing enough carbon to change the CO_2 content of the atmosphere by several parts per million in a few weeks. The massive destruction of forests following an exchange of nuclear weapons can be expected to contribute a further surge in the rate of release of CO_2 from the biota and soils into the atmosphere, compounding the growing problem of a CO_2-caused climatic warming. Such analyses, however, are sufficiently complex and uncertain to be speculative, and require a much more elaborate analysis than can be offered here.

The important primary effect of the fall-out field, apart from the direct hazards to man, would be the destruction of forests over very large areas. This destruction would become apparent in the weeks following the attack. It would also affect the amount and quality of runoff water as deforestation always does, and would result in flooding, erosion of uplands, siltation of streams and lakes, and serious losses in the quality of water. Water supplies of cities would be contaminated, not only with radioactive debris but with the host of contaminants that accompany any serious destabilization of the landscape. These problems would be aggravated by fires which would start at the time of the attack and continue through the following weeks as trees died and the forests dried out, becoming unusually flammable. No aspect of life would remain untouched in this dust-filled, radioactive world.

Agricultural crops are also vulnerable not only to heat and blast but to ionizing radiation. The extent of their vulnerability

138

varies with a complex set of factors, including the stage of development of the crop at the time of exposure (earlier stages are commonly more vulnerable) the species, and the organ used for food. (Seed production has a different pattern of sensitivity than root or tuber production, for example). It is almost impossible to predict the full range of effects, except to note that none would improve yields or render the crop safer or more nutritious. Residual radioactivity, especially from cesium and strontium, would present a further hazard to survivors through ingestion and incorporation of the radionuclides into the body.

THE IMPORTANCE OF MUTATIONS AND INTERNAL EMITTERS FOR MAN

The most important biotic effect of ionizing radiation is the production of mutations, a general term that refers to changes in the complement of genes in an organism. Mutations are necessary for evolution, and we might ask whether the sudden surge in the rate of mutation following a nuclear holocaust might have the benefit of causing a surge in the rate of evolution, with some potential for the development of beneficial new forms of life.

Unfortunately even this hope is unrealistic. Evolution does indeed depend on mutations, but it depends on many other factors as well, including relentless selective pressures over many generations. An increase in the mutation rate alone is unlikely to have any effect on the rate of evolution. It is more likely simply to increase the rate of mortality, especially at the time of reproduction, because most mutations are deleterious and result in serious genetically-caused deficiencies. Man is especially vulnerable to an increased rate of mutation because he is long-lived, reproduces slowly, and tends to protect individuals. These factors may result in the accumulation of mutations in the human population to the point where there is a serious loss of quality in the gene pool, and thus a decrease in the health of successive generations.

Man is unique in this respect. All other species remain subject to rigorous selection, and mutations are lost within one or two generations. This fact alone means that ionizing radiation presents a special hazard to man; thus the protection of man from enhanced exposures in the general environment assures the protection of all other organisms.

The other long-term effect of ionizing radiation on man is the increased production of cancers. The increase in the incidence of cancers due to radiation is usually thought to be one case per 1000–10 000 man-rems (4). Those who survived the immediate hazards of the initial blast, heat, and radiation from the fireballs, and the longer-term hazards of overlapping radiation fields and the ubiquitous radioactive dust, would discover the virtual impossibility of avoiding the long-lived radionuclides which would contaminate almost all water and food not previously stored. The cumulative exposure from these internal emitters would result in additional deaths among those struggling to live on a landscape impoverished beyond detailed description.

CONCLUSION

The broad pattern of ecological effects is clear enough, although the list of effects, interactions, and secondary hazards to man is virtually infinite. In a world where such bombs could be used, the additional details of further complications for survivors mean little. There would be survivors, as there would be surviving plants, other animals, and, here and there, an un-

touched forest and an uncontaminated agricultural plot. But a realistic look at the earth after a nuclear attack leaves one guessing that a quick, merciful roasting in a personal fireball might be the better way.

References and Notes

1. Dose is the energy absorbed in tissue; it is often measured as rads, or "radiation *absorbed* dose". Exposure is an indication of the intensity of the field; it is usually measured as roentgens (R), defined as the number of ionizations produced in air. The relationship between the rad used in other articles and the roentgen is not simple; it depends on the physical properties of both the radiation and the medium through which it passes. For the gamma rays likely to occur in nuclear warfare and for doses measured in air, 1 R = 0.87 rad. For water and soft tissue 1 R = 0.96 rad. However, although they have nearly the same numerical value, it should be remembered that the rad and the roentgen are units of different quantities.
2. C F Miller, *Physical damage from nuclear explosions, in:* Ecological Effects of Nuclear War, G M Woodwell, Editor. Brookhaven National Laboratory, U.S.A.E.C. pp 1–10 (1963).
3. G M Woodwell and A H Sparrow, *Effects of ionizing radiation on ecological systems, in* G M Woodwell, *op cit* pp 20–38.
4. Even for the same physical dose, the biological effect may be different for different types of radiation. For our purpose radiations can be roughly divided into two groups, low and high linear energy transfer (LET). LET refers to the ionizing powers of the radiation. Of the radiations encountered in nuclear warfare, beta-rays, gamma-rays, and X-rays are classified as low-LET, while neutrons and alpha-particles are high-LET radiations. For the same dose, the high-LET radiation generally produces more biological damage than low-LET radiation. The dose of low-LET radiation which is estimated to be equivalent in biological effect to a given dose of high-LET radiation is called the "dose equivalent" of the latter and is measured in rems. One rem of high-LET radiation, or any mixture of radiations, is thus assumed to be equivalent in its effect to one rad of low-LET radiation. The collective dose is the product of the dose and the number of people exposed to it; thus, it is a measure of the total burden on the population due to the exposure to radiation. The collective dose is measured in man-rads and the collective dose equivalent in man-rems.

THE PROCESS OF RECOVERY

It might seem that biotic recovery following nuclear devastation could be expected to follow more or less the normal patterns of ecological succession for the region in question—that is, to run its course over a period of decades or even centuries. However, this is not entirely the case. For one thing, vegetational recovery would be hindered to the extent that seed sources would no longer be available in a region, this being a function of the severity and geographical extent of the attack.

Another serious concern would be the question of ecosystem stability. The numerous plants and animals occurring in any region would differ widely in their relative radio-sensitivities as well as in their susceptibility to the other factors of a nuclear attack. As a result, many subtle and some not-so-subtle imbalances could be created in the predator/prey, host/parasite, and endless other biotic interactions, that form the very basis of an ecosystem. In particular, troubles might arise as a result of the relative radio-resistances exhibited by insects, bacteria, and fungi. Moreover, the tendency for some radionuclides to become more concentrated as they are transferred up a food-chain would provide a disproportionate stress on the carnivores at the top.

"Nutrient dumping" would result in an impoverished pioneer stage of succession and hence in a far longer-than-usual tenure of the early successional stages or communities. Moreover, the biomass of these early stages would be even lower than expected, inasmuch as trees are in general more radio-sensitive than shrubs, high shrubs more than low shrubs, woody plants more than herbaceous plants, and Angiosperms more than mosses and lichens. A reduced biomass would result in reduced ecosystem productivity—reduced, for example, by as much as 80 percent in a change from forest to grassland.

In short, ecological succession would proceed following nuclear devastation, but far more slowly and less predictably than otherwise.

Arthur H Westing

Excerpted from *Environmental Conservation*, Vol 8, No. 4, 1981.

ELEVEN

ECONOMIC CONSEQUENCES: BACK TO THE DARK AGES

YVES LAULAN

After the bombs fall there will be no such thing as a world "economy". The millions of dead and wounded in the North would multiply to 1 billion or more in the Third World from starvation and disease brought about by the total collapse of the international system of trade and exchange. The author argues that we would be returning to an economic "dark ages" with emphasis on basic necessities: food, clothing, shelter and medical care.

Conventional warfare is generally limited to the destruction of human resources and wealth. Societal and economic infrastructures remain more or less intact. One of the ironies of history is that war—as we have known it—is often followed by an economic renaissance and renewed prosperity. Germany and Japan make good examples of this: 30 years after the Second World War the "losers" look like the real "winners". This apparent paradox can be explained by the simple fact that in certain circumstances, conventional wars can lead to a better use of resources, full employment, a change in demographics, and the renewal and improvement of plants and equipment.

That disturbing fact can be explained by separating the effect of war on people from its effect on material well-being. So long as the basis of economic activity is not completely destroyed, under certain circumstances a conventional war can be a stimulant to a nation's economy, as World War II was to the economy of the US. Under other circumstances protracted wars involving catastrophic loss of life—like the Thirty Years War in Europe and the current war in Cambodia—can bleed a nation dry, leaving a weakened and exhausted economy.

A nuclear war, however, falls into neither category. The nuclear war outlined in our Reference Scenario, given the extensive amount of damage to the Northern Hemisphere, would probably trigger a drastic decline in — if not the near total disappearance of — any form of economic activity except the barter system. We would be returning to the dark ages.

This stark conclusion is based on the following assumptions. A nuclear conflict will pit the largest industrialized countries of Western Europe, Japan and North America against the Soviet Union and Eastern Europe. The combatants would include not only the possessors of the enormous nuclear arsenals, they also represent most of the real economic power in the

world. The consequences for the combatants—and thus for the largest economies in the world—can be gauged according to a rather simple formula based on the total number of people killed.

If the loss of human life is limited to less than 10 percent of the total population of any given country the economic consequences can be compared to those of a severe conventional war: after a relatively short period of time, both the economy and even the population recover. A good example is Berlin after World War Two.

However, if 50 percent or more of the populations of the belligerent countries are destroyed, the result could be the end of these particular societies or civilizations as we know them. Since 50 percent is the *minimum* average of deaths for the population centers hit in this scenario, it is safe to predict that this would result in the total disintegration of organized social and economic activities in the Northern Hemisphere. Anthropological and historic evidence have documented time and again that there is a point of no return, beyond which human or animal social groups simply cannot recover, and beyond which their societies cannot long survive.

For purposes of discussion, let us take a medium position, postulating a population loss in the range of 10 to 50 percent— somewhat less than this scenario projects. Even with such an "optimistic" outlook, our society would still go through tremendous convulsions, giving rise to fundamental changes in our patterns of cultural and economic behavior.

First of all it is necessary to recall that humankind's basic needs consist of food, water, clothing and shelter. At a more advanced level, society requires a system of exchanging goods and services, a communications network, medical care, and the possibility of travel. At an even more advanced state, people need higher education, cultural activities, and leisure time. The aim of economic activity is to meet these needs on various levels, by producing goods and services. The excess not needed for immediate consumption can be saved, and those savings can be used to finance further investments intended to maintain or expand the means of production—plants and equipment. Keeping in mind the various elements of the reference scenario, it is possible to sketch out the economic consequences of a global nuclear war. First, investments would completely disappear because all remaining production would be used to meet only the most basic and urgent needs: food, water, shelter, clothing and medical care. Second, money would also disappear. Traditionally money is used as a means of exchange—a sort of yardstick of value—and as a store for the future. In a post nuclear war society (or what is left of it), all modern means of economic exchange would more or less disappear and we would see a rapid demonetarization of the economy characterized by a return to the most elementary form of exchange used by primitive societies—the barter system. And here we are touching a very raw nerve. The international division of labor, along with the commercial and financial means of exchange, has made possible an extraordinary increase of resources and wealth, especially for the industrialized countries, over the past four decades. Commercial and monetary exchange is therefore instrumental for economic growth. Consequently it is most likely that a nuclear world war of the kind envisioned in this issue would result in the total disappearance of organized large and medium scale economic activity at both the national and international levels. This would have dire consequences far beyond the "mere" destruction of physical wealth and human lives, and it is necessary to discuss the impact of a nuclear war both on the means of production and exchange and on economic agents not only in the belligerent countries but in the non-belligerents as well, especially in the Third World.

ECONOMIC CONSEQUENCES FOR THOSE COUNTRIES DIRECTLY INVOLVED

The dead and the wounded

We must realize that aside from immediate and delayed deaths, the casualties in a nuclear attack will also include vast numbers of wounded and incapacitated people. Medical services will be wholly inadequate to deal with the flood of injured, but the attempt must be made, and the attempt will involve massive outlays of scarce resources.

Assuming that about 50 percent of the population is killed outright and another 25 percent are injured or otherwise incapacitated, the remaining 25 percent would be left with the task of attempting some form of recovery. The most immediate result would be a drastic decline in the number of producers and a corresponding rise in the number of consumers—the sick, injured and incapacitated. There would be a fundamental change in the volume and structure of labor as well as of consumption.

In the period immediately following the war, consumption would emphasize medical supplies and services. Under the force of circumstances these services would become highly specialized—skin grafts for burns, plasma, antibiotics and so on. There would be a change in both quantity and quality of consumption. And certain types of consumption will vanish; most notably leisure activities, travel, education, the performing arts *etc.* Collective needs will overshadow all else, focusing on the procurement of food, water, medicine, basic transportation, and civil protection.

Economic Consequences

In less industrialized societies a nuclear war would have a devastating impact, but would be limited in scope, mainly affecting the area directly involved. However, the more industrialized the society, the more destructive will be the results of nuclear warfare. The vulnerability of a society to a nuclear war is much greater if there is a concentration of people in big cities and a dependence on sophisticated economies based on specialized skills in automation, computers, communications, microelectronics *etc*. Because of the near total destruction of these systems, war in these societies would have a considerable "multiplying" effect.

Indeed, whereas a conventional war can destroy resources but leave relatively intact the communication networks and the basic economic infrastructure, a nuclear war's destruction is immediate, complete and indiscriminate. Its concentration on population and strategic centers would utterly destroy organized economic activity.

The ensuing paralysis would be all the more widespread because destruction would be instantaneous, and would thus impede the rapid substitution of new systems of production and exchange. Under such conditions, it is probably impossible for highly technological societies, like those of Europe and North America, to ever really recover in any meaningful sense of the word. The destruction would be irreversible, at least for a very long period of time.

It is also clear that industrial and agricultural production would collapse, since the survivors will not have adequate substitutes for the machines that previously performed an array of vital economic functions.

In agriculture, for example, horse and tractor power would probably not be available to pull heavy agricultural machinery or to fertilize the land. Fuel would be unavailable and horses mostly unobtainable, if only because many of those that survive would be butchered for their meat. There is also the problem of radioactive fallout,

which would render thousands of hectares of arable land useless for food production for some years after the war. As a result, agricultural production will be reduced to primitive levels.

The same applies to firewood. Most modern houses and flats have no fireplaces. If there is no electricity or fuel for cooking and heating and it is impossible to return to the days of the wood stove, how will people be able to cook or keep warm?

In summary, immediately after the conflict our societies would undergo drastic and fundamental changes. Consumption of services would be highly specialized (*eg* medical care) while many activities we now take for granted would simply disappear. There would be an extraordinary drop in the resources available for consumption, which would precipitate an instantaneous drop in the standard of living. It might be like going from the 20th Century back to the dark ages at the snap of a finger. We would be reduced to bare subsistence, and it is clear that this situation would continue for a long time.

CONSEQUENCES OF THE WAR ON COUNTRIES NOT DIRECTLY INVOLVED

Following a nuclear war, the non-combatants, especially those in the Third World, would not suffer as badly as the combatants. But they would still suffer. Developing countries in Asia, Latin America, Africa and the Middle East, with their overflowing populations, dwindling natural resources, lack of arable land and primitive agricultural practices would find themselves in the middle of an overpowering economic and human crisis. Most of these countries cannot now produce enough food to feed their teeming populations; they are heavily dependent on massive imports of food and technology to keep their people fed and their economies running. With the source of vital foodstuffs and technology in ruins, it is likely that the non-belligerents will be more severely affected by a nuclear war than those directly involved. In this case the weapons of death are not nuclear bombs, but widespread starvation, sickness and urban unrest, which would spread over much of the Third World as the total collapse of the international network of trade and exchange became apparent. The 750 million deaths in the Northern Hemisphere would become 1–3 billion in tropical regions and the Southern Hemisphere. Why so many?

Basic Dichotomy Between Population and Resources

Over the past 40 years the world's population has undergone spectacular growth. In 1900 there were only 1.5 billion people in the world. By 1960 this figure doubled to 3 billion and in 1980 it had already jumped to 4.3 billion. It is expected that the global population will be 5.1 billion people by 1990 and 6.1 billion in the year 2000 (1).

Despite the recent downturn in demographic growth, most of that population growth is in developing countries. Africa and Latin America report annual population growth rates over 2.5 percent; in much of Asia it is 2 percent. But while the population of the less-developed countries has been increasing dramatically, there has been a corresponding drop in agricultural production due to loss of cropland, erosion, desertification *etc.* Population growth is simply outstripping food production (see Figure 1).

The resulting deficit has been balanced by massive imports of foodstuffs. International food and technological aid reached $ 36 billion in 1980—an amount corresponding to the accumulated GNP of 31 developing countries. What happens when the flow of aid ceases altogether?

The world trade in grain is a case in point. Just five countries (US, Canada, France, Argentina and Australia) sold 91 million tons of wheat and rice to deficit countries in Asia (34 million tons), Latin America (9 million tons), Africa (15 million tons), plus Brazil (5 million tons), the USSR (16 million tons), and China (12 million tons) (2). The major exporters—Canada, the US, and France—would be prime targets in a nuclear war.

Yet another important consideration is the international trade in oil, or to be more exact, the international barter system that has evolved: oil to the North in exchange for food and technology for the South. Oil importing countries like the USA, Europe and Japan buy 235 million tons of oil a year

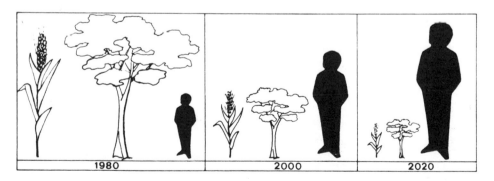

| 1980 | 2000 | 2020 |

Figure 1. If current rates of land degradation continue, nearly one-third of the world's arable land (symbolized by the stalk of grain) will be destroyed in the next 20 years. Similarly, by the end of this century (at present rates of clearance) the remaining area of unlogged productive tropical forest will be halved. During this period the world population is expected to increase by almost half—from just over 4000 million to just under 6000 million. Source: IUCN/Strategy for World Conservation/Robert Allen, 1980.

145

from Africa, 866 million tons from the Middle East, 83 million tons from Latin America and 56 million tons from Indonesia (3). In turn, the hard currency from oil sales enables these developing countries to purchase food, agricultural machinery and industrial technology from the West. If the world market for oil should suddenly collapse, as a result of a nuclear war, oil exporting developing countries would find themselves unable to produce the food to feed their burgeoning populations, or the technology to keep their modest industrial infrastructures running. Also many of their investments are in the West. It doesn't take much imagination to foresee the dire consequences for their fragile economies.

GREEN REVOLUTION LARGELY A MYTH FOR THIRD WORLD

Miracle strains of wheat, corn and rice have been developed over the past twenty years, increasing production of these crops by 120–180 percent in the USA, Canada, Europe and Argentina. However the same new varieties produced an increase of only 50 percent in Africa and Asia. And the improved efficiency in agricultural production noted in some Third World countries is highly dependent on continuing purchases of agricultural machinery, fertilizers, pesticides and related technologies from the West. For example, in 1980 the OECD countries sold $ 1 million worth of tractors to Africa, $ 650 million worth to the Middle East and $ 600 million worth to the Far East (4).

Developing countries also imported some $ 2 billion worth of fertilizers—$ 1 billion in Asia alone. What marginal progress has been made in increasing crop yields in tropical or arid countries is dependent upon huge injections of capital, fertilizers and machinery. Take away this economic prop and the Third World's economy will collapse, resulting in widespread starvation and violence.

CONCLUSION: WHAT WILL A POST-NUCLEAR WAR SOCIETY LOOK LIKE?

Economics involves the management of scarce resources, and historically it has been applied to sustain our material needs, and to create powerful bases of economic and military domination. In a post-nuclear war society economics would be devoted to managing very scarce resources indeed. The survivors would find themselves confined to specialized societies with highly planned economies contained inside rather authoritarian regimes. War economics geared to sheer survival, with no regard for growth, would be the dominant configuration. In other words we would be returning to a sort of economic dark ages: inward looking, and locked up in an autocracy that would be primarily agricultural. These societies would most likely be self-supporting and independent of the outside world.

After returning to a certain equilibrium of stagnation, these economies would probably evolve towards an unforeseeable future. We can imagine however, that deep psychological changes would be felt. We would probably see the total breakdown of our present values and motivations. There would be no reason for economic progress as we know it, no will to innovate, invest or invent. Mankind would be moving towards some kind of unprecedented economic pattern. Perhaps we would end up in monastic-like social and economic groupings with the primary emphasis on meditation, introspection and menial labor.

References and Notes

1. *World Population: Monthly Bulletin of Statistics* (United Nations, New York, NY, 1981).
2. International Trade of Grains, *FAO Monthly Bulletin of Statistics*, 4, no. 10 (FAO, Rome, October 1981).
3. World Supply and Demand of Oil, *Petrole 80: Elements Statistiques, Activité de l'Industrie Petroliere* (Comité Professionnel du Petrole, Paris, France, 1980).
4. *International Trade of Agricultural Machinery and tractors: Statistics of Foreign Trade* (OECD, Paris, 1981).

TWELVE

THE IMPACT ON GLOBAL FOOD SUPPLIES

HOWARD W. HJORT

Agricultural practices would revert to those of the 19th Century, with mostly human and animal power to till the soil and harvest crops. The tremendous number of deaths in the Northern Hemisphere, both human and animal, would lower the need for food and the production of animal products. Still, survivors would have to move to the food areas that remained. And millions would perish in the developing world because of the breakdown of the world food trade.

The world food system has been subjected to considerable shocks before, during wars and when weather reduced production. But prior experience is of only limited use in assessing the impact of a nuclear war of the magnitude outlined in the Reference Scenario (1), because the shock to the world food system would be so much more massive.

Other authors in this book discuss the effects of a global nuclear war on population, the economy, the atmosphere, freshwater and ocean systems, terrestrial ecosystems, and agricultural systems. These studies have important implications for the global food system; however, the full impact of a nuclear war on global food supplies is essentially beyond comprehension, or at least is not subject to precise quantification. It is the summation of a number of lesser impacts, some of them direct, others indirect.

The essential element in any estimate of global food supplies following a nuclear war is the destruction of people in relation to the destruction of animals and crops. Food stocks will no doubt be damaged and extensive croplands rendered radioactive. Furthermore, problems of distribution will almost certainly result in pockets of starvation in regions where local supplies are inadequate.

In this chapter, the proportion of the human population which would survive in each region has been estimated by comparing population densities with the account of likely targets which accompanies the Reference Scenario. The damage to food production from blast, fires and initial fallout was estimated by comparing maps of the target areas with maps showing their crop and animal densities. The damage to agriculture due to global fallout was estimated by comparing the estimates given in Table 2 of the Reference Scenario with data on the patterns of global agricultural production.

PREVIOUS STUDIES

Previous studies on the relative vulnerability of population and agriculture are helpful in guiding judgments about the relative decline in the production of food. Brown (2) believes that agriculture in the United States is approximately as vulnerable to a nuclear attack as is population. He calculated survival rates following a 1300 Mt nuclear attack at about 80 percent for humans, 70 percent for milk cows, 75 percent for beef cattle, and 76 percent for swine. He also concluded that about 85 percent of the corn and soybeans, 75 percent of the potatoes and sugar beets, and 65 percent of the wheat would survive a June 15 attack. He also presented convincing evidence that June 15 would be at or near the most vulnerable time for crops produced in the United States.

However Neal (3) concluded that a severe food shortage would exist in the United Kingdom after a nuclear exchange. In an attack in which an estimated 75 percent of humans would survive, an estimated 64 percent of sheep, 67 percent of dairy cattle, 68 percent of beef cattle, and 72 percent of pigs also survived, assuming the animals were sheltered; for unsheltered animals the survival rates were 53 to 55 percent for sheep and cattle and 69 percent for pigs. The lack of experimental data on the impact of beta radiation on crops forced him to give a wider range for damage to crop yields. He concluded that cereal crop yields would be reduced by 25–50 percent, pasture production about 25 percent, and potato yields only slightly. Neal also noted that, assuming a June attack, cereal stocks would be quite low, which would add to short supply problems.

Findings from a large number of experiments conducted to determine the sensitivity of animals and plants to radiation were reported in 1971 (4). The findings of particular interest to this assessment are these:

• Poultry are more resistant to radiation than swine, and swine more resistant than cattle and sheep, especially if the latter are on pasture.

• Poultry are appreciably less sensitive than humans, swine a little less sensitive, cattle and sheep about as sensitive when in pens and barns, but considerably more sensitive when on pasture.

• Resistance to radiation effects has been found in sheep and swine, with the resistance quite long lasting in the latter.

• Relatively little negative impact has been found on animal productivity, but beta irradiation of the gastrointestinal tract of cattle and sheep severely reduces feed intake and weight. Survivors usually return to normal feed consumption within 60 days but considerably more time is required to recover the weight loss. Iodine-131 can destroy thyroid tissue, which reduces lactation in dairy cattle.

• Radiation has relatively little effect on reproduction, but bone deformities can result if the exposure occurs when limb buds are just starting to form.

• Surviving animals could be used for food under emergency conditions. Muscle meat would be the safest. Milk should be avoided until Iodine-131 levels have declined to a relatively low level.

Effects on Plants

Little is known about the effects of beta radiation on plants. Most of the experimental results have involved gamma radiation. The major findings from one such experiment (5) are as follows:

• Plants are more resistant to gamma radiation than animals (including man) and can survive exposures that would be fatal to human populations. But an exposure which kills only 10 percent of the plants reduces the yield by 50 percent.

• Sensitivity to radiation varies greatly between different plant species (by at least 100-fold) and also varies considerably according to age (by over 50-fold within a single species). A plant near harvest is more resistant than at an earlier stage, and species with small cell nucleus volumes and large numbers of chromosomes are more resistant. Only 1370 rads administered at the seedling stage were required to achieve a 50 percent reduction in barley yield, while 4570 rads were required to achieve the same result in maize. Each crop has its own characteristic period of peak sensitivity.

• Among the major crops, the ranking from most to least sensitive is barley > rye > oats > wheat > maize > groundnuts >sunflower > alfalfa > sorghum > cotton > sugar cane > soybean > rice. Yields for barley were reduced 50 percent by exposure to 500–600 rads; a similar reduction in rice yields required 14 000 rads, about 25 times as much.

IMPACT ON FOOD SUPPLIES

The availability of food after a nuclear war will be affected by a number of factors, apart from the demand for food, as determined by the number of people who survive, and the production of food, as determined by the damage to crops and animals. For example, the expected disruptions of the internal transportation and processing systems would have an important impact on food supplies; merely moving agricultural products from areas of surplus to areas of shortages—either within countries or between countries—would be a problem of immense magnitude. And the reduction in supplies of fertilizers and agricultural chemicals used to produce and protect food would have a substantial impact on production.

The Reference Scenario used for this book targets a higher proportion of nuclear warheads on oil refining installations than on agricultural chemical plants. As a result, it is assumed in the calculations that fuel supplies are more restricted than supplies of agricultural chemicals. Since the reference scenario indicates ports would be particularly hard hit and some straits would be closed, it is assumed that it would be impossible for the most heavily-targeted areas to either import or export agricultural products or chemicals for some time after the war.

Previous studies (6) have concluded that industrial capacity would suffer proportionately more damage than the human population, and this is assumed to be the case for purposes of this paper. In the most heavily-targeted countries the ability to process agricultural products would be reduced to a small fraction; much of the previous capacity would be destroyed, and there would be little fuel for the plants that escaped destruction.

Global food supplies would also be seriously affected by changes in the atmosphere and in climate. Crutzen and Birks (7) believe the impact on the atmosphere of uncontrollable fires would pose a major threat to agricultural production. In combination with the potential changes in climate due to a nuclear war (8) the effect on food supplies could be substantial, although these considerations are beyond the scope of this assessment.

The impact of all of these factors on food supplies would vary greatly from region to region. So far as food production is concerned, the most heavily-targeted regions, which will be described as "high intensity target regions," are Western Europe, Eastern Europe, the USSR, North America and Japan. The "medium intensity target regions" are the Asian centrally planned economies, South Asia, the Middle East, and several countries in East Asia. The "low intensity target regions" are Latin America (except Cuba), Africa (except South Africa), and Oceania (except Australia).

High Intensity Target Regions

Agricultural productivity in the high intensity target countries is far above the world average. With only one-fourth of the

1985 world population, they will produce about 65 percent of the coarse grain, 60 percent of the wheat, 50 percent of the oilseed, and 40 percent of the cotton. They also produce a disproportionate share of the meat and other animal products.

North America exports massive quantities of animal feeds to the other high intensity target countries, and this trade would come to an abrupt halt. Large quantities of wheat and vegetable oil are also exported from North America and the European Economic Community to the other countries in the high intensity target region, but even larger quantities are exported to countries in the medium and low intensity target regions. All the high intensity target countries import large quantities of tropical products from the Third World, and their inability to import would have important economic consequences for the exporting countries.

Most of the world's fertilizer and agricultural chemicals are produced in the high intensity target countries. They trade large quantities of these products among themselves, but many developing countries also depend upon them for these important agricultural supplies.

North America

In North America, according to the analysis reported by Brown (2), adjusted to include Canada and to account for heavier targeting of cities, the survival rate for humans would be about the same as that for beef cattle and swine, and proportionately, about the same as the damage to the potato and sugar beet crops. Survival rates would be lower for milk cows and wheat, but higher for corn, soybeans and poultry than for humans.

As a result, per capita meat supplies (including poultry) would be slightly higher after the attack than before, even after accounting for the cessation of meat trade. Per capita supplies of dairy products would be lower, egg supplies higher. Sugar supplies would be cut sharply due to the absence of imports, and coffee, tea and cocoa supplies would soon cease to exist. Grain and oilseed supplies would be in excess of the domestic consumption requirement, unless yields were reduced by the lack of fuel and chemicals or because of atmospheric changes. Grain and oilseed stocks would be relatively low, but well above levels in Europe, the USSR or Japan.

About five percent of the 1985 wheat crop would have been harvested by June 11, and a month later 60 percent would have been harvested. Fuel supplies to harvest this wheat and to perform a significant share of the farming operations over the balance of the season would be in the hands of farmers.

North America produces much more wheat, rice, corn, sorghum and oilseed than is needed at home. Most of the grain and oilseed—used for animal feed—is exported to other high intensity target countries. Those exports would stop. By the time spring crops are due to be harvested, fuel supplies in North America would be very tight. Animals and humans would have to be used to harvest crops. Processing soybeans and other raw agricultural products would be impossible.

However foodgrain supplies might be adequate. In 1985, North America is expected to harvest over 100 million tons of wheat and rice; 70 or 75 million tons are scheduled for export. June stocks alone would be more than enough to provide for domestic use for a year, assuming they were not destroyed or contaminated by fallout.

There would be excess supplies of food in rural areas and the people would have to go to them instead of supplies going to the people. The diet would contain a much higher proportion of unprocessed foods.

The USSR

Survival rates for both humans and crops are expected to be slightly higher in the USSR, but the proportions of humans, different species of animals, and crops sur-

viving should be similar to those in North America. However, wheat and barley are the major grains, while sunflower is the major oilseed. These crops are more sensitive to radiation than the major crops produced in the United States (corn, soybeans and wheat). Further, the USSR is a net importer of sugar, other tropical products, meat, wheat, rice, coarse grain and oilseeds. Therefore per capita food supplies would be tighter in the USSR than in North America. Supplies of fuel, fertilizer and other agricultural chemicals would probably be at least as short as in North America, but harvesting the damaged crops may not be as big a problem. A higher proportion of the people work in agriculture and live in rural areas than in North America, so employing "man power" to harvest crops may not be as difficult as it would be in North America or Europe.

Western Europe

Western Europe has high human and animal population densities, and wheat and barley are the major grains. Severe food shortages are expected. Survival rates are likely to be even lower than in North America. Western Europe, especially the European Economic Community, is a net exporter of wheat. But grain stocks would be lower than in North America, and because wheat and barley are more sensitive to radiation the decline in grain production may be proportionately greater than the decline in the human population. Massive quantities of animal feeds are imported by Western Europe, and surviving animals would have to be slaughtered to bring their numbers in line with the feed supply. This would provide a temporary boost in meat supplies, but lead to shortages later. The threat to yields from inadequate inputs of fertilizer and other chemicals and harvest problems would be similar to those in North America. The inability to import tropical products would soon reduce supplies sharply.

151

Eastern Europe

Eastern Europe also has a relatively high density of humans and animals, so survival rates would be low. The region is a net importer of agricultural products, especially animal feeds, wheat and tropical products. Per capita food supplies would be inadequate. Problems due to inadequate inputs of chemicals and fertilizers and the difficulties in harvesting crops would be similar to those in Western Europe.

Japan

Japan has a very high population density, and relies upon imported agricultural products to a very great degree. Survival rates would be very low, but the rice crop would suffer less than the human population. Even so, supplies would be inadequate, and after the forced slaughter of surviving animals the threat of starvation would be real.

Medium Intensity Target Regions

The medium intensity target countries rely upon plants for food to a much greater degree than the more industrialized nations. Animals are a much less important source of food. In Asia, rice, which is highly resistant to radiation, is the dominant foodgrain. Reliance upon manufactured fertilizer and agricultural chemicals has been increasing rapidly, but by 1985 will still be far lower than in the high intensity target countries. Mechanization of agriculture has also been rising at a rapid pace, and while fuel shortages would be a problem they would not cause the same difficulties as the high intensity target countries would experience. Fewer cities are targeted, and industrial and military targets are much fewer in number. Delayed global fallout levels are relatively high, but still only 25 to 30 percent of the levels expected in Europe or the USSR after one month, and about 40 percent of the levels expected there after ten years. The exceptions are northeast China and North Korea, where fallout accumulations

152

are higher, and Southeast Asia, where they are much lower. The impact on people and agriculture would be much less than in the high intensity target countries.

Asian Centrally Planned Economies

The Asian centrally planned economies have very high population densities, but the intensity of the attack would be much lower. Survival rates would be well above those in Japan or Europe; survival rates for humans and swine would be about the same, but crops should fare better than humans, mainly because rice is the dominant foodgrain. These countries import wheat and agricultural chemicals, mainly fertilizer. But imports are a relatively small percentage of domestic production. Inadequate supplies of manufactured fertilizer and agricultural chemicals would slow progress in agriculture but would not have a major impact on food supplies.

South Asia

South Asia, dominated by India, uses animals primarily as a source of power rather than as a source of food. Rice is the dominant foodgrain but wheat is important in India and Pakistan. However, the 1985 wheat crop would have been harvested by June. Population density is very high and even though only cities with 500 000 people or more are targeted, the percentage surviving is expected to be lower for humans than for food. The need for food imports would therefore decline. The region exports rice and imports a slightly larger quantity of wheat in a normal year. Oilseed meals, sugar and other tropical products are exported, but imports of vegetable oil are very large. A relatively high proportion of the fuel, fertilizer and other agricultural chemicals used in the region is imported. Tight world supplies of vegetable oil and wheat would have an impact on food supplies, but the major shortages are likely to occur in subsequent years, the consequence of inadequate supplies of agricultural inputs. The most serious lack is likely to be the shortage of fuel.

The Middle East

The Middle East relies on imports for a significant share of its food supply. Imports of a large number of agricultural products are climbing at a rapid rate. Agricultural production would be adversely affected by a nuclear war and some of the people would be killed. On balance, the percentage reduction in people may be about the same as the reduction in agricultural production. The inability to obtain food and agricultural inputs from other countries would be the major problem facing the Middle East countries after the initial effects of a nuclear war had been dealt with.

East Asia

The East Asian countries have relatively high population densities, but except for South Korea they are not heavily targeted. Survival rates may be about the same for animals and humans, but crops would suffer somewhat less damage. These countries are net importers of wheat and coarse grain but are becoming self-sufficient in rice, their major foodgrain. They are major exporters of vegetable oils and significant exporters of other tropical products. The East Asian countries would be hurt by the loss of markets for their export products and would have a difficult time obtaining both wheat and the animal feed needed for a rapidly-expanding livestock industry. Restricted availability of agricultural inputs would be a problem, but of relatively moderate proportions.

Low Intensity Target Regions

Survival rates in the low intensity target countries would be very high compared with the high intensity target countries. The primary impact on food supplies would result from the disruption of trade in food and in agricultural inputs.

Latin America

Latin America is now a net importer of wheat and coarse grain, an exporter of meat, oilseeds and oilseed oils and meals, and a major exporter of sugar and other tropical products. Imports of fertilizer exceed domestic production. The inability to obtain fertilizer (and other agricultural chemicals) following a nuclear war would lower yields in subsequent years. However much of the fertilizer is used on tropical crops, and because prices for these crops would be seriously depressed by the inability of the high intensity target countries to import, they would not be fertilized or harvested anyway. Oilseed meals would be in excess supply, but there would be a demand from South Asia and other countries for the region's vegetable oil. Coarse grain and wheat supplies would be inadequate, and changes in diet would have to take place.

Africa

Africa is an important importer of foodgrains and exporter of coffee and cocoa. Export markets would be destroyed and imports would not be available. Existing economic problems would become even more severe. The lack of food aid and agricultural development assistance would also make an already difficult situation much worse. Food shortages would be quite widespread.

Oceania

Oceania is a net exporter of most agricultural products. There would be a strong market for the region's grain, expecially wheat, but sugar and other tropical products, and meat and dairy products are likely to be in excess supply. The agricultural economy would turn even more to grain production, away from animal and tropical agriculture.

153

CONCLUSIONS

In the immediate aftermath of a nuclear exchange, blast would destroy some food crops, those in cities and at ports. Fire would destroy food stocks, and thousands of hectares of crops would burn. Some crops would be killed from radiation, and surviving crops near targets would yield much less than expected. Lower yields would be the major cause of lower crop production, death the major cause of lower animal product production. The threat to plant yields comes from several directions: initially from radiation, then from atmospheric changes due to uncontrollable fires, inadequate levels of fertilizer, reduced ability to control weeds, insects and diseases, and possibly from changes in climate.

On a global basis, the problem associated with harvesting the crops that survive may be the greatest of all. Global fuel supplies would range from very tight to inadequate, and it may be necessary to use animal and human labor to harvest an abnormally large share of the crops. The transition back from modern agriculture to traditional agriculture would be beyond the experience of surviving farmers in the highly industrialized economies but would be a less difficult transition elsewhere.

The impact of a global nuclear war on food supplies begins with the war and continues for years into the future. The death of millions of people would reduce the need for food but the death of millions of animals would reduce the production of food. Plants would be killed and those that survive would have reduced yields. The destruction of the capacity to produce fertilizers and chemicals to control weeds, plant and animal pests, and insects would seriously affect agricultural production on a global scale. The demolition of the oil refining industry and chaos in oil and gas fields would eliminate energy-intensive agricultural production and processing systems. Fires raging out of control over vast areas and the effect they would have on atmospheric conditions may have both a direct and indirect effect on the yield and production of food. Even changes in climate and world weather patterns are possible. Damage to the food processing systems in high intensity target countries would mean a much smaller range of products for survivors. Disruptions in electrical power and in the communications systems would also disturb the food system. Damage to the internal transportion systems in the heavily-targeted countries and regions would mean excess food and supplies in some areas and severe shortages in others. People would have to move to food instead of food moving to people.

The impact of a global nuclear war would be much more severe in some countries and regions than in others. Closing the straits and demolishing the major ports would stop the flow of food from formerly industrialized countries, and to them from the Third World food exporters. Surviving populations in Japan, South Korea, Europe, and the Middle East would probably face more severe food shortages than those in the United States, Canada or even the USSR. Conditions in Sub-Saharan Africa would deteriorate further, while Oceania would become a more important source of food supplies.

References and Notes

1. Reference Scenario, Chapter 3.
2. Stephen L Brown, in *Proceedings of a Symposium on the Survival of Food Crops and Livestock in the Event of Nuclear War*, (CONF-700909, National Technical Information Service, Springfield, Virginia, USA, December 1971), pp 595–607.
3. W T L Neal, In *Proceedings, op. cit.*, pp 616–625.
4. MC Bell, in *Proceedings, op. cit.* pp 656–669.
5. A H Sparrow, S S Schwemmer, P J Bottino, in *Proceedings, op. cit.*, pp 670–711.
6. *The Effetcs of Nuclear War*, US Arms Control and Disarmament Agency (ACDA), 1979.
7. Paul J Crutzen and John W Birks — see Chapter 6.
8. G M Woodwell — see Chapter 10.

THIRTEEN

EFFECTS ON HUMAN BEHAVIOR

E. I. CHAZOV AND M. E. VARTANIAN

At least one third of the survivors of a nuclear war will suffer from severe mental and behavioral disturbances. For the vast majority of these psychiatric casualties, no adequate medical treatment will be possible.

It is difficult to predict the possible effects of a global nuclear war on mental health and human behavior, but a number of authors have made attempts in recent decades (1, 2, 3). Most use an analysis of data from the atomic attacks on Hiroshima and Nagasaki (2, 4, 5), or attempt to make extrapolations by analyzing individual and group behavior in other, non-nuclear, mass disasters (6, 7, 8). It should be noted that such extrapolations are suspect, since non-nuclear disasters—earthquake, flood, fire—can scarcely equal the impact of a nuclear war on the human organism.

It is usually acknowledged that the disturbances of behavior and mental activity which would follow a nuclear war can be divided into two classes: disorders arising directly from the explosions, and more remote effects. The direct disorders may include acute brain syndromes, protracted anxiety states, and reactive psychoses, and the behaviors which are manifested as a result of these disorders may range from massive panic reactions, psychomotor excitation and flight to reactive depressive states, adynamic conditions and conflict behavior. However, it has frequently been observed that mass catastrophes do not cause a marked increase in cases of psychosis (9, 10), and in a number of catastrophes the initial stages of the disaster result in more organized patterns of behavior, as the survivors mobilize and concentrate in places where first aid, food, and assistance is available.

Nevertheless, behavioral and mental disturbances will present one of the main after-effects of a nuclear war. In the first instance, such disturbances will be associated with the emergence of anxiety reactions in large numbers of the survivors. It is expected that one-third of the survivors will be in a state of marked anxiety (11), characterized by fear, apprehensiveness, irritability and confusion. Those emotional reactions will be heightened by the effect of encountering large numbers of casualties.

Sensory deprivation, as a consequence of isolation and the absence of customary environmental stimuli, may play an essential role in prompting behavioral disturbances, and a form of sensory deprivation psychosis may be seen following the large-scale destruction of a nuclear explosion. D K Kentsmith notes (12) that disorientation results from the sensory deprivation caused by the isolation and destruction of the immediate surrounding in a major disaster. Restlessness, boredom, irritability and increasing anxiety are common signs of this disorientation. The individual frequently feels separated from his environment and depersonalized. There is often an impairment in the ability to solve simple problems, difficulty in concentrating, and in some cases abnormal visual sensations, including hallucinations.

K T Erikson singles out three common behavioral changes in the survivors of catastrophes (13). First, the survivors suffer from severe demoralization, reflected in a profound apathy, a feeling that the world has more-or-less come to an end and that there is no longer any sound reason for doing anything. Second, the survivors suffer from a prolonged sense of disorientation. They are likely to be unable to locate themselves meaningfully in space or time. Places and objects seem transitory. Time seems to stop. They are frequently unable to remember such everyday details as the names of close friends, their own telephone number, *etc.* Third, the survivors frequently exhibit what might be described as a loss of connection—a sense of separation from other people.

The survivors of Hiroshima and Nagasaki also displayed a form of "survivor guilt." In their flight from the cities, most survivors could not avoid ignoring appeals for help from other victims, because of the impossibility of helping the large numbers of casualties and the need to escape the fires. The feelings aroused by that situation become a long-term source of emotional stress (14); the survivors associated the disaster with chaos, helplessness and death, and the feelings of personal insignificance that arose from it remained troublesome for a long period of time.

The overwhelming majority of the survivors of the nuclear attacks on Japan still exhibit signs of mental disturbances, including permanent fear, uncertainty, and various psychoneurological disorders. One source of those fears is exposure to radiation. The health of the survivors is threatened by the emergence of remote radiation effects, and they fear diseases and malformations in their children. They are also concerned about the cost of treatment, the decrease in their working capacity, their unstable financial circumstances, and by the discrimination shown by other members of the community.

It seems clear that the psychological reactions of the survivors of a nuclear war will continue for months or years after the disaster. These remote effects may include chronic neurotic conditions, massive apathy, a drastic reduction in working capacity and a thorough disorganization of interpersonal relations.

Long-term personality changes such as increased aggressiveness, irritability, nightmares and irrational behavior are also typical of persons who have spent two weeks in a locked, underground space (15). There are obvious parallels with people forced to spend long periods in an air-raid shelter under nuclear bombardment.

The question of the help that can be afforded the survivors of a nuclear attack naturally arises, and the following factors must be considered in attempting to answer it: first, the number of individuals with mental and behavioral disturbances and the duration and severity of these disturbances; second, the number of psychiatrists and psychologists who might be available to provide treatment following a nuclear attack; third, the amount of time required for treatment; fourth, the availability of treatment facilities following a nuclear attack; and fifth, the availability of psychotropic and other drugs for treatment.

It is immediately obvious that no adequate treatment would be possible for the vast bulk of the psychiatric casualties. Let us assume, in accordance with a number of studies, that approximately 20–25 percent of the urban population of European countries would survive a nuclear attack. About one third of the survivors would be in a state of acute anxiety; about 20 percent of the survivors would be so incapacitated by psychological and pathopsychological conditions that they would be unable to care for themselves or others. In an urban area of one million population, with 200 psychiatrists and psychologists, it would require 120 hours to examine each person in need of treatment for 10 minutes. If the mental health professionals suffered the same rate of casualties as the population at large, it would require 25 days before each patient could be seen for 10 minutes— assuming in both cases that the psychiatrists and psychologists worked 24 hours per day.

In addition, a patient load of such dimensions would exceed even the peacetime capacity of the mental hospitals in both the USSR and the US. The US has about 1.6 beds per 1000 population in psychiatric hospitals, the USSR has about 1.5 per 1000 population, and those beds are already well used. In peace-time, some five to seven percent of the urban population is in need of psychiatric treatment. Even if all of the psychiatric hospitals escaped damage in a nuclear attack—an unlikely prospect—the number of psychiatric casualties would exceed the number of beds for treatment by about 50 times. It is also unlikely that the drugs necessary for effective treatment would be available. There is no hope of adequate treatment for the wide range of behavioral disorders, including profound neuropsychic disturbances, which would be incurred in a nuclear war.

Any attempt to calculate the extent of

psychiatric casualties following a nuclear war is of necessity based to a large extent on guesswork. Experience in military catastrophes indicates that there are no individual characteristics which predispose a person to a breakdown; the most critical factor appears to be the duration of the stress (12), but it is impossible to predict who will become a casualty. It is equally impossible to predict the pattern of casualties, including psychiatric casualties, following a nuclear war; it follows that the only rational alternative is to prevent such a war from occuring. As the Pugwash Medical Working Group notes in its statement: "As doctors of medicine and scientists in health-related fields, we conclude therefore that nuclear weapons are so destructive to human health and life that they must never be used. Prevention of nuclear war offers the only possibility for protecting people from its medical consequences. There is no alternative."

References and notes

1. F Hocking, Extreme Environmental Stress and its Significance for Psychopathology, *Medical Journal of Australia* **2**, 477 (1965).

2. W Kinston and R Rosser, Disaster: Effects on Mental and Physical State. *Journal of Psychosomatic Research* **18**, 437 (1974).

3. J G Edwards, Psychiatric Aspects of Civilian Disasters, *British Medical Journal* **1**, 944 (1976).

4. R J Lifton, *Death in Life: Survivors of Hiroshima* (Random House, New York, 1967).

5. J L Janis, *Air War and Emotional Stress* (McGraw-Hill, New York, 1951).

6. G J Newman, Children of Disaster: Clinical Observation at Buffalo Creek, *American Journal of Psychiatry* **133** (3), 306 (1976).

7. G C Gleser, B L Green and C N Winget, Quantifying Interviewed Data on Psychic Impairment of Disaster Survivors, *Journal of Nervous and Mental Disease* **166**, 209 (1966).

8. K J Tierney and B Baisden, *Crisis Intervention Programs for Disaster Victims*. DHEW Publication (USA); 79–675, 1979

9. R R Dynes, *Organized Behavior in Disaster*, Monograph Series 3 (The Disaster Research Center, Ohio State University, Columbus, Ohio, 1974).

10. J G Edwards, Psychiatric Aspects of Civilian Disaster, *British Medical Journal* **1**, 944 (1976).

11. G W Baker and D W Chatman, *Man and Society in Disaster* (Basic Book Inc, New York, 1967).

12. D K Kentsmith, Minimizing the Psychological Effects of a Wartime Disaster on an Individual, *Aviation, Space and Environment Medicine*, pp. 409–413, 1980.

13. K T Erikson, Loss of Communiality at Buffalo Creek, *American Journal of Psychiatry* **133** (3), 302 (1976).

14. A Hedge, *Surviving a Nuclear War* (Proceedings of the Medical Association for Prevention of War v. 3, P. 5 1981) p. 185–199.

15. A Ploeger, A 10-year follow up of miners trapped for two weeks under threatening circumstances, in: *Stress and Anxiety* vol 4, pp. 23–28, (1977).

16. R R Rogers, On Emotional Responses to Nuclear Issues and Terrorism, *Psychiatric Journal of the University of Ottawa*, **5** (3), 1980.

THE PARADOX OF THE ARMS RACE: INCREASED THREAT, BUT DECREASED RESPONSE

The potential for psychological damage in a nuclear attack is obviously catastrophic. But the continuing arms race between the two superpowers also contributes — together with other factors — to psychological distress and the intensification of mental and emotional tension in large numbers of people. The damage is less obvious, but all the more insidious for that.

A number of investigators have tried to clarify the concrete mechanisms by which the threat of nuclear war has its psychological impact (16). It should be noted that no convincing proof of the part played by such a threat in psychological disturbances was obtained, perhaps in part because the investigations were limited and did not include examinations of large numbers of people, and did not attempt to identify the remote effects of such a threat.

After the bombing of Hiroshima and Nagasaki, popular movements against the use of nuclear weapons developed in many countries. But this public response to the horrors of nuclear war gradually fell off during subsequent decades, despite the increasing numbers of weapons in the nuclear arsenals and therefore the increasing threat of nuclear war.

In an attempt to explain this apparent paradox — an increased threat, but a decreased public response to that threat — concepts of denial, suppression and adaptation were borrowed from theories of individual psychology. Explaining the failure of public response to the nuclear threat as a denial phenomenon arising from an adaptive response of individuals to an unpleasant situation can seem tempting, but these extrapolations are essentially speculative, without any basis in direct studies of large groups. And they fail to explain why the public response to the threat of nuclear war suddenly became more active at the beginning of the 1980s.

Suppression has also been suggested as an adaptive response to a continuing threat, a phenomenon which implies a loss of ability to respond to constant stimuli which are lost in the flood of other stimuli that make up our daily lives. Little by little, the horrors of Hiroshima and Nagasaki are forgotten in the joys and sorrows of everyday life.

And because of the length of time that has passed since the nuclear attacks on Japan, many people — and especially the young — view the nuclear threat as an abstraction, divorced of any real force. One result is that many people fail to perceive the qualitative difference between nuclear weapons and others. Some authors view this process of abstraction, arising from a lack of experience, as one possible mechanism leading to an underestimation of the realities and consequences of a nuclear war.

But the explanations for the absence of public response to the nuclear threat in the 1960s and 1970s are perhaps less interesting than the reasons behind the sudden explosion of public concern at the beginning of the 1980s. It is well known that behavioral reactions become stronger as a given threat becomes more real, and it seems clear that events in the armaments race developed in such a way — particularly in Europe — that they created a more serious threat to the balance of forces in this region. The public has reached a level of comprehension that recognizes changes in the nuclear balance — both because of increased quantities of weapons and because of more effective weapons — as a concrete threat to their security. This in turn has prompted a marked increase in the protests against nuclear weapons. Widespread discussion of the possibility of a "limited" nuclear war, of the deployment of neutron bombs, and the acceleration of the arms race have all created and increased the psychological pressure felt by the public at large. There is considerable fear for the continued existence of man on earth; in the end that fear, as it gathers force, may well lead to more effective measures for the prevention of a nuclear catastrophe.

FOURTEEN

CONCLUSIONS

AMBIO ADVISORY GROUP

The disastrous consequences of a nuclear war, as described in this book, should make it clear that any such war is unwinnable.

In such a war no nation on earth will remain undamaged. The industrialized societies of the Northern Hemisphere will be totally destroyed, and hundreds of millions of people will die, either directly or from the delayed effects of radiation. Even greater numbers may ultimately perish there and in Third World countries as a result of the collapse of their societies and of the international exchange of food, fertilizers, fuel and economic aid. The environmental support system on which man is dependent will suffer massive damage.

In this book, we have chosen to emphasize the environmental aspects of the aftermath of a nuclear war. The scenario on which the issue is based is not one which would result in the maximum number of human casualties in the short term; in fact the scenario assumes that a substantial part of the nuclear arsenals remains unused. Despite this, the contributors as a whole show that when environmental consequences are included in the study, many more people will ultimately be affected by nuclear war than are directly killed by bombing and radiation.

Each chapter deals with the impact of the war on a different aspect of the human environment. The authors emphasize the uncertainties associated with their estimates of possible consequences, and readers of the following summary should keep this in mind. Because of these uncertainties, many of the estimates are on the low side. Even with this conservative assessment, the full range of possible effects is so overwhelming as to be almost inconceivable.

IN SUMMARY

The number of immediate or early deaths resulting from the effects of blast, fire, and heat in the nuclear exchange described here will approach 750 million (slightly more than half of the population of the cities bombed) and about 340 million will be seriously injured. To these casualties must be added those who will succumb to or be incapacitated by fire and heat. A considerable proportion of those who survive the blast, fire and heat will suffer from acute radiation sickness as a result of exposure to fallout. In addition, sublethal levels of ionizing radiation will lower resistance to infection, and diseases such as cholera and dysentery will spread rapidly in the absence of proper water and sanitation facilities.

About one-third of the urban survivors will be in a state of acute anxiety, and about 20 percent of the other survivors will be so incapacitated by psychological and pathopsychological conditions that they will be unable to care for themselves or others. Those who have witnessed the annihilation of their societies may suffer from profound apathy and disorientation. The staggering numbers of corpses to be cleared away and the pressing need to care for the wounded and ill will absorb much of the time and energy of those who are still capable of purposeful action.

Survivors in urban and suburban areas will probably disperse to the countryside in a desperate search for the basic necessities of life —relatively safe food, water and shelter. But rainwater, and surface water, (streams and lakes) will be contaminated, and many of the water supply systems destroyed, although water in deep aquifers should remain safe to drink. Rainwater in early fallout areas will contain such a high concentration of toxic material that it will be a lethal poison. Those caught in such areas will experience burns through the full thickness of the exposed skin.

Faced with food shortages, people will almost certainly be unable to avoid eating food contaminated with radioactivity. Even in areas remote from "local" fallout, the radioactivity levels in diet and in human tissue will be about 20 times higher than during the weapons-testing period of the 1960s. Increased incidences of cancer, sterility and genetic defects can be expected among the survivors.

Enormous amounts of light-absorbing and light reflecting particulate debris will cloak the atmosphere in a dark veil which will hinder sunlight for weeks and perhaps months. In the Northern Hemisphere vast fires will almost certainly sweep over expanses of forest land and agricultural fields, and these fires along with those in oil and gas fields ignited by the thousands of nuclear explosions will load the lower atmosphere with tiny particles of tar, soot and ash. When the fires burn out and the particles eventually fall to the ground, the changed chemistry of the atmosphere would be such that a severe photochemical smog could form over much of the Northern Hemisphere. This smog, together with a shortage of all types of supplies and a state of chaos, will tend to make agriculture extremely difficult. A large reduction of the stratospheric ozone layer is also possible. It would last for several years and lead to an increased intensity of solar UV-radiation received at the earth's surface, with serious consequences for humans, plants and animals.

Agricultural and natural ecosystems weakened by radiation and other environmental stress will be vulnerable to attack by pests that thrive on ailing plants. Cockroaches and rats, carrion birds and organisms of decay will increase in frequency. Pests, those small-bodied, fast-multiplying organisms that are often in competition with human beings, are relatively resistant to radiation, and will thrive in the conditions of the aftermath.

All these factors will cause enormous problems for the survivors in the Northern Hemisphere and severe food shortages will persist in large areas for months or years following the war. Widespread famines will return to areas where they have long been absent.

Although the impact of radioactive contamination of the marine environment will probably be less than on terrestrial ecosystems, (primarily because of the dilution factor), the reduction of sunlight could have serious consequences for marine ecosystems. Fisheries in shallow coastal areas will be particularly vulnerable.

Societies will be drastically changed. The economies of the Northern Hemisphere will collapse and there will be a return to the barter system. Commodities and services now taken for granted will no longer exist. No modern economic system based on economies of scale, specialization and international exchange would be likely to survive the war. Decades, or even centuries might pass before any social and economic recovery could be possible.

Industrially less developed countries with large populations and inadequate food production—even if not directly involved—will be swept by waves of famine, disease and social unrest. The complete breakdown of the system of international trade in fertilizers, fuel, farm machinery and technology and funds, would also deprive many Third World countries of resources that are currently needed to sustain them, thus creating a lethal gap between the number of people and the resources available to support them.

In the face of such anarchy, post-nuclear "governments" would most likely be highly authoritarian, and of necessity dependent on Draconian laws. Surviving "societies" would have to be highly restricted, dedicated to the virtually impossible task of managing scarce resources, and closely governed by the exigencies of survival.

ADDITIONAL CONSIDERATIONS

Although the authors have emphasized the environmental impacts of a nuclear war, time has not allowed sufficient study of secondary ecological effects. It may well be that the massive damage to the environment caused by a nuclear war would result in large-scale and long-term effects on ecosystems in different parts of the globe. One of the conclusions that may be reached from this study is that the short-term effects for which we have relatively reliable calculations — fire, blast, and radioactive contamination — may be matched or even vastly overshadowed by longer-term, less-predictable environmental effects.

Although the basic scenario did not include the bombing of nuclear reactors, we decided that a sub-study should be included which would show the consequences of such a targeting plan. The results of that special case study included in Chapter 3 show that if nuclear power plants were systematically targeted in a large-scale nuclear war, the long-term effects of radioactive contamination would be significantly increased. After an initial period, radioactivity released by the destruction of reactors would dominate over that released by the detonation of nuclear weapons.

FINALLY...

Although the impact of the nuclear war we have described would be widespread and terrible, there would probably be survivors. Their fate, however, is extremely uncertain. The human and social environment in which they will have to live will be changed far beyond our comprehension. In addition to wartime destruction and poisoning, the natural environment might suffer such grave long-term changes as to severely threaten the survivors' fight for recovery. In any case societies as we know them today will most certainly cease to exist.

FIFTEEN

THE CONSEQUENCES OF A "LIMITED" NUCLEAR WAR IN EAST AND WEST GERMANY

WILLIAM ARKIN, FRANK VON HIPPEL AND BARBARA G. LEVI

This chapter which describes two variations of a "limited" nuclear war in East and West Germany, is based on scenarios that differ from the one on which the rest of the book is based. The authors demonstrate that even the most limited of militarily significant uses of nuclear weapons in the two Germanies would have catastrophic consequences, with many millions of fatalities, and the likelihood of escalation to full scale, global nuclear war.

As we have seen, the use of a significant fraction of the US and Soviet strategic weapons arsenals could result in enormous destruction throughout the Northern Hemisphere. It is their ability to invoke this murder-suicide pact that the superpowers consider their ultimate deterrent against nuclear attack.

The strategic warheads which the US and Soviet Union are prepared to rain down upon each other comprise, however, less than half of the number of nuclear warheads in their arsenals. The remainder of their nuclear weapons are intended for naval warfare and for the deterrence of attacks against their "vital interests" in regional confrontations around the world.

The most heavily nuclearized regional confrontation is that between the NATO and Warsaw Pact forces in Europe, involving over 10 000 so-called "theatre" nuclear warheads. Currently there is a great debate going on in Europe about the benefits and dangers which are associated with the presence of these weapons. Frequently discussed in this debate are scenarios for the "limited" use of nuclear weapons in Europe. The purpose of this chapter is to provide some estimates of the consequences for the civilian population of such possible "limited" nuclear wars.

Our finding is that any use of nuclear weapons which would have militarily significant effects against targets in the densely populated and developed continent of Europe would result in the deaths of many millions of civilians. Similar estimates have previously been obtained for the consequences of limited nuclear exchanges between the superpowers (1).

Since some strategists will probably point out the "good news"—that, for the very limited and controlled attacks discussed in our scenarios, the majority of the population of Europe would survive—it is important to emphasize how unlikely it is that a nuclear war would be stopped after such initial attacks. By the time warheads

were used against large fractions of significant classes of military targets (hundreds of nuclear warheads against fixed military targets and more than a thousand against battlefield targets), it is likely that the exchange of nuclear blows would be building up with such great rapidity that all-out nuclear war would be inevitable. Each side would be under enormous pressure to use its nuclear forces for fear that its weapons or command and control abilities were about to be lost due to enemy attacks (2).

The first use of nuclear weapons in Europe would probably be an act of desperation—an attempt either to reduce the strength of an apparently imminent nuclear attack by the other side or to prevent a major defeat or irreversible loss of territory in a war being fought with non-nuclear weapons. In the following two sections we will, therefore, describe and consider the consequences of two hypothetical, strictly "limited" nuclear attacks:

A) preemptive attacks by each side against the nuclear weapons and nuclear weapons delivery vehicles of the other side, and
B) the battlefield exchange of nuclear weapons between the NATO and Warsaw Pact armies.

Our analysis restricts itself to a study of consequences of these nuclear exchanges for East and West Germany because a comprehensive analysis of the consequences for all of Europe was not feasible. Our choice of the two Germanies was hardly by chance, however. Across the boundary dividing their small combined area (356 000 square kilometers—equal to only 4 percent of the area of the US or 1.5 percent of the area of the Soviet Union) large fractions of both the nuclear and non-nuclear military forces of the NATO and Warsaw Pact alliances confront each other "nose to nose." As a result, should war break out in Europe, it is most likely that the Germanies would be at its focus and, should nuclear weapons be used, it is likely that they would be used both first and most intensely on these same small territories.

It is unlikely that any nuclear exchange would long remain limited to the Germanies, however. It would make little sense, in particular to conduct a preemptive attack against the nuclear weapons in the Germanies without attempting to destroy the other nuclear weapons which are controlled by the alliances in Europe. Ultimately, it would make little sense to destroy the nuclear weapons deployed by a superpower in Europe without trying to destroy the associated nuclear weapons on that superpower's home territory. Nothing but labeling prevents these weapons from being targeted against the nuclear forces of the opposite alliance—either in Europe or at home. Our analysis of the consequences of such preemptive attacks should therefore be thought of as an examination of what might occur as a result of the first nuclear exchanges in one small part of what would probably grow rapidly into a global nuclear battlefield.

Both the attacks which we will discuss are assumed to be purely countermilitary. In neither case do we assume that there is a deliberate attempt to destroy populations or their support systems. In other words, all civilian deaths would be purely "collateral" (unintentional). By focussing on the smallest plausible military use of nuclear weapons in the Germanies (apart from "demonstration" attacks), we hope, therefore, to make clear the *least* damage which would result to the population and society of this one area of Europe following any actual implementation of the doctrines of limited nuclear war on that continent.

In what follows, we will discuss for each of the hypothetical attacks in turn: the targets of the attack; then the nuclear warheads which might be used in those exchanges and their individual effects; and finally, the consequences for the populations of East and West Germany of the full exchanges.

PREEMPTIVE ATTACKS AGAINST NUCLEAR FORCES

The Targets. While the introduction of nuclear weapons into Europe has made a large scale "conventional" (World War II type) war less likely, it has made nuclear war more likely. Specifically, in a period of crisis, if one side believed—correctly or mistakenly—that the other was considering using even a few nuclear weapons, there would be enormous pressure to attempt a "preemptive" attack on those weapons.

The superpowers have gone to great lengths to protect their strategic arsenals against surprise attack by placing them in thousands of widely separated underground concrete silos, in many submarines hidden in the depths of the ocean, and in bombers prepared to take off given 5–15 minutes notice. Almost all of the many thousands of nuclear warheads and delivery systems in the Germanies are, however, grouped during peacetime at about 135 known and relatively vulnerable sites. (Efforts would be made during crisis or wartime to further disperse these weapons) (3). In some situations such a dispersal might be interpreted by the other side as preparation for "going nuclear," however, and could, therefore, be the trigger for a preemptive attack before dispersal could be completed).

In addition to nuclear weapons and delivery systems, there are other classes of facilities and locations in Europe which are discussed as appropriate targets for nuclear weapons. According to one recent official listing, these include: "IRBM/MRBM [Intermediate and Medium Range Ballistic Missiles] sites; naval bases; nuclear and chemical storage sites; airbases; command, control, and communications centers; headquarters complexes; surface-to-air missile sites; munitions and petroleum storage areas and transfer facilities; ground forces installations; choke points; troop concentrations; and bridges" (4).

Although Appendix I to this chapter categorizes more than 1 100 such targets in the two Germanies, it does not include all the target categories on this list.

For the targets of the hypothetical preemptive exchange discussed in this article, we have limited ourselves to the 171 locations shown in Figure 1a which are the sites of the greatest offensive nuclear threats in the Germanies: 91 bases for military aircraft, 56 sites where surface-to-surface nuclear missiles are based, and 24

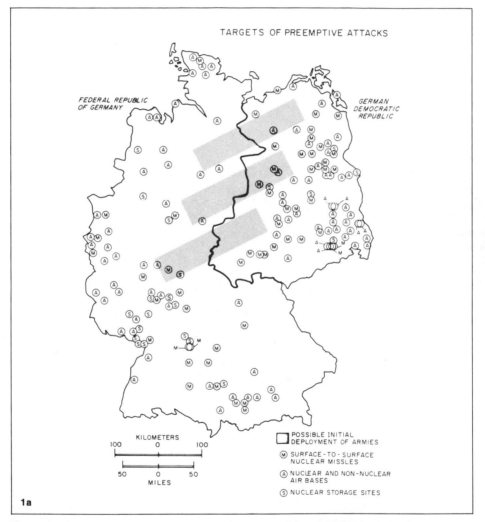

TARGETS OF PREEMPTIVE ATTACKS

FEDERAL REPUBLIC OF GERMANY

GERMAN DEMOCRATIC REPUBLIC

KILOMETERS
100   0   100

50   0   50
MILES

☐ POSSIBLE INITIAL DEPLOYMENT OF ARMIES

Ⓜ SURFACE-TO-SURFACE NUCLEAR MISSLES

Ⓐ NUCLEAR AND NON-NUCLEAR AIR BASES

Ⓢ NUCLEAR STORAGE SITES

1a

Figure 1 a. The locations of 92 military airbases in the Germanies are indicated by the circles containing the symbol "A", 56-surface-to-surface missile sites by a circle with an "M", and 24 known and inferred nuclear weapons storage depots by a circle with an "S". These are the assumed targets of the preemptive attacks discussed in the text. The area of each circle is 180 square kilometers, the estimated equivalent "area of death" below a 200 kiloton warhead exploded at an altitude of 2 kilometers.

The shaded rectangles show the sizes of the areas which might be covered in a confrontation along the border by three Soviet Armies and the opposing NATO forces. Battlefield nuclear weapons would be used against the forces in such areas.

known or inferred nuclear weapons storage depots. Military airfields which are not known to host nuclear armed aircraft during peacetime are included in this list because history suggests that, under crisis conditions, nuclear armed aircraft would be dispersed for their protection to all military airfields and probably to some civilian airfields as well. During the Cuban missile crisis, for example, some US strategic bombers were even dispersed to major metropolitan airports.

All of the targets shown in Figure 1a could, of course, be attacked with non-nuclear weapons but with much less assurance of success than could be achieved with a nuclear attack. Storage sites for nuclear weapons and their delivery vehicles, as well as airbases and many support facilities, have been "hardened" against attack by conventional explosives. Furthermore, important installations are defended against bomber attack by surface-to-air missiles, anti-aircraft guns and fighter air-

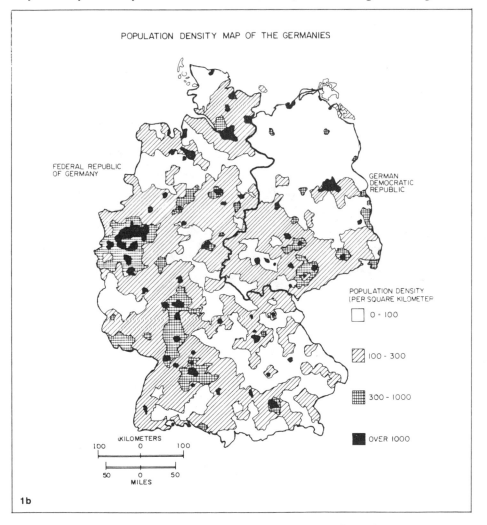

POPULATION DENSITY MAP OF THE GERMANIES

FEDERAL REPUBLIC
OF GERMANY

GERMAN
DEMOCRATIC
REPUBLIC

POPULATION DENSITY
(PER SQUARE KILOMETER

0 - 100

100 - 300

300 - 1000

OVER 1000

KILOMETERS
100   0   100

50   0   50
MILES

1b

Figure 1b. The pattern of population density in the two Germanies.

169

craft (5). The ballistic missiles which would probably be used to penetrate these defenses are equipped exclusively with nuclear warheads.

It is likely that an attacker would try to eliminate the reconnaissance and communications systems of the enemy and try to destroy his air defenses and command facilities at the beginning of a preemptive attack. Nevertheless, in describing the smallest plausible preemptive attack, we have excluded as targets: radar early warning sites, high level headquarters, communication centers, and the locations of air defense missiles. We have also excluded 38 nuclear-capable artillery unit locations from the preemptive attack because the short range (less than 30 kilometers) of such weapons limits the area which they can immediately threaten.

The Attacking Weapons. The nuclear weapons which are committed for use in an attack against fixed targets in Europe include approximately 2500 warheads on short to medium range missiles plus the

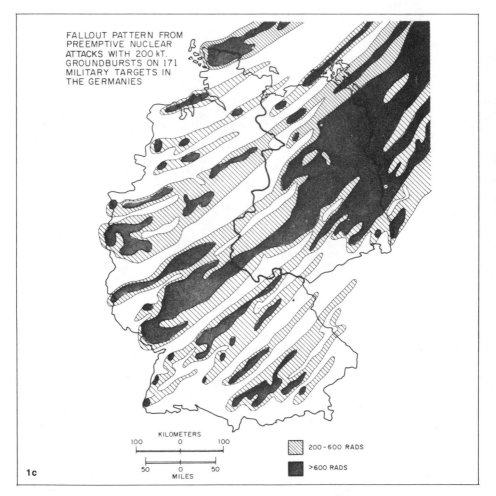

Figure 1c. The fallout pattern, given "typical June winds," for an attack against the targets shown in Figure 1a with surface-burst 200 kiloton weapons.

170

bombs carried by an estimated 2 500 nuclear-capable fighter-bomber aircraft and medium range bombers. These delivery vehicles are located in Europe, the United States, the Soviet Union, and the waters surrounding Europe (see Appendix II). The number of nuclear weapons and delivery vehicles on each side is so large that, even if a preemptive attack by one side against the other throughout Europe were 90 percent successful, the attacked side would retain enough nuclear weapons to execute a symmetrical counter-attack without resorting to strategic weapons.

The estimated yields of the warheads on the short to medium range delivery vehicles targeted on Europe range from one to over one thousand kilotons (a nuclear weapon with a one kiloton yield produces a blast equivalent to the explosion of one thousand tons of TNT). For simplicity, we will assume that all weapons used on the targets shown in Figure 1a have a yield of 200 kilotons. This is close to the yield of 150 kilotons which is ordinarily assumed for each of the three warheads on new Soviet SS-20 missiles. It is also the yield of each of the three Polaris warheads on Britain's ballistic missile submarines. (These submarines are under NATO control.) It is considerably more than the 40–50 kilotons which is the estimated yield of each of the 400 Poseidon warheads which the US has committed to NATO but it is also considerably less than the 1 100 kiloton yield of the most powerful weapons carried by NATO bombers and fighter bombers. In short, it seems a reasonable mid-range choice.

The Weapons Effects. A principal determinant of the "collateral" effects of the explosion of a nuclear warhead is whether or not it is exploded close enough to the ground to cause local fallout.

If a 200 kiloton warhead were exploded at an altitude greater than about one half kilometer, the nuclear fireball would not touch the ground and therefore would create relatively little local fallout. At or above such an altitude it would still be possible to maximize the areas covered by overpressures up to about 15 atmospheres (6). Missiles and aircraft could be destroyed by much less overpressure than this. Conceivably, therefore, preemptive attacks in the Germanies might involve relatively few bursts at low enough altitudes to result in local fallout. However, if the attacker wished, for example, to make an airport unusable by cratering its runways or by blanketing it with intense fallout— both options are discussed in the military literature (7)—then lower altitude or surface bursts would be used. The predictability and relative immunity to countermeasures of contact fuses, could also introduce a strong bias in favor of surface bursts (8). In the 1980 NATO "Square Leg" exercise, which involved a hypothetical nuclear attack on strategic and other targets in the United Kingdom, it was assumed that most "time urgent" military targets would be attacked by *both* surface burst and air burst weapons (9).

Surface Bursts: A 200 kiloton surface burst would pulverize and vaporize vast amounts of soil and rock. A considerable amount of this material would mix with the radioactive fission products from the explosion and be carried by the rising fireball to a height of about 10 kilometers. In the following hours, the larger particles in the resulting cloud of radioactive dust would filter back to the surface creating a swath of radioactive "local" fallout—typically stretching for hundreds of kilometers downwind from the explosion. Figure 2 shows contours of radiation dose for such a swath while Figure 1c shows the summed effects of 200 kiloton groundbursts landing on the targets shown in Figure 1a. Both patterns were calculated assuming "typical June day" wind conditions (10, 11). These conditions are highly simplified in that the wind speed (which is about 50 kilometers per hour averaged from the earth's surface

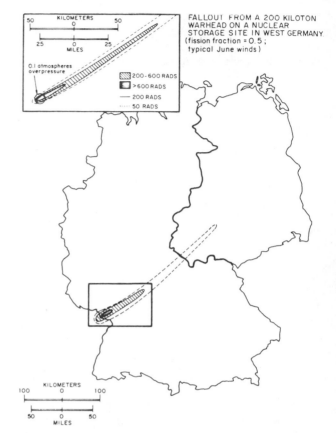

FALLOUT FROM A 200 KILOTON
WARHEAD ON A NUCLEAR
STORAGE SITE IN WEST GERMANY.
(fission fraction = 0.5;
typical June winds)

KILOMETERS
50   0   50

25   0   25
        MILES

0.1 atmospheres
overpressure

▨ 200-600 RADS
▩ >600 RADS
— 200 RADS
···· 50 RADS

**Figure 2. The fallout pattern
for one of the 171 weapons
whose summed effects are
shown in Figure 1c.**

KILOMETERS
100   0   100

50   0   50
        MILES

to the 10-kilometer cloud height) and wind directions are assumed to remain constant, rainfall is assumed to be absent, and the effects on the wind of hills and mountains are ignored. If these oversimplifications were corrected, a much more complex fallout pattern would result. Also, of course, the winds of one day are quite different from those of another. Our calculated fallout patterns are therefore merely indicative of the magnitudes of the areas which would be covered by fallout at various levels of intensity.

The contours in Figures 1c and 2 measure the peak level of radiation damage at the time when the intensity of the fallout radiation field has declined to the level where the rate of biological repair exceeds that of further biological damage. This damage, the "equivalent residual dose"

(ERD), is measured by the equivalent dose of radiation in units of "rads" of a single short burst of gamma radiation which would cause an equal amount of biological damage. Deaths from radiation illness would begin to occur at equivalent doses of less than 200 rads and, in the absence of access to hospital facilities, few people would survive for much more than two months after receiving equivalent doses greater than about 600 rads (see Figure 3) (12, 13). Persons spending most of their time indoors would have radiation doses only about one third as large as those shown in Figures 1c and 2. Persons able to find and stay in below-ground basements for periods on the order of one month would accumulate radiation doses only about one tenth as large.

Sheltering would be especially important for dose reduction in the early period immediately after fallout began to arrive. Twenty kilometers downwind from the 200 kiloton nuclear explosion, more than one half of the dose shown in Figure 2 would accrue in the first eight hours of exposure. Unfortunately, this is just the period during which much of the population might be caught on the roads trying to evacuate, searching for missing children, or trying to equip a basement for a lengthy stay.

For that part of the population away from areas affected by blast and fire and who had access to shelter in basements, conditions would still be quite grim. This sheltered population would be confined mostly to cramped quarters, without adequate ventilation or sanitary arrangements, without adequate supplies of uncontaminated water and food, and would often have its resistance to disease reduced by significant radiation doses.

With no access to medical help, it is quite likely that the level of serious illness and illness-caused deaths would increase more rapidly with dose than indicated in

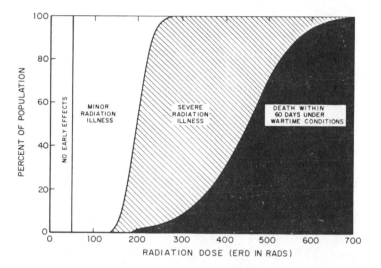

Figure 3. The expected early (within two months) outcome from radiation illness for populations exposed to various levels of radiation from fallout. Reference 6 (pp. 583–584) describes the development of severe radiation illness in the 200–1000 rad dose range as follows:
"The initial symtoms are . . . nausea, vomiting, diarrhea, loss of appetite and malaise . . . After the first day or two the symptoms disappear and there may be a latent period of several days to 2 weeks . . . Subsequently there is a return of symptoms, including diarrhea and a steplike rise in temperature which may be due to accompanying infection . . . Commencing about 2 or 3 weeks after exposure, there is a tendency to bleed into various organs, and small hemorrhages under the skin . . . are observed . . . Particularly common are spontaneous bleeding in the mouth and from the lining of the intestinal tract. There may be blood in the urine due to bleeding in the kidney . . . [These effects are due to radiation induced] defects in the blood-clotting mechanism . . . Loss of hair, which is a prominent consequence of radiation exposure, also starts after about 2 weeks . . . Susceptibility to infection of wounds, burns, and other lesions, can be a serious complicating factor [due to] loss of the white blood cells, and a marked depression in the body's immunological process. For example ulceration about the lips may commence after the latent period and spread from the mouth through the entire gastrointestinal tract in the terminal stage of the sickness . . . ."

Figure 3 (14). Under these circumstances, many members of the sheltered population would have strong desires to leave the shelters early and search for help. Unfortunately, few would have adequate information to estimate the risks associated with leaving their shelters or information as to where help might be found—if at all.

Air Bursts: For a 200 kiloton weapon exploded at a high enough altitude to avoid local fallout, the area of destruction would be determined primarily by the effects of the blast wave and by the flash of light and heat from the fireball (15). In Figure 4 we show the areas exposed at different levels to the heat and blast wave from a 200 kiloton nuclear warhead exploded at an altitude of 2 kilometers.

The inner circle on Figure 4 has an area of approximately 80 square kilometers (30 square miles). Here, the experience in Hiroshima indicates that the collapse of buildings would crush and trap most of the population and that most of those trapped would die in the subsequent fires. For those outdoors or indoors near windows, the danger of being crushed and trapped would be less—but there would be greater danger of injury or death from shards of glass and other projectiles and from burns due to the flash of the fireball. Many fires would be started by the heat of the fireball and additional fires might be started by sparks and pilot lights igniting leaking gaseous and liquid fuels and other flammable materials in the wreckage caused by the blast. In Hiroshima many fires merged about 20 minutes after the explosion into a firestorm and completely burned an area corresponding, for the yield of the Hiroshima bomb (12.5 kilotons) to that of the inner circle in Figure 4 (16).

Over the area of the outer circle the effects would be somewhat less intense with the level of destruction declining as the outer boundary was approached. Even at a distance of 10 kilometers, however, the fireball would cover an area of the sky more than 100 times larger than the sun

174

and the associated flash would be correspondingly brighter (17).

Figure 5 gives a more detailed representation of the probability of being killed or injured as a function of distance from ground zero for populations in various locations: outdoors near buildings, indoors but above ground, in basements, and in reinforced basement shelters. The results shown are based on a model developed by Phillip Sonntag (18). Naturally, models of this type involve considerable uncertainties due to the small data base and the variability in the numerous factors that determine the severity of blast or fire effects. This particular model assumes a surprisingly small reduction in risk associated with being in basement shelters. The reason given is that, close to the point under the nuclear explosion ("ground zero"), the overpressures would be great enough to crush even reinforced basement ceilings. Further out, where basement ceilings could survive the overpressure, the people underneath would still frequently be trapped by the debris above and would therefore be unable to escape the effects of the subsequent fires.

The consequences. Sonntag assumes that the population would have some warning of an imminent nuclear attack and that most would seek refuge in basements (75 percent in ordinary basements, and 5 percent in reinforced basements). He assumes that, of the remaining 20 percent of the population, half would be indoors above ground and half outdoors. Clearly there is no definite area such that people within it would die and people outside would not. As Figure 5 shows, the probability of death decreases to zero over a large radius. However, one may select a radius so that the number of people dying outside that area equals the number who survive inside the area. That radius determines the equivalent "area of death" in the present context. With the population sheltered as assumed by Sonntag, a single 200 kiloton airburst would kill the equivalent of the population of 180 square kilometers (70 square miles). This corresponds to the area of a circle 15 kilometers (9 miles) in diameter which would fall half way between the inner and outer circles in Figure 4. The circles in Figure 1a show this equivalent "area of death" around each of the targets of the hypothetical preemptive attacks. Together they cover almost ten percent of the area of the two Germanies. These could, therefore, hardly be called "surgical" strikes.

Figure 1b shows the population distribution of the Germanies (19). Their com-

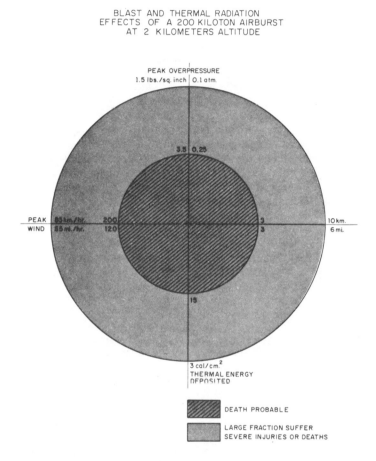

BLAST AND THERMAL RADIATION
EFFECTS OF A 200 KILOTON AIRBURST
AT 2 KILOMETERS ALTITUDE

PEAK OVERPRESSURE
1.5 lbs./sq. inch | 0.1 atm.

3.5 | 0.25

PEAK   85 km./hr.   200 | 3   10 km.
WIND   55 mi./hr.   120 | 3   6 mi.

15

3 cal/cm^2
THERMAL ENERGY
DEPOSITED

DEATH PROBABLE

LARGE FRACTION SUFFER
SEVERE INJURIES OR DEATHS

Figure 4. Blast and thermal radiation intensities at 5 and 10 kilometers from the point on the surface beneath a 200 kiloton explosion at 2 kilometers altitude. Blast damage results from the combined effects of peak overpressure (which at 0.25 atmospheres would exert a force equal to the weight of 2.5 metric tons per square meter) and the drag of the wind accompanying the blast shock wave. The thermal radiation would cause burns on exposed areas of skin (ranging from first degree burns for a deposited energy of about 3 calories per square centimeter to third degree burns at about 9 cal/cm^2) and would set fire to various materials (leaves at about 5 cal/cm^2, clothes and curtains at about 15 cal/cm^2, etc.) (See Reference 6.) In an environment of broken gas lines and spilled fuels of various types, a conflagration and possibly a firestorm would ensue.

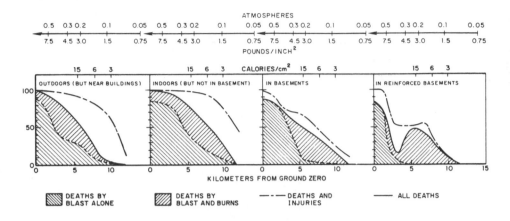

EFFECTS OF A 200 KILOTON EXPLOSION AT 2 KILOMETERS ALTITUDE (SONNTAG'S MODEL)

Figure 5. The probabilities of death and injury (according to a model put forward in Reference 13) as a function of distance from the point on the surface ("ground zero") beneath a 200 kiloton warhead exploded at 2 kilometers (1.2 miles) altitude. It will be seen that, within a radius of 5 kilometers, the probability of death by blast or burns is high—even for a population sheltered in residential basements. Outdoors the hazard from burns is associated primarily with direct exposure to the fireball. Indoors the hazard is due primarily with being trapped inside a collapsed building which subsequently burns.

bined population is about 76 million (59 million in West Germany and 17 million in East Germany). Their population density averages about 200 persons per square kilometer overall and about 3 000 persons per square kilometer in large urban areas. A 200-kiloton airburst would therefore kill about 40 000 people in an area of average population density and about 500 000 in an average urban area. For comparison, the 12.5 kiloton airburst over Hiroshima killed about 70 000 persons and seriously injured approximately the same number (20).

The area of death from blast and heat associated with a ground burst would be somewhat less than for an airburst but there would be additional casualties downwind due to the associated fallout. As noted above, Figure 1c shows our calculated distribution of fallout radiation doses in the Germanies associated with surface bursts on each of the targets shown in Figure 1a—given the winds of "a typical June day."

In order to estimate the casualties which would result in the affected areas shown in Figures 1a and 1c, it is necessary to take into account the population densities in each target and fallout area. At the time of this writing, we have not completed this task. The results of calculations done by Sonntag (13) for West Germany will serve, however, to indicate ranges within which our results will likely fall.

Sonntag's results, shown in Figure 6, were derived as follows: The area of West Germany was divided into squares 10 kilometers on a side. High and low estimates of the number of casualties which would result from the explosion of a given number (N) of airbursts were then calculated by assuming respectively that they were exploded over the (N) least densely and (N) most densely populated squares of West Germany.

For the 86 two hundred kiloton airbursts over West Germany assumed in our minimal preemptive attack, the dashed curves in Figure 6 show between 0.5 and about 10 million fatalities. Since the average population density of East Germany is comparable to that of West Germany (160

176

vs. 240 per square kilometer), it is reasonable to assume a similar range of fatalities for the same sized preemptive attack on that nation. The total number of fatalities in the Germanies following a preemptive attack using 200 kiloton airbursts would therefore lie somewhere in the range 1–20 million. A comparison of Figures 1a and 1b shows that many of the targets are in densely populated areas. As a result, the number of fatalities for a preemptive attack on these targets would be many

times greater than Sonntag's lower limit, *ie*, many millions. In addition, similar numbers of individuals would be severely injured (21).

Sonntag also calculated ranges for the numbers of the deaths and injuries which would result from varying numbers of groundbursts in West Germany, using the same approach outlined above for airbursts. The upper two curves on Figure 6 show that in this case it was estimated that 2–20 million people or up to 30 percent of

FATALITIES FROM A
NUCLEAR ATTACK ON WEST GERMANY

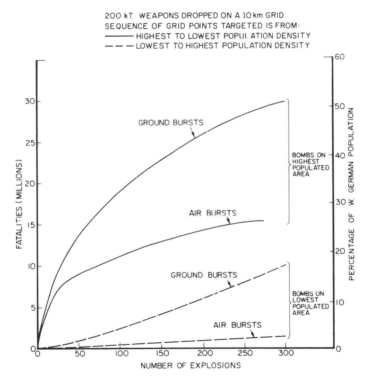

200 kT WEAPONS DROPPED ON A 10 km GRID
SEQUENCE OF GRID POINTS TARGETED IS FROM:
———— HIGHEST TO LOWEST POPULATION DENSITY
— — — LOWEST TO HIGHEST POPULATION DENSITY

BASED ON SONNTAG (1970)

Figure 6. Maximum and minimum estimates from Reference 13 of the fatalities which would result from attacks on West Germany with 200 kiloton bombs as a function of the number of weapons. Both airburst (at an altitude of 0.7 km.) and surface burst were considered. For the fallout from the surface bursts, it was assumed that all the energy yield is due to fission and that winds of 20 kilometers per hour are blowing. The maximum (minimum) estimates of fatalities are obtained by assuming that the weapons are exploded in the N most (least) densely populated areas of the country. A spacing between explosions of at least 10 kilometers was assumed.

the population would die from the consequences of 86 two hundred kiloton groundbursts on West Germany—even assuming that 80 percent of the population was able to stay for weeks in basement fallout shelters. The total population of East Germany is only 17 million so that one would expect somewhat lower casualties from the same number of groundbursts in that country. The fallout fatalities in adjoining nations—Poland in particular—would, however, probably considerably raise the total.

Thus we have found that a preemptive nuclear attack using 200 kiloton weapons against the targets shown in Figure 1a would probably result in between 1 and 40 million fatalities in the Germanies and surrounding areas and a similar number of severely injured persons. It appears likely that more exact estimates will yield numbers in the middle of this range, ie, on the order of 10 million killed and a similar number seriously injured.

BATTLEFIELD USE OF NUCLEAR WEAPONS

The Targets. A preemptive nuclear attack against key nuclear and other military targets is one way in which a nuclear war might start in central Europe. Another possibility is that war would cross the nuclear threshold via the use of "battlefield" nuclear weapons—because one side in a confrontation limited to non-nuclear weapons was about to suffer a serious defeat or because the attacking side was not able to achieve its objective without the use of nuclear weapons. Both NATO and the Warsaw Pact have integrated into their armed forces thousands of nuclear warheads deliverable by artillery, aircraft, or short-range missiles. These weapons would be used against the ground forces of the opposing side, including nuclear capable units, tank concentrations, artillery batteries, field level military headquarters, and structures such as bridges (22).

The use of battlefield nuclear weapons would probably be authorized by the political authorities, initially at least, in "packages." According to NATO doctrines, all the warheads within a given package are intended to explode approximately simultaneously—both to maximize the shock effect and to create a "pause" for negotiations or force movements (23). A single nuclear warhead would, however, typically kill the crews of only a few tanks (see Box 3). It would, therefore, require hundreds of battlefield nuclear explosions to destroy a significant fraction of the 20 000 tanks which might be involved in a full scale battle between NATO and the Warsaw Pact in the Germanies (24).

Since a tank could drive across either East or West Germany in a single day, the use of tactical nuclear weapons could occur almost anywhere in the Germanies. In order to be specific, however, we show on Figure 1a, areas where these weapons might be used if the nuclear threshold were crossed while the battle was still raging at the border between the two nations. The rectangles spanning the border correspond to the areas where three Soviet armies in East Germany might confront NATO troops in West Germany (25). The size of these rectangles was chosen on the basis of the stylized descriptions of US and Soviet formations in US defense literature (26). Although the combined area of these three rectangles is 45 000 square kilometers, or one-eighth the combined areas of the two Germanies, they would contain only about one-half of the military forces deployed in those countries. The 60 kilometer widths of the rectangles are such that they almost cover the entire north-south section of boundary dividing the two Germanies. The depth of the nuclear battlefield on each side of the border, 125 kilometers, corresponds to the expected depth of deployment of the military units on which battlefield nuclear weapons would be delivered: by artillery at short range, and by missiles and aircraft at longer range (26).

Mobile artillery and missiles, due to their short range, would be concentrated near the "battlefields." (Figure 1a does not show the locations of nuclear capable artillery batteries).

The Attacking Weapons. The types of nuclear weapons which are designed only for battlefield use—low yield bombs, nuclear artillery shells, nuclear land mines, and short-range missiles—generally have explosive yield in the range of 0.1 to 100 kilotons of TNT equivalent. For simplicity, in the discussion below we will describe the consequences of their use in terms of the consequences of the use of a similar number of "enhanced radiation" or neutron warheads of one kiloton yield (see Appendix III).

The Weapons Effects. The area of destruction by blast for a one kiloton weapon exploded at the surface is 1–2 square kilometers. For nuclear weapons in this range of explosive yield, however, the area bathed by intense "direct" or "prompt" nuclear radiation (*ie* from the explosion itself, in distinction to the "indirect" or "delayed" radiation associated with fallout) exceeds the area affected by severe blast effects. In the case of a one kiloton enhanced radiation weapon, the effective "area of death" by radiation illness for exposed soldiers and civilians would be approximately 5 square kilometers (2 square miles).

The Consequences

In a war involving the use of battlefield nuclear weapons there would probably be both attempts to spare towns and a perceived necessity to attack some. Towns could be largely spared if the enemy were to be found in the countryside outside. However, much of the time that would not be the case. On average there is one populated place in the Germanies per 4 square kilometers, hence, the well known complaint of nuclear weapons officers in Europe: "The towns and villages in Germany are only 1–2 kilotons apart" (27).

Roads naturally pass through towns, so presumably would the tanks and convoys which would be the principal targets of battlefield nuclear weapons. In addition there is considerable discussion in the military literature of the possibility of both attackers and defenders using towns as protective cover (28). It would be difficult under these circumstances to use a large number of battlefield nuclear weapons without causing a great number of civilian deaths.

A reasonable estimate is that the net effect of all these countervailing pressures bearing on the targeting of battlefield nuclear weapons would be that the resulting casualties would accumulate as if the nuclear weapons were exploded over areas with an average population density of 200 persons per square kilometer. After multiplying by the 5 square kilometer "area of death" for a neutron bomb, this leads to the estimate that, in addition to the occupants of perhaps 0–15 armored vehicles, an average of about one thousand civilians would die from radiation illness as a result of each nuclear explosion. If one thousand nuclear weapons were used, the number of deaths could be on the order of one million. These people would suffer the various stages of radiation sickness for up to two months before they eventually died.

LONGER TERM EFFECTS

The use of one thousand small battlefield nuclear weapons in the Germanies could lead to the deaths of a million and the use of 170 larger nuclear weapons against fixed military targets would result in the deaths of perhaps ten million. Similar numbers of people would be seriously injured. What about the people who survived? What type of future could they look forward to?

After a nuclear war involving the explosion of hundreds to thousands of nuclear weapons in the Germanies, in Europe or worldwide, the survivors would not be as "lucky" as the survivors of Hiroshima and Nagasaki. The Hiroshima and Nagasaki bombs were exploded at great enough alti-

179

tudes so that there was little residual radioactive fallout and the cities were surrounded by a damaged but still functioning society which could supply them with medical treatment, food, and shelter. Perhaps most importantly, there was no fear of further bombings.

There is no experience of a modern society whose technical and social infrastructure has both broken down to the degree which would prevail in the Germanies following the preemptive attack which we have described and where there would be so little hope of outside help. And, with the recent emphasis on developing the capability of fighting a nuclear war lasting months or longer, it is not clear when the postwar struggle to survive could begin.

Most likely, the future would appear as described in the accompanying articles in which the consequences of a global nuclear war are dicussed. It is difficult to imagine that such a holocaust as we have described in the Germanies could be prevented from turning into a global nuclear conflagration.

CONCLUSION

Nuclear weapons are so terrible that their existence has a sobering ("deterrent") effect on leaders who might otherwise pursue military options. With nuclear weapons leaders can no longer dream that battles can be fought far from home. They must face the facts that no one is out of range and that the physical and human fabric of the social organizations which support them could easily be destroyed in a nuclear war. In this way, as Herbert York has stated, the "placing at risk of the entire future of the continent and its people" has bought "the current happy political stability in Europe" (29).

Unfortunately, while the catastrophic consequences of a deliberate attempt to destroy Eastern or Western Europe with nuclear weapons are generally understood, both sides are prepared to use nuclear weapons against "purely military" targets, if it is necessary to avoid defeat in a major conflict. Europe, however, is densely

180

populated; the intermixing of military and civilians is intimate; and the areas of death which would be caused by the use of even "small" battlefield nuclear weapons are very large. In this article it has been shown that, as a result, even the purely military use of nuclear weapons in Europe on any scale large enough to achieve militarily significant results would result in the unintentional deaths of many millions of civilians.

Political and military leaders must be made to understand, therefore, that, to the extent that they develop security policies which depend upon the use of nuclear weapons in Europe, they are committing themselves to a policy which involves the mass slaughter of civilians *no matter how purely military the nominal targets of attack!*

References and Notes

1. Sidney Drell and Frank von Hippel, "Limited Nuclear War," *Scientific American*, p 27 (November 1976).
2. See Desmond Ball, *Can Nuclear War Be Controlled?* (London International Institute for Strategic Studies) Adelphi Paper #169, 1981; and John Steinbruner, "Nuclear Decapitation" in *Foreign Policy*, Winter 1981–'82, p. 16.
3. See the discussion in US Senate Armed Services Committee Hearing, *Department of Defense Authorizations for Appropriations for Fiscal Year 1981*, Part 5, pp. 2827–2828, 3019.
4. US Senate Foreign Relations Committee and US House Committee on Foreign Relations, Joint Committee Print, *Fiscal Year 1981 Arms Control Impact Statements*, (May 1980) p. 243.
5. See reference 4, p. 235; and US Senate Armed Services Committee Hearing, *Department of Defense Authorizations for Appropriations for Fiscal Year 1981*, Part 3, p. 872.
6. US Departments of Defense and Energy, *The Effects of Nuclear Weapons*, 3rd edition (Samuel Glasstone and Philip J Dolan, eds. 1977), Fig. 3.73a.
7. See US Defense Intelligence Agency, *Physical Vulnerability Handbook: Nuclear Weapons* (AP-550-1-2-69-INT, revised 1976).
8. See Richard L Garwin, "Defense of Minuteman Silos Against ICBM Attack," reprinted in *Effects of Limited Nuclear Warfare*, Hearing before the Subcommittee on Arms Control, International Organizations and Security Agreements of the US Senate Committee on Foreign Relations, September 18, 1975, pp. 56–59.
9. Duncan Campbell, "World War III: An Exclusive Preview", in *Britain and the Bomb* (London, The New Statesman, NS Report #3, 1981) p. 65.
10. We have used the WSEG-10 Fallout Model which is used in US government assessments of fallout effects. This model is documented in Leo A

Schmidt, Jr., *Methodology of Fallout-Risk Assessment* (Washington, DC, Institute for Defense Analyses, Paper P-1065, 1975) and has been incorporated in a set of computer programs which are described by the same author in *Development of Civil Defense Damage Assessment Programs* (Washington, DC, Institute for Defense Analyses, Paper P-1526, 1980). We have adapted the program GUISTO to our needs.

The wind data used in this program are summarized in two sets of parameters: wind vectors averaged from ground level to the level from which the fallout is descending (10 kilometers for a 200 kiloton weapon); and a "wind shear" which provides a measure of the rate of change of the wind vector with height at that level. The wind vector determines the direction and the distance that the fallout is carried while the transverse wind shear determines the rate at which the fallout cloud grows in a direction transverse to the direction in which it is being carried.

11. Northern Hemisphere wind data for a "typical day" in each month of the year have been compiled by the Defense Communications Agency Command and Control Technical Center of the US Defense Department (unclassified tapes EA 275 and EB 275.)

12. Figure 3 is adapted from Figure 5.36–1 of reference 13.

13. Phillip Sonntag, "Matematische Analyse der Wirkungen von Kernwaffen Explosionen in der BRD," in *Kriegsfolgen und Kriegsverhutung*, (Carl Friedrich von Weizsacker, ed., Munich, Carl Hanser, 1971).

14. See the discussion by Herbert L Abrams, "Infection and Communicable Diseases," in *The Final Epidemic: Physicians and Scientists on Nuclear War* (Ruth Adams and Susan Cullen, eds., Chicago, University of Chicago Press, 1981), p. 192.

15. Because absorption by the atmosphere of neutrons and gamma rays is quite strong, the radii at which radiation doses from these forms of nuclear radiation exceed a given level, grow much more slowly than do the radii of blast and flash effects. For neutron radiation, for example, the distance at which the dose exceeds 100 rads only approximately doubles (from 1.1 to 2 kilometers) in going from a 1 kiloton fission weapon to a 200 kiloton thermonuclear weapon. The growth of the corresponding radius for gamma radiation is from 1.1 to 2.5 kilometers (reference 6, pp. 332–335, 345–348). As a result, while, for a one kiloton weapon, nuclear radiation has a larger lethal radius than blast or heat, the situation is reversed for a 200 kiloton weapon.

16. *Op cit* 6, pp. 300–304.

17. Figure 4 is based on material in reference 6—especially that on pp. 71, 115, 123, 178–184, 219, 291, 300–304, 554–555, 564.

18. *Op cit* 13, pp. 75–198. The minimum shown for the probability of death in a reinforced shelter at 3 kilometers reflects Sonntag's assumptions that, at that distance, the shelter would survive but that the debris above would be so flattened that it would not support an intense fire.

19. Figure 1b is derived from data given in: (West Germany) *Bevolkerung und Kultur, Reihe 1, Bevolkerungsstand und -entwicklung, 1969* (FGR, Statistisches Bundesamt, Wiesbaden, Verlag W Kohlhammer), and (East Germany) *Bevolkerungsstatistiches Jahrbuch der Deutschen Demokratischen*

Republik, *1977* (DDR, Staatliche Zentralverwaltung für Statistik).

20. *Op cit* 6, p. 544.

21. In calculating fatalities from airbursts, Sonntag assumed an altitude of burst of 700 meters for a 200 kiloton warhead, while the results shown in Figures 4 and 5 are for an airburst at an altitude of 2000 meters. Sonntag's casualty estimates for airbursts are therefore probably significantly smaller than we would calculate. On the other hand, in calculating the casualties which would result from the fallout from groundbursts, Sonntag assumed that 100 percent of the explosive yield of a 200 kiloton weapon would come from fission while, in Figures 1c and 2, we have made the more conventional assumption of 50 percent. This difference would tend to lower our estimate of casualties from fallout relative to those of Sonntag. In all fallout calculations, Sonntag assumed a constant 20 kilometer per hour wind blowing from south to north with a 0.3 kilometers per hour per kilometer altitude transverse wind shear, while we have used wind data at 5 altitudes at each of 9 points spaced on an approximately 400 kilometer grid over and around the Germanies to construct an interpolated wind field for a "typical June day" (see note 11). The median wind (averaged from ground level to 10 kilometers) for this day is about 50 kilometers per hour and the median transverse wind shear is about 0.36 kilometers per hour per kilometer altitude.

22. "Critical combat units that might be targeted for nuclear strikes include the following:
(a) Nuclear capable units.
(b) Tanks and mechanized units.
(c) Conventional artillery units.
(d) Other units or locations such as command and control headquarters, nuclear supply points, or bridges."
[US Army, Staff Officers' Field Manual, *Nuclear Weapons Employment Doctrine and Procedures* (FM 101-31-1, 1977), p. 5.]

23. John P Rose, *The Evolution of US Army Nuclear Doctrine, 1945–1980* (Boulder, Colorado, Westview Press, 1980), p. 172.

24. Within the area of 5000–10000 square kilometers covered by one typical Soviet Army formation, the numbers of military equipment would include 3020 tanks, 2230 armored fighting vehicles, 930 artillery guns, and 425 air defense weapons. This considerable amount of military equipment gives some insight into the number of neutron weapons which might be used in an attempt to immobilize it. See US Senate Armed Services Committee, *Department of Defense Authorizations for Appropriations for Fiscal Year 1981, Part 5*, pp. 3054–3060.

25. John M Collins, *US—Soviet Military Balance, Concepts and Capabilities, 1960–1980*, (New York, McGraw-Hill Publications, 1980) pp. 311, 315.

26. See the discussion in reference 24.

27. Based on the numbers of names of populated places listed in US Board of Geographic Names, Gazetteer Numbers 47 (*Germany—Federal Republic and West Berlin*, 1960) and 43 (*Germany—Soviet Zone and East Berlin*, 1959).

28. See Paul Bracken, "Urban Sprawl and NATO Defense," in *Survival* Vol. 18, #6, p. 254 (1976); and "Collateral Damage and Theatre Warfare," *ibid.* Vol. 22, #5, p. 203 (1980).

29. Herbert York, "The Nuclear 'Balance of Terror' in Europe," *Ambio* **4**, 203 (1975).

APPENDIX I. TARGETS FOR NUCLEAR WAR IN THE GERMANIES

	Number of targets		Hardness
	West Germany	East Germany	
A. NUCLEAR THREAT			
* Surface-to-surface missile sites	23	33	low-moderate
* Nuclear air bases	9	8[a]	low-moderate
Nuclear artillery battalions	38	0	low
* Nuclear storage sites	18[a]	6	moderate-intermediate
	88	47	
B. OTHER MILITARY			
National/International hq.	12	6	low
Command/Communications centers	31	13	moderate-intermediate
Army/Corps/Division hq.	31	34	low
* Air bases (non nuclear)	37	40[a]	low-moderate
Naval bases	7	8	low
Ground forces bases	256	137	low
Radar/Early warning sites	21	10	low
Surface-to-air missile sites	90	100	low
Munitions/Petroleum storage areas	75	63	moderate
Logistic installations	27	15	low-moderate
Chemical storage sites	1	6	moderate-intermediate
	588	432	
TOTAL	676	479	

* Targets attacked in our scenario for a preemptive attack.
[a] At the time of this writing we have not obtained the coordinates of one of these sites. An attack on it is therefore not shown on either Figures 1a or 1c.

Sources for Table: The numbers of targets were derived by counting known locations and infer-ring additional locations via analysis of force structure and military organizations. While specific numbers may be inaccurate, the ratio of targets in each class and on each side are thought to be accurate enough to represent the nature of the military presence in the two countries. Estimates of target hardness were derived from the US Departments of Defense and Energy, *The Effects of Nuclear Weapons*, 3rd Edition, (Samuel Glasstone and Philip J Dolan, eds., Washington, DC, US Government Printing Office, 1977).

The theory of nuclear deterrence, as practiced by the superpowers, requires not only that they be able to destroy each other's societies, but that they also be able to use nuclear weapons against purely military targets should the nu-clear threshold be crossed (1). As nu-clear weapons delivery systems have be-come lower yield, more diverse, flexi-ble, and accurate, so that they are effective against particular targets with less (but still enormous) damage to the surrounding civilian society, the list of military targets against which nuclear weapons could be used has become steadily longer. The Table in this Appen-

dix categorizes more than 1 100 sites in the Germanies which have been desig-nated by military authorities as appr-opriate targets for nuclear weapons.

Much more is known about NATO's nuclear targeting plans in Europe than those of the Warsaw Pact but NATO's plans are probably indicative of the thinking on both sides. NATO's "Nu-clear Operations Plan" includes two attack plans: the "priority strike plan" and the "tactical strike plan" (2). The priority strike plan includes the "nu-clear threat targets" which are targets which are assumed in the preemptive attack scenario discussed here.

The tactical strike plan includes other military and urban industrial installations.

The targets for nuclear weapons in Europe are much "softer" than the underground silos in which intercontinental ballistic missiles are housed. These silos are designed to withstand overpressures of 140 to 400 atmospheres. Virtually all of the targets listed on the Table would be destroyed by overpressures of less than 20 atmospheres and most of them (*eg* aircraft and above ground military office buildings) would be destroyed by "low" overpressures (less than 0.3 atmospheres for equipment disablement, up to one atmosphere for essentially complete destruction). The hardest targets in Europe are probably buried and partially buried structures with steel reinforced concrete arches which occur at nuclear weapons storage sites and some command centers. These might require "intermediate" overpressures (less than 15 atmospheres overpressure for disablement and up to 20 for destruction). The remaining targets would require overpressures falling in the "moderate" range (less than 3 atmospheres for disablement and up to 4 atmospheres for destruction).

Because of the superior accuracy of delivery vehicles such as the Pershing II and cruise missiles which have been proposed by NATO for deployment in Western Europe and the relative softness of their targets, the warheads which would be deployed on these vehicles have yields in the tens rather than in the hundreds of kilotons range. Many of the targets listed in the Table are spread over considerable areas, however, and therefore may continue to require large yields for their destruction.

References and Notes

1. Targeting and target categories are discussed in: Ball, Desmond, "Counterforce Targeting: How New? How Viable?" *Arms Control Today*, February 1981; Geoffrey Kemp, *Nuclear Forces for Medium Powers: Part 1; Targets and Weapons Systems* (London: Institute for Strategic Studies, Adelphi Paper #106, 1974); US Congress, Senate Armed Services Committee Hearing, *Department of Defense Authorizations for Appropriations for Fiscal Year 1980*, Part 3, p. 871; and US Congress, Senate Armed Service Committee Hearing, *Department of Defense Authorizations for Appropriations for Fiscal Year 1981*, Part 5, p. 2721.
2. NATO's strike plans are discussed in US Congressional Budget Office, *Planning US General Purpose Forces: The Theater Nuclear Forces* (Washington, DC, US Government Printing Office, January 1977).

APPENDIX II. NUCLEAR WEAPONS COMMITTED FOR USE IN EUROPE

The listing in the Table which comprises Appendix II indicates that both NATO and the Warsaw Pact have a great enough diversity of nuclear weapons and delivery vehicles to assure themselves that they will always have a "nuclear option" available for virtually any contingency (1). The warhead explosive yields range from as little as 0.01 kilotons for some nuclear land mines to 1 100 kilotons for some bombs.

Almost all the missiles or aircraft listed in the Table could be used in the preemptive attack discussed in the main text. Missiles have the greatest probability of reaching their targets (there is no defense today against incoming missiles) but they are generally less accurate than nuclear bombs and must be pre-targeted. The best indication of which weapons would actually be used in a preemptive attack is the weapons which are kept constantly on alert. These are indicated in the Table. NATO has approximately 580 warheads on constant alert in Europe (2), but the number that the Warsaw Pact has on alert is unknown.

Artillery and pre-positioned land mines could be used in addition to ballistic missiles and aircraft for the delivery of nuclear weapons on the battlefield. On the NATO side, neutron warheads are being produced for delivery by both artillery and the short-range Lance missiles.

References and Notes

1. Comprehensive discussions of the nuclear weapons in Europe appear in Jeffrey Record, *US Nuclear Weapons in Europe: Issues and Alternatives* (Washington, DC, The Brookings Institution, 1974); and Stockholm International Peace Research Institute, *Tactical Nuclear Weapons: European Perspectives* (London, Taylor & Francis, Ltd., 1978).
2. Our estimates of the NATO warheads on alert include 400 Poseidon submarine launched ballistic missile warheads, 48 Polaris submarine launched ballistic missile warheads, 45 Pershing missiles, 48 bombs on long range aircraft (F-111 and Vulcan bombers), and 40 bombs on medium range aircraft (F-4, F-104, Jaguar and Buccaneer fighter aircraft).

Weapons Class and Type	Number of Delivery Vehicles Deployed for Possible Use in the Germanies (as of 1/82)	Number of Warheads Per Delivery Vehicle × Estimated Yield (in kt)	Range (km)	Primary Uses
Ballistic Missiles				
Submarine Launched				
Polaris A3 (NATO)	64 (400 *warheads*)	3×200	4600	Pre-targeted, Portion on Alert
Poseidon C4 (NATO)		(10–14)×(40–50)	4500	Pre-targeted, Committed to NATO, on Alert.
Intermediate Range				
SS-20 (Warsaw Pact)	190	3×150	5000	Pre-targeted, Possibly on Alert
SS-4/SS-5 (WP)	255	1×1000	1900/4100	Pre-targeted, Possibly on Alert
Short Range				
Pershing 1A (NATO)	180[a]	1×(60–400)[b]	720	Pre-targeted and Battlefield Use, Portion on Alert.
SS-12 (WP)	65[a]	1×low kt	900	Pre-targeted, Possibly on Alert
SCUD (WP)	460[a]	1×low kt	150–450	Battlefield Use and Pre-targeted
Lance (NATO)	100[a]	1×(1–100)[b]	135	Battlefield Use.
FROG (WP)	120[a]	1×(1–10)	120	Battlefield Use.
Nuclear Capable Aircraft				
Long Range Bombers (NATO)	213	(≈2)×1–1100	1900–2800	Pre-targeted and Battlefield Use, Portion on Alert.
Long Range Bombers (WP)	500	(1–4)×low-high kt	1600–4025	Pre-targeted and Battlefield Use.
Medium Range Aircraft (NATO)	680	(1–2)×1–1100	720–950	Battlefield Use and Pre-targeted, Portion on Alert.
Medium Range Aircraft (WP)	1000	1×low-high kt	600–720	Battlefield Use and Pre-targeted
Other Weapons				
Artillery (NATO)	700	(av. ≈3)×<1–10	14–29	Battlefield Use.
Atomic Demolition Munitions (NATO)	300	1×<1–15	–	Battlefield Use and Pre-targeted

[a] Does not include reloads
[b] Variable yield

Sources: William M Arkin, "Nuclear Weapons in Europe: What are They, What are They For?", in *Disarming Europe* (Mary Kaldor and Dan Smith, eds., London; Merlin, 1982); and IISS, *The Military Balance, 1981–82* (London: International Institute for Strategic Studies, 1981). These and other sources differ in detail but not in the order of magnitude of the totals.

185

APPENDIX III. THE EFFECTS OF NEUTRON BOMBS

The attributes of nuclear weapons make them uniquely effective for destroying large area targets such as cities and industrial complexes. On the battlefield, however, the indiscriminate nature of these weapons has continually put their usability into question. This has led to an effort to design nuclear weapons which minimize "collateral damage" for a given level of military effectiveness. The most recent products of this effort are enhanced radiation warheads ("neutron bombs"). In the diagram we compare areas of radiation and blast effects of one of these weapons with those of an ordinary fission bomb which releases the same amount of energy (one thousand tons TNT equivalent) (1).

The larger lightly shaded circle indicates the area within which people not protected by thick shields of concrete or dirt could receive large enough doses of neutron and gamma radiation from the blast to result in death by radiation illness in the short term and cancer deaths in the longer term (2).

The smaller darker shaded circle indicates the area of the desired military effect: a radiation dose sufficient to render the occupants of tanks at most "partially effective" due to vomiting, diarrhea, and other radiation sickness symptoms during the hours to days before they died (3).

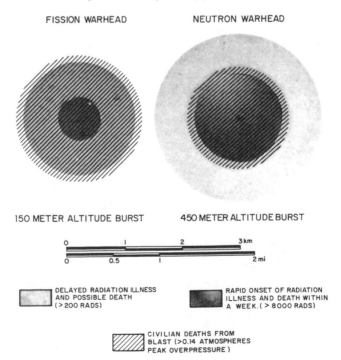

FISSION WARHEAD   NEUTRON WARHEAD

150 METER ALTITUDE BURST   450 METER ALTITUDE BURST

0   1   2   3 km
0   0.5   1   2 mi

DELAYED RADIATION ILLNESS AND POSSIBLE DEATH (>200 RADS)

RAPID ONSET OF RADIATION ILLNESS AND DEATH WITHIN A WEEK.(> 8000 RADS)

CIVILIAN DEATHS FROM BLAST (>0.14 ATMOSPHERES PEAK OVERPRESSURE)

Finally, the crosshatched area indicates the area subjected to blast sufficient to cause some fatalities among the above ground occupants of residential structures (greater than 0.14 atmospheres peak overpressure) (4).

It will be seen that the larger amount of radiation emitted by the neutron bomb increases the area of its military effect almost fourfold—to about 2 square kilometers (0.8 square miles). The larger radius of this military effect also makes it possible to explode the neutron warhead at a greater altitude, reducing the area of its blast damage somewhat. More important to any civilians in the environs, however, is likely to be the fact that the area covered by doses leading to longer term radiation illness and death is more than doubled—to 6 square kilometers (2.5 square miles) (5).

The expected density of tanks in an attack in the Germanies is a column or row in which the spacing would be 100 meters or greater (6). The average population density of the Germanies is about 200 per square kilometer. And the area of lingering civilian deaths following the explosion of a neutron bomb would be about three times that of prompt effects on tank crews. Given these facts and the likelihood that a large fraction of battlefield nuclear weapons would probably be mistargeted under the conditions which would prevail on a nuclear battlefield, a crude calculation suggests that there might be on the order of two hundred civilian deaths for every tank crew that is rendered "partially effective" by a neutron bomb, or a million civilian deaths per five thousand tank crews so affected.

References and Notes

1. This figure is based on a table of numbers given by S T Cohen in "Enhanced Radiation Warheads: Setting the Record Straight," *Strategic Review*, Winter 1978, p. 9, and on a figure in Samuel Glasstone and Phillip Dolan (eds), *The Effects of Nuclear Weapons*, 3rd Edition (US Departments of Defense and Energy, 1977), p. 115.
2. According to Glasstone and Dolan (Ibid, p. 583), "For doses between 200 and 1000 rems [rems equal rads for the present purpose] the probability of survival is good at the lower end of the range and poor at the upper end." Assuming a relative biological effectiveness for cancer induction of 10 for neutrons relative to X-rays, the likelihood of cancer death due to a 200 rad dose of neutron radiation would be 20 percent or greater. [US National Academy of Sciences, *The Effects on Populations of Exposure to Low Levels of Ionizing Radiation* (1980), pp. 141, 147].
3. US Army Field Manual, *Operations*, Chapter 10 "Tactical Nuclear Operations," p. 10-3 (FM 100-5, 1976).
4. Glasstone and Dolan (*op cit* 1 p. 180).
5. The military, however, compares the 1 kt neutron bomb to a 5-10 kt fission warhead which would have a comparable military effect. In this context the neutron bomb would exact a somewhat lower human toll.
6. See S T Cohen and W R Van Cleave, "Western European Collateral Damage from Tactical Nuclear Weapons," (*Royal United Services Institute (RUSI) Journal*, June 1976, p. 323).

GLOSSARY

Acronyms:
ALCM, GLCM,
ICBM, SLBM,
MIRV

ALCM: Air-launched Cruise missile.
GLCM: Ground-launched Cruise missile.
ICBM: Inter-continental ballistic missile.
SLBM: Submarine-launched ballistic missile.
MIRV: Multiple, independently-targetable re-entry vehicle; a method of delivering several warheads with a single rocket.

Circular error
probable (CEP)

A measurement of the accuracy of ballistic missiles. The radius of a circle drawn with the target at its centre within which a given missile has a 50 percent chance of landing. Some US inter-continental ballistic missiles now have a CEP of 350 meters; by 1985, a CEP of less than 100 meters may be possible.

Critical mass

The smallest mass of fissile material which will support a self-sustaining chain reaction, and hence a nuclear explosion. The amount varies with the material used, its purity, and the presence of materials which reflect neutrons back into the fissile material. The Nagasaki bomb used about eight kilos of plutonium, surrounded by reflecting material. For a bare sphere of pure ^{239}P in its densest form, the critical mass is about 10 kilos, which would be a sphere roughly the size of a grapefruit. If a suitable reflector is used, the critical mass is about 4.4 kilos, roughly the size of an orange. If a technique known as implosion is used to compress the mass about two kilos— roughly the size of a tennis ball—will cause a nuclear explosion. Since World War II the total global production of highly enriched uranium for nuclear weapons is estimated at about 1500 tons; the global production of plutonium in the same period is estimated at 150 tons.

Half life;
half residence
time;
biological half
life

Half life is the time required for half of the nuclides in a radioactive substance to undergo disintegration, and thus the time required for the level of radioactivity to be reduced by 50 percent. Half residence time is the time required for half of the radioactive particles in atmospheric fallout to return to earth. Biological half life is the time required for a substance (usually radioactive) contained in the body or in a particular organ to be decreased by half through natural biological processes.

LD-50

Lethal dose for 50 percent. The dose of radiation required to kill 50 percent of a given population within a specified period of time.

Measurements of radiation and its effects: roentgens, rads, rems and curies.

The *roentgen* (R) is the unit of ionizing radiation actually emitted (and thus of *exposure*) as measured by its ability to induce an electrical charge in a given quantity of air. The *rad* (roentgen absorbed dose) is a measurement of the effect of ionizing radiation (and thus of the *dose*) as measured in terms of the energy absorbed in tissue. Since this varies with both the type of radiation and the medium through which it passes, the relationship between the rad and the roentgen is not simple. For the gamma-rays likely to occur in nuclear warfare and for doses measured in air, 1 R = 0.87 rad; for water and soft tissues, 1 R = 0.96 rad. Different types of radiation produce different biological effects; the *rem* is the unit of dose equivalent designed to permit the effects of different types of radiation to be compared. One rem is assumed to be equivalent to one rad of the type of radiation (beta, gamma and X-rays) to be expected in nuclear warfare. The rate at which a given dose of radiation is received has an important bearing on its biological effects; the *dose rate* is measured in rads per unit of time. In describing the total burden of ionizing radiation on a large group of people, the *collective dose* (in man-rads) and *collective dose equivalent* (in man-rems) are used. The level of radioactivity of a given substance is measured in *curies* (Ci), which is defined in terms of the number of atomic transformations per unit of time. 1 Ci = 3.7×10^{10} transformations per second. An international system (SI) of units has also been developed. The SI unit of exposure is the *coulomb/kilogram*, (c/k), the amount of radiation required to induce a charge of one coulomb in one kilogram of air. 1 c/kg = 3876 R. The SI unit of dose is the *gray* (Gy), which is the absorption of one joule per kilogram of tissue. 1 Gy = 100 rads. The SI unit of dose equivalent is the *sievert* (Sv), also one joule per kilogram. 1 Sv = 100 rems. The SI unit of radioactivity is the *becquerel* (Bq) equal to one transformation per second; thus 1 Ci $= 3.7 \times 10^{10}$ Bq. 1 Bq $= 27$ pCi.

Megaton and kiloton

Measurements of the explosive power of nuclear weapons. One megaton (Mt) is defined as 4.187×10^{15} joules, or approximately the equivalent of one million tons of TNT. One kiloton (kt) is approximately equivalent to 1000 tons of TNT. The bomb dropped on Hiroshima yielded about 12.5 kt; the Nagasaki bomb yielded about 22 kt; all of the bombs dropped during the eight most violent years of the Vietnam War were the equivalent of approximately four Mt, the largest modern nuclear weapons yield about 20 Mt; the Soviet and US arsenals combined contain about 12 000 Mt.

Overpressure

The increase above normal atmospheric pressure of the blast wave from a nuclear explosion. For a 1 Mt explosion, the overpressure in a circle with a radius of 1.5 miles from ground zero would be more than 20 psi, sufficient to destroy reinforced concrete buildings and giving rise to winds in excess of 800 km per hour.

Tactical nuclear weapons; theatre nuclear weapons; strategic nuclear weapons

Tactical nuclear weapons generally have a relatively short range (less than 100 km) and relatively small yields. Strategic weapons have long ranges and large yields. US and Soviet intercontinental ballistic missiles have ranges of more than 10 000 km. Theatre weapons are medium range and medium yield. The distinctions between the three, never sharp, have become blurred with the development of new weapon systems like the US Pershing II and Cruise missile, the Soviet SS-20, and so-called Euro-strategic missiles.

191

NOTES ON AUTHORS

WILLIAM A ARKIN is a military analyst with the Institute for Policy Studies in Washington, DC. He has been an intelligence analyst with the US Army in Berlin and a senior staff member of the Center for Defense Information. His areas of expertise include military organization and infrastructure, nuclear weapons, and military research and analysis. Mr Arkin has a Bachelor of Science Degree in Government and Politics from the University of Maryland (European Division) and is a graduate in National Security Studies at Georgetown University (MA). He is the author of *Research Guide to Current Military and Strategic Affairs* (Washington, DC: IPS, 1981) and numerous articles on military issues. He is completing a book on *Nuclear War in Europe.* His address: Institute for Policy Studies, 1901 Q Street NW, Washington DC 20009, USA.

FRANK BARNABY is guest Professor of Peace Studies, Free University, Amsterdam, and Consultant to the Stockholm International Peace Research Institute (SIPRI). Between 1971 and 1981 he was the Director of SIPRI; earlier he was the Executive Secretary of the Pugwash Conference on Science and World Affairs, a research nuclear physicist at University College, London, and worked at the Atomic Weapons Research Establishment, Aldermaston. He is the author of *Man and the Atom, The Nuclear Age,* and *Prospects for Peace,* and has written or edited numerous books and articles on disarmament issues and military technology. His address: Brandreth, Station Road, Chilbolton, Stockbridge, Hants SO20 6AW, England.

JOHN W BIRKS is Associate Professor in the Department of Chemistry and Fellow of the Cooperative Institute for Research in Environmental Sciences (CIRES) at the University of Colorado, Boulder, Colorado, USA. He earned his Ph D in chemistry at the University of California, Berkeley. His principal research interest is reaction kinetics. His address: Department of Chemistry and Cooperative Institute for Research in Environmental Sciences, Campus Box 449, University of Colorado, Boulder, Colorado 80309, USA.

ERNEST A BONDIETTI is the Research Manager of the Toxic Substances Program, Environmental Sciences Division, at Oakridge, Tennessee. He obtained his Ph D in soil science from the University of California (Riverside). His research interests include environmental biogeochemistry with a specialization in the artificial radioactive elements: Plutonium, Americium, Neptunium and Technetium. He has also conducted studies of these elements in groundwater to assist both siting and safety assessment requirements for the development of high-level radioactive waste repositories. His address: Toxic Substances Program, Environmental Sciences Division, Oakridge National Laboratory, Oakridge, Tennessee 37830, USA.

EVGENI I CHAZOV is a medical doctor and the deputy Minister of Health of the USSR. He is also Director-General of the National Cardiology Research Centre and a member of the Presidium of the Soviet

Academy of Sciences. His address: USSR Academy of Medical Sciences, Zagorodnoe shosse 2, Moscow, USSR.

JOHN E COGGLE, MSc, PhD, is senior lecturer in radiation biology at the University of London in St Bartholomew's Hospital Medical School and the author of a standard textbook on radiation biology. His address: Department of Radiobiology, The Medical College of St Bartholomew's Hospital, Charterhouse Square, London EC1M 6BQ, UK.

PAUL J CRUTZEN has been Director of the Air Chemistry Division of the Max Planck Institute for Chemistry in Mainz, Germany, since July 1980. Prior to that he was Director of the Air Quality Division of the National Center for Atmospheric Research in Boulder, Colorado, USA. He obtained his doctorate in meteorology at the University of Stockholm. His main research interest is the study of the role of air chemistry in biogeochemical cycles. His address: Max Planck Institute for Chemistry, Box 3060, D-6500 Mainz, Federal Republic of Germany.

FRANK VON HIPPEL is a senior research physicist at Princeton University's Center for Energy and Environmental Studies. He received his doctorate in theoretical physics from Oxford University in 1962 and did research in elementary particle physics until 1973. His book, *Advice and Dissent: Scientists in the Political Arena,* co-authored with Joel Primack, was published in 1974. Since that time his research has related primarily to problems of energy policy including: reactor safety, the narrowing gap between civilian and military nuclear technologies, and the energy inefficiency of automobiles. In 1976 von Hippel co-authored with Sidney Drell an article in *Scientific American* on the consequences of "limited" nuclear wars between the superpowers. He is currently the elected chairman of the Federation of American Scientists. His address: Center for Energy and Environmental Studies, Princeton University, Princeton, New Jersey 08544, USA.

HOWARD W HJORT is president of Economic Perspectives, Inc, a food and agriculture consulting firm. Previously he was economic advisor to the US Secretary of Agriculture (from 1977 to 1981) and vice-president and partner in a Washington DC economic consulting firm. He also served with the Ford Foundation in India, and with the US Department of Agriculture. He completed his undergraduate and graduate training in agricultural economics at Montana State University and North Carolina State University. His address: c/o Economic Perspectives Inc., 6723 Whittier Avenue, Suite 101, McLean, Virginia 22101, USA.

YVES LAULAN is the Chief Economist at Société Générale, the largest French bank. He also teaches at the Institut d'Etudes Politiques de Paris. In addition, M. Laulan is a corresponding editor of Newsweek Magazine, an editor with Hachette Publications and a regular lecturer at the Institut des Hautes Etudes de Défense Nationale et Ecole Supérieure de Guerre in Paris. From 1969 to 1974 he was Director of Economic Affairs and Chairman of NATO's Economic Committee. His speciality is the economics of defense and he has published several books in this area, most notably *Visa Pour un Désastre.* Another recent title is *The General Theory of Employment, Interest and Cheating.* His address: Société Génerale, Service des Etudes et Renseignements, 7 Place Edouard VIII, 75009 Paris, France.

BARBARA G LEVI, who currently works at the Bell Telephone Laboratories, was, until recently, on the research staff of the Center for Energy and Environmental Studies at Princeton University. She also writes research news stories for *Physics Today* magazine and has consulted for the Congressional Office of Technology Assessment on such studies as *Nuclear Proliferation and Safeguards.* She received a doctorate in high energy physics from Stanford University in 1971. Before coming to Princeton in 1981, she taught physics at the Georgia Institute of Technology and at Fairleigh Dickinson University. Her address: Bell Telephone Laboratories, WBID 216, Holmdel, New Jersey 17733, USA.

PATRICIA J LINDOP, PhD, DSc, FRCP, is professor of radiation biology at the University of London and head of the department of radiobiology at St Bartholomew's Hospital Medical College. She has been investigating the biological effects of radiation since 1958, and was a member of the British Royal Commission in Environmental Pollution from 1974 to 1979. Her address: Department of Radiobiology, The Medical College of St Bartholomew's Hospital, Charterhouse Square, London EC1M 6BQ, UK.

HUGH MIDDLETON, MD, is a lecturer at the Clinical School in Cambridge. He qualified in medicine in 1974 and began specialized training in respiratory medicine. A doctoral thesis on pulmonary hypertension and chronic obstructive airways disease was completed in 1980. Since then he has devoted his time to publicizing the medical consequences of the use of nuclear weapons. He is a founder-member of the Medical Campaign Against Nuclear Weapons and is co-author of their pamphlet, and has also written several other publications on the subject of nuclear weapons and their medical consequences. He also took part in organizing the 1982 Congress of International Physicians for the Prevention of Nuclear War. His address: Department of Medicine, Addenbrook Hospital, Hills Road, Cambridge, UK.

JOSEPH ROTBLAT is Emeritus Professor of Physics at the University of London. During World War II he worked at Los Alamos on the atom bomb project; as a result of this he turned from nuclear physics to medical physics and radiation biology. He is a founder of the Pugwash Conference on Science and World Affairs and was its Secretary-General from 1957 to 1973. He is a past President of the British Institute of Radiology and of the Hospital Physicists Association. For many years he was Editor-in-Chief of *Physics in Medicine and Biology.* His address: c/o Pugwash, Great Russell Mansions, 60 Great Russell Street, London SC1B 3BE, UK.

ALLYN H SEYMOUR is a marine biologist and Professor Emeritus, University of Washington (Seattle). He is a former Director of the Laboratory of Radiation Ecology, and instructor at the College of Fisheries at the University of Washington. His academic and professional interests are aquatic radioecology and fishery biology. He was chairman of the committee which prepared the National Academy of Science-National Research Council volume *Radioactivity in the Marine Environment,* and a committee member for the NRC report *Long Term Worldwide Effects of Multiple Nuclear Weapons Detonations.* His address: Fisheries Center, WH-10, University of Washington, Seattle, WA 98195, USA.

M E VARTANIAN is Deputy Director of the Institute of Psychiatry of the Soviet Academy of Medical Sciences. His address: C30 Institute of Psychiatry, USSR Academy of Medical Sciences, Zagorodnoe shosse 2, Moscow, USSR.

KLAUS GUENTHER WETZEL has been since 1971 the director of the Central Institute of Isotope and Radiation Research of the Academy of Sciences in Leipzig, German Democratic Republic. He holds two doctorates, in chemistry and in natural science, and was previously head of the Department of Isotope Separation by Chemical Methods in the Institute he now directs. His professional interests include isotope geochemistry, separation of stable isotopes, applications of stable isotopes in agriculture and medicine, and the applications of ionizing radiation. His address: c/o Central Institute of Isotope and Radiation Research, Permoserstr. 15, 7050 Leipzig, German Democratic Republic.

GEORGE M WOODWELL is Director of the Ecosystems Center of the Marine Biology Laboratory at Woods Hole, Massachusetts. He holds a Ph D in ecology from Duke University, and was previously Senior Scientist at the Brookhaven National Laboratory and a professor at Yale University. His professional interests include the biotic effects of ionizing radiation, and the effects of toxic substances on the structure and function of forests, estuaries and other terrestrial ecosystems. His address: c/o The Ecosystems Center, Marine Biological Laboratory, Woods Hole, Mass. 02543, USA.

Ambio, first published in 1972, is the international journal of the human environment published by the Royal Swedish Academy of Sciences in Stockholm, Sweden.

Ambio is regarded as one of the world's foremost environmental publications. Its six issues a year are read by people in more than 100 countries, and cover a wide range of environmental subjects, including: air and water pollution, acid rain, toxic substances, loss of tropical forests, species extinction, urbanization, over-population, desertification, loss of agricultural land, low-level radiation, and health effects of heavy metals. At least once a year *Ambio* publishes a special issue devoted to an in-depth presentation of one broad topic, such as "Nuclear War: The Aftermath," the double issue on which this book is based. For subscription information, write: *Ambio,* Royal Swedish Academy of Sciences, Box 50005, S-104 05 Stockholm, Sweden.